The Theory of Monetary Institutions

The Theory *of* Monetary Institutions

LAWRENCE H. WHITE
University of Georgia

First published 1999

2 4 6 8 10 9 7 5 3 2 1

Blackwell Publishers Inc.
350 Main Street
Malden, Massachusetts 02148
USA

Blackwell Publishers Ltd
108 Cowley Road
Oxford OX4 1JF
UK

Library of Congress Cataloging-in-Publication Data

White, Lawrence H. (Lawrence Henry)
    The theory of monetary institutions / Lawrence H. White.
        p.   cm.
    Includes bibliographical references and index.
    ISBN 1-55786-236-2 (hardbound   :   alk. paper).
    – ISBN 0-631-21214-0 (pbk.   :   alk. paper)
        1. Free banking.   2. Monetary policy.   I. Title.
    HG1811.W47   1999
    332.1'01–dc21   98-46425
                                                                CIP

British Library Cataloguing in Publication Data

A CIP catalogue record for this book is available from the British Library.

Typeset in 10½ on 12 pt Times
by Ace Filmsetting Ltd, Frome, Somerset

This book is printed on acid-free paper.

Contents

List of Figures and Tables   ix

Preface   xi

Acknowledgments   xiii

1 The Evolution of Market Monetary Institutions   1
    The Mystery of Money   1
    Menger's Theory Restated   3
    Some Implications of the Theory   7
    From Simple Commodity Money to Coins   9
    Bank-issued Money   11
    Regular Par Acceptance   14
    Clearing Arrangements   16
    The Path to Fiat Money   18
    Spontaneous Separation between the Media of
        Redemption and Account?   20
    Questions   24

2 Commodity Money   26
    Determining the Price Level   27
    The Simple Stock-flow Analytics of Gold Supply
        and Demand   28
    The Historical Sources of Gold Supply Disturbances   37
    The Benefits of a Gold Standard   39
    The Resource Costs of a Gold Standard   42
    Is a Gold Standard Worth the Resource Cost?   48
    Questions   50

3   **Money Issue by Unrestricted Banks**   53
The Purchasing Power of Money   54
Bank Optimization and the Equilibrium Quantity
   of Bank-issued Money   56
Correcting Over-issue by an Individual Bank   60
Correcting Over-issue by the System as a Whole   61
Responding to Shifts in Demand   64
Shifts between Deposits and Currency   67
Questions   68

4   **The Evolution and Rationales of Central Banking**   70
Central Banking Roles and CHAs   71
The Origins of Government Central Banks   80
Historical Cases   81
Questions   86

5   **Should Government Play a Role in Money?**   88
Is Some Aspect of Money a Public Good?   89
Are There Relevant External Benefits in the
   Choice of Which Money to Use?   92
Are There Relevant External Benefits to the Choice
   of How Much Money to Hold?   105
Is the Supply of Base Money a Natural Monopoly?   116
Questions   119

6   **Should Government Play a Role in Banking?**   121
The Problem of Bank Runs   121
Inherent Fragility in Theory:
   The Diamond–Dybvig Model   123
The Fragility of the Diamond–Dybvig Bank:
   A Numerical Example   126
Deposit Insurance in the Diamond–Dybvig Model   127
Criticism of the Diamond-Dybvig Model   127
Are Deposit Contracts Inherently Fragile?   128
Historical Evidence on Inherent Fragility   132
Is There a Natural Monopoly in Bank-issued Money?   133
Can Government Produce Currency More Efficiently?   134
Questions   135

7   **Seigniorage**   138
The Sources of Seigniorage   139
Maximizing the Take from Seigniorage   143

Reserve Requirements   150
Other Legal Restrictions   153
The Dynamics of Hyperinflation   155
The Transition between Steady States: Is Honesty
     a Government's Best Policy?   158
How Well Does Seigniorage-maximization Explain
     Actual Governments' Behavior?   163
Questions   165
Appendix   166

8   **Central Bank as Bureaucracy**   173
Bureaucratic Explanation of the Fed's Operating
     Procedures   173
Bureaucracy and "Inflationary Bias"   176
Questions   179

9   **Political Business Cycle Hypotheses**   180
The Nordhaus–MacRae Model   180
The Rational Expectations Critique   187
An Alternative Formulation: Wagner's Political
     Seigniorage Cycle   188
The "Partisan" Political Business Cycle Theory   189
Questions   192

10   **Discretion and Dynamic Inconsistency**   193
The Kydland–Prescott Model   194
Positive Implications: Using the Model to Explain
     Changes in Inflation   199
Policy Implications Under Discretion   202
Rules Versus Discretion   204
Subsequent Literature   207
Questions   208
Appendix: An Algebraic Version of the Model   210

11   **Monetary Rules**   215
Benefits and Burdens of Counter-cyclical Policy   215
Independence for the Central Bank   217
Arguments for Rules   218
Friedman's Proposals   219
McCallum's Case for a Feedback Rule   223
Simple Versus Complicated Rules   225
Questions   226

12 **Competitive Supply of Fiat-type Money** 227
Klein's Model with Perfect Foresight 228
Klein's Model with "Imperfect Foresight" 231
Is the Equilibrium Rate of Inflation Bounded
    under Imperfect Foresight? 233
Conclusion 238
Questions 239

13 **Cashless Competitive Payments and Legal Restrictions** 240
The Greenfield–Yeager Proposal 240
Is Bundles-worth Redemption Workable? 242
Other Concerns About the GY Proposal 243
The Legal Restrictions Theory 244
Historical Evidence on the Non-coexistence Prediction 246
Questions 247

References 249
Index 260

Figures and Tables

Figure 2.1 Stationary equilibrium in the markets for gold   29
Figure 2.2 An increase in the monetary demand for gold   32
Figure 2.3 An increase in the flow supply of gold   35
Figure 2.4 Ongoing steady growth in the monetary
                demand for gold   45
Figure 3.1 The probability of illiquidity   58
Figure 3.2 An in-concert expansion   64
Figure 7.1 Maximum seigniorage and the *h* demand curve   147
Figure 7.2 The Bailey curve   150
Figure 7.3 Required reserve ratio   152
Figure 7.4 Restrictions on *H* substitutes   154
Figure 7.5 Steady state convergence   156
Figure 7.6 Runaway monetary expansion   157
Figure 7.7 Raising the expansion rate   159
Figure 7.8 A "dishonest" government raising the expansion rate 161
Figure 9.1 Long-run and short-run Phillips curves
                (LRPC and SRPCs)   182
Figure 9.2 Electoral popularity isoquants   183
Figure 9.3 The Nordhaus political business cycle   183
Figure 9.4 Myopic long-run equilibrium at point M   186
Figure 9.5 Partisan post-election results   191
Figure 10.1 Long-run and short-run Phillips curves
                (LRPC and SRPCs)   195
Figure 10.2 Social indifference (isomisery) curves   196
Figure 10.3 Time-consistent equilibrium M versus optimal
                outcome G   199
Figure 12.1 Unbounded monetary expansion   237

Table 3.1   A simplified balance sheet   56
Table 6.1   The life history of the DD bank   125

Preface

This book grows out of my lecture notes from teaching graduate and under-graduate courses in monetary and banking theory and monetary policy. No available book discussed in detail what I consider the most interesting and fundamental issues in monetary economics, so I wrote this one. I have field-tested early drafts in more than one course. However, I haven't tried to make this a "textbook" in the usual sense of an inclusive (much less neut-ral!) survey of the field as conventionally defined. It focuses, instead, on a particular (perhaps idiosyncratic) set of theories and evidence concerning monetary institutions and monetary policy regimes. For that reason, it may find wider use as a supplement than as a main text – if anyone assigns supplemental texts these days in money-and-banking or monetary theory courses.

Actually, though, I hope that this book's audience will not be limited to students who have it assigned to them. I hope my fellow economists will find something of interest here. I also invite the "educated layman". Parts of the subject matter are challenging, but I have tried to make the exposition accessible by holding algebra to a minimum, and by relegating it whenever possible to chapter appendices.

There are four basic parts in this book. The first four chapters explore, theoretically and historically, how market monetary institutions evolved and operated through most of modern history, before the era of fiat money, and how central banks came on the scene. The next two chapters are normative, critically evaluating the most prominent rationales for government involve-ment in the payments system. The following four chapters present what I consider the leading theories of how the monetary policy regime we pres-ently have – a fiat standard operated by a government central bank acting at its own discretion – may behave, depending on the central bank's objectives. The final three chapters consider how some proposed alternative regimes might work: simple or complex monetary rules, competitive fiat-type monies, or a "cashless" payment system that divorces the medium of redemption from the (multi-commodity) medium of account. Regardless of the ultimate verdict of any of these proposals, understanding them is useful because, by contrast, they bring crucial features of our current regime into sharp relief.

These are interesting times to study monetary regimes. While central banks in the developed world have become much less inflationary than they were in the 1970s, the desirability of having a central bank is no longer being taken for granted in the post-socialist, post-kleptocratic and post-hyperinflationist monetary reconstruction of Central and Eastern Europe, Asia, Africa, and Latin America. This book is not a reformist tract about what should be done, but it aims to contribute to a better understanding of what the alternatives are.

Lawrence H. White
Professor of Economics
University of Georgia
July 1998

Acknowledgments

I am grateful to the John M. Olin Foundation for a research grant that allowed me to begin this project in 1988–90. Mac Boot and the Department of Economic History at the Australian National University provided a hospitable environment for writing in the fall of 1989. The Terry Fellowship program of the Terry College of Business, University of Georgia provided research support over several summers. Charles Hickson has given me several valuable opportunities to present the material contained herein at the Queen's University of Belfast. I have received very useful comments from George Selgin, Bryan Caplan, and three readers: Tyler Cowen, George Mason University; Marvin Goodfriend, University of Virginia; and Jan Lemmen, London School of Economics. Lois Allen provided efficient research assistance. My editors at Blackwell have been more than patient.

Most of all, I am indebted to the graduate and undergraduate students over the years who have asked questions, raised objections, and demanded better explanations. I particularly want to thank Louann Ahlgren, Fernando Alvarez, Michele Fleming, Natalie Janson, Curtis Melvin, Kevin Rogers, Kurt Schuler, Christopher Sorrow, Richard Shedenhelm, and John Turner.

Athens, Georgia
July 1998

1

The Evolution of Market Monetary Institutions

In the beginning, goods were bartered directly for other goods. A theoretical account of the evolution of monetary institutions naturally begins with an attempt to explain how the earliest money emerged from a non-monetary or barter economy. "Money" here, following standard usage among economists, means a *commonly accepted medium of exchange*. A "medium of exchange" means a good that people acquire through trade with the intention of trading away later (rather than consuming for its own sake or using up in a production process). "Commonly accepted" means that the money good is routinely offered and taken in trade for other goods, and so appears on one side of nearly every transaction. The theory that follows aims to explain why, and how, some good should acquire these characteristics.[1]

The Mystery of Money

The Austrian economist, Carl Menger (1892), developed the classic explanation of the origin of money. Menger showed how money can emerge from barter without anyone *inventing* it, or to use Adam Smith's phrase, "as if by an invisible hand." In his account, money emerges through a series of steps, each based on self-seeking actions by individual traders, without the resulting social order (monetary exchange) being part of anyone's intention. This

---

[1] For a further teasing out of these defining terms see White (1989, ch. 11). There I used the modifier "generally accepted"; here, following Wärneryd (1990), I use "commonly accepted" in the same sense. The present chapter draws on Selgin and White (1987) and White (1989, ch. 9). For complementary accounts of these issues, see Glasner (1989, ch. 1) and Dowd (1996, ch. 1).

is a satisfying mode of explanation because it does not require heroic assumptions about the knowledge possessed by any trader.

A number of writers before Menger expressed the idea that money was an undesigned or spontaneously emerged institution. Among them are Adam Smith, the French economists Etienne de Condillac and Destutt de Tracy, and the British monetary pamphleteers, Thomas Hodgskin and Samuel Bailey. Menger was certainly aware of Smith's writings, though he does not cite Smith in this context. However, none of these earlier writers spelled out the emergence of money step by step. The typical modern textbook discussion of the origin of money is plainly inadequate.[2] It lists the problems of barter exchange, and shows that monetary exchange overcomes these problems. A prototype can be found in Aristotle (*Nichomachean Ethics*, Book 5): "All the things which we exchange need to be comparable. This need led to the invention of money to serve as a medium giving value to every thing." Unfortunately, the simple contrast between problems and solution does not explain how the solution (money) was arrived at, any more than a list of the advantages of standard time zones would explain how they came about. One is left with the impression that barterers, one morning, suddenly became alert to the benefits of monetary exchange, and, by that afternoon, were busy using some good as money. In one version of the story, a wise head of state introduced the idea that a certain commodity was to be sanctioned as a general medium of exchange.

Taken seriously as a theory of the origin of money, this account would suggest that the idea of money was fully grasped before money existed. Money would be an invention, like the telephone, which existed in someone's mind before a prototype was produced. In fact, money is not a product of technological advance brought forth by a single mind or a research laboratory. This is evident from the fact that gold dust or salt, used as money, is not technologically different from gold dust or salt, not used as money. What transforms gold dust or salt into a money is not some physical change, but rather the development of a *social convention* concerning the use of that good. The use of any particular item as money is a social convention, in the same sense that the use of particular utterances or gestures to communicate particular ideas is a social convention. Each of us (in an English-speaking group) calls a certain fruit an "apple" because that is what everyone around us calls it, and we wish to communicate with them. Likewise, each of us uses item x as a medium of exchange because nearly all others in our society do, and we wish to trade with them.

A money could not spring forth full-blown from barter unless people throughout a society simultaneously arrived at the idea of using x as a medium of exchange, *and* each person knew that he could count on others to

---

[2] Notable exceptions are McCulloch (1982) and Goodhart (1989b).

do so too. Such a scenario begs too many questions. It invokes the realization of money in the attempt to explain how money was realized. It attributes knowledge of the benefits of money to people who would not have such knowledge in a barter economy.

Menger begins by emphasizing the "mystery" of money: why is everyone willing to trade truly useful goods and services for mere tokens? In Menger's day (a century ago), these tokens were otherwise practically useless disks of gold and silver, or slips of paper (banknotes) representing claims to such disks. Today, the mystery is even greater, as the tokens are otherwise completely useless disks of cupro-nickel and slips of paper interchangeable with them.[3]

Menger's approach does not apply only to commodity money, though it was originally framed to explain such money. It emphasizes that the use of a commodity money has a "conventional" aspect, the convention being one that develops through a historical process. By extension, the use of a fiat money rests on the prior development of a commodity money convention, because fiat money is launched by suspending the redeemability of claims to a commodity money. However, we are getting ahead of the story.

It is worthwhile restating Menger's theory in detail for several reasons. Our immediate interest, here, is its usefulness in explaining the origin of money. Later in the book, we will return to the theory because it has implications for the viability of projects to establish a new money, or a payments system without money. The theory also draws out certain "essential features" of money that have implications for the macroeconomic properties of a monetary economy (Yeager 1968). Finally, the theory holds a general interest to students of the social sciences because it provides a paradigmatic example of an invisible-hand explanation of a social institution.[4]

Menger's Theory Restated

A simple barter economy faces each trader with the problem of finding a trading partner with preferences and endowments reciprocal to his own. (This has come to be known as the problem of finding a "mutual coincidence of

---

[3] In recent years, a number of monetary economists have offered non-evolutionary models of money as solutions to the mystery of a positive value being accorded to "intrinsically useless" and inconvertible fiat money: in particular, the overlapping generations model (Wallace 1980) and search-theoretic models (Kiyotaki and Wright 1989, Ritter 1995). Menger's solution is different, and is less subject to the cogent criticisms made of the overlapping generations model (Tobin 1980, McCallum 1983), of other general equilibrium models of money (Bryant and Wallace 1980), and of search-theoretic models (Selgin 1997b). Of course, it is subject to other criticisms.

[4] It has been cited as such by Nozick (1974, p. 18), though Nozick actually cites a restatement of Menger's theory by von Mises (1980).

wants.") For Alanis to trade the asparagus she brings to market for the bacon she prefers to take home and consume, via a direct pairwise exchange, she must find some other trader ("*B*") who both has what Alanis wants (bacon), and wants what Alanis has (asparagus). It may be difficult or even impossible to find such a match, even when a unanimously preferred reallocation of goods could be arranged in another way. McCulloch (1982, ch. 1) offers a simple example: imagine three individuals and three indivisible goods, where *A* has good 1 and prefers good 2 (but not good 3) to good 1, *B* has good 2 and prefers only good 3, and *C* has good 3 and prefers only good 1. Clearly, all are better off if good 1 goes to C, good 2 goes to A, and good 3 goes to B, but there is no pairwise exchange that makes both traders better off. More generally, even where a pairwise trading partner *could* be found, it may be difficult and time-consuming to find that trader among the many in the marketplace.

A trader who is frustrated by her inability to find a rare or non-existent matched trading partner need neither continue the effort fruitlessly nor give up and go home. There is an alternative. Consider the three-agent case just described. Suppose that each pair of individuals has met, and has quickly discovered that only one party wants to make each possible pairwise trade. Alanis has discovered that Bjork, who is selling the good that Alanis prefers (bacon), does not prefer what Alanis has to offer (asparagus). In this situation, it would not take too much cleverness on Alanis's part to ask Bjork what good Bjork *would* prefer. Learning that Bjork prefers cabbage, which Coolio has offered to Alanis in exchange for asparagus, Alanis will be led by self-interest to trade with Coolio, even though Alanis does not want to consume cabbage. Alanis will then be in a position to make an offer for Bjork's bacon that Bjork will accept.

The general point illustrated by this example is that, potentially, a barterer can economically achieve a preferred holding of goods by exchanging her initial endowment for some good which can then be turned around and exchanged for the good(s) she ultimately wants to consume. This practice is known as *indirect exchange*, in contradistinction to the *direct exchange* of simple barter. In the example, individual A has used good 3 as a vehicle for indirect exchange or, as it is usually put, as a *medium of exchange*.

Now consider a larger barter market, such as a trade fair, with anonymous traders selling many goods. (As noted below, such a fair would not historically have been found in a barter economy, because specialization and trade could not develop far where trade remained so difficult to accomplish.) To keep the discussion simple, assume that each trader still arrives endowed with a single indivisible good and desires to take home some one other good, though several traders may now be selling each good. As before, every trader besides Alanis is trying to use direct exchange, and will agree to trade only for the one good she wishes to consume. Alanis, again coming to market with asparagus, will find that her trading problem is now more difficult. With a larger number of traders, it may take more time to discover a trader B who is selling the bacon that Alanis wants to buy. The probability that this B wants to take home asparagus is smaller than before. Once Alanis learns what good j this trader B *will* agree to accept in exchange, it will take more time to find which (if any) among the sellers of j will accept asparagus in exchange. In this setting, it can easily be the case that Alanis acquires the desired bacon most economically neither by direct exchange, nor by waiting until she meets a seller of bacon to learn what goods can potentially be used as a medium of exchange. Instead, Alanis's best trading strategy is to exchange her asparagus for a good k which any seller of bacon (and, for that matter, of good j) that Alanis may happen to meet is *relatively likely* to accept.

Here Menger introduces the concept that different goods have different *degrees of marketability*. Marketability is a "non-Walrasian" concept: in a Walrasian general equilibrium model, with costlessly coordinated trade, and with a single price at which a good may be either bought *or* sold, every good is perfectly marketable. In a world of costly trade, it takes some amount of time, effort, and expense to sell for a good price. (Anyone who has ever tried to sell a used car knows this.) A more highly marketable good is a good that is easier (less costly) to sell for a good price. A "good price" here means a price close to the best price that could potentially be found with full information on both sides of the market. (Menger calls this best price, an "economic price.")[5]

A perceptive barterer will exchange her initial endowment goods for more highly marketable goods, which can then easily be exchanged for the goods he or she wants to consume. She wants to maximize her expected gains from trade, which obviously depend on the prices at which trade takes place, net of the costs of finding trading partners (costs of search), and of the costs of consummating trade (costs of transportation, contracting, and the like). Indirect exchange requires two trades, instead of one. It is therefore more likely to be advantageous to the extent that:

1   the good to be used as a medium of exchange is more widely consumed, and traded, than the endowment good, and hence trading partners offering a good price in it, and for it, are easier to find; and
2   the costs of buying, holding, and reselling it (costs of contracting, spoilage, and transportation) are relatively small.

---

[5] Because marketability has at least three dimensions (time cost, other selling costs, and percentage of economic price realized), it may not always be possible to rank the marketability of different goods unambiguously.

Where indirect exchange is advantageous, it pays a trader to accumulate an inventory of highly marketable items for use as media of exchange.[6] Having highly marketable items on hand allows a trader to find good buying prices more easily for the things she wants to consume.

Other alert traders in the market, facing the same situation, will adopt the same strategy of indirect exchange. Menger notes that some individuals may not catch on to the advantages of indirect exchange immediately or on their own. Eventually though, they will notice the success enjoyed by those who are trading their produce for a medium of exchange rather than persisting in attempts at direct exchange. They are then likely to imitate the practice of using indirect exchange.

Once many individuals are using indirect exchange, the stage is set for social convergence toward a *common* medium of exchange. One perceptive trader, say M, will learn from experience which commodities are *most* marketable, and best suited for use as media of exchange. The knowledge that he can unload them easily will lead him to accept these commodities all the more readily, and in preference to other commodities. M's greater acceptance of a good k incrementally reinforces its usefulness as a medium of exchange for other traders, $A \ldots L$ and $N \ldots Z$, because they can count on one more place to spend it. Its marketability for them has increased. They may learn of good k's improved suitability as a medium of exchange, either through communication, or from trial-and-error experience, or as a last resort by imitation of the successful traders. Traders N, O, and the others will then accept good k more readily, just as M did earlier. Again, each trader who does so reinforces its usefulness for the others. With every trader preferring more marketable to less marketable media of exchange, ultimately one good (or at most a few, covering different sets of transactions) is elevated to the status of being *commonly* or *generally* or *routinely* accepted as a medium of exchange. It becomes money.

This theory is not meant to suggest that extensive specialization and market trade historically antedated the emergence of money. On the contrary, it helps to explain why specialization and trade developed simultaneously with money, a fact Leijonhufvud (1981, pp. 229–30) has emphasized. Pre-monetary communities were basically autarkic (Dingle 1988). Direct exchange is so difficult that the scope of specialized production "for the market" is limited by the

---

[6] This was pointed out long ago by Adam Smith (1981, pp. 37–8): "In order to avoid the inconveniency of such situations [in which the seller of a desired good does not want the produce the would-be buyer has to offer], every prudent man in every period of society, after the first establishment of the division of labor, must naturally have endeavoured to manage his affairs in such a manner, as to have at all times by him, besides the peculiar produce of his own industry, a certain quantity of some one commodity or other, such as he imagined few people would be likely to refuse in exchange for the produce of their industry."

scope of indirect exchange. Thus Adam Smith's dictum, that the division of labor is limited by the extent of the market, may be supplemented by the observation that the extent of the market is limited by the extent of money's use.

Some Implications of the Theory

The Mengerian theory helps us to understand the important characteristics of a monetized economy that are the result of these evolutionary origins of money. Menger emphasized the following three.

1   Everyone in a monetary economy routinely accepts money, and routinely attempts to trade output or endowment goods for money before acquiring consumption goods.
2   The ability to purchase goods at "the going rate" with money is not at all doubtful, even in anticipation of dealing with an anonymous seller. There is virtually no risk of meeting a seller who refuses to accept money, or accepts it only at a discount.
3   Sellers are reluctant to accept goods of lesser marketability than money, with the result that the marketability of the money good is discontinuously greater than that of any other good. A buyer (with money) has markedly less difficulty trading at close to economical prices than does a seller (of a non-money good). As Menger notes, being forced to sell on short notice imposes much more of a burden than being forced to buy on short notice.

The theory also establishes that *no collective decision* or legislative act is necessary for money to emerge. Menger emphasized this point with respect to the defining characteristic of money: its general acceptance as a medium of exchange. Money did not originate from, or fail to perform its medium-of-exchange function fully until endorsed by, the legal decrees of rulers.

By extending Menger's theory, we can see that the role of money as a "unit of account" also arises spontaneously. The "unit of account" means some definite quantity of a good used as a pricing and accounting unit. Strictly speaking, as Jurg Niehans (1978) has pointed out, it is not proper to say that *money* is a unit of account, because money as such is not a unit. Money is rather a *medium* of account. The *unit* of account is a specific quantity of the good constituting the medium of account. For example, silver may be the money and medium of account, while the "ducat" (defined as so many grams of standard-fineness silver) is the unit of account.[7]

[7] The ducato d'argento of Venice, 1201–1355, was 96.5% fine and weighed 2.18 grams.

The medium of account in an economy will naturally coincide with its commonly accepted medium of exchange or money. A seller pursues his self-interest by posting prices in terms of the good or goods he is routinely willing to accept in exchange. If this seller were to post prices in terms of some other good, he would incur the extra trouble, for himself and for his customers, of keeping track of and figuring in the current exchange rate between the pricing medium and the payment medium he is willing to accept. An accountant could not calculate profit and loss as easily, or as clearly, were she to keep books in units of a commodity other than the commonly accepted medium of exchange in which the income actually accrues, liabilities come due, transactions balances are held, and for which other assets can most readily be exchanged.

Accordingly, some common unit of money naturally becomes the unit of account. It may be an early popular coin (e.g. the Spanish dollar), a simple bullion weight (e.g. the "pound sterling"), or a natural unit (one standard-sized cowry shell). No official proclamation is necessary to establish a standard unit of account, any more than to establish a standard building brick. Commercial practice can converge on a conventional unit, without any collective decision being taken, in much the way that it converges on a money commodity. Each seller will discover that he does best for himself by posting prices in the unit most popular with his potential trading partners. Court decisions can, and historically did, follow trade custom in deciding how much of what fineness of what metal would legally satisfy a contractual obligation to deliver a "ducat" (or whatever money unit). The courts did not *create* customary units.

There is no denying, of course, that governments often have played a role in pushing a new money or unit of account. The point is that no collective deliberation or action is needed for money to emerge fully, or was historically instrumental in its original emergence.[8]

Money only makes sense, given its origin in indirect exchange, in a world with certain features. There must be three or more traders, and at least two goods besides money, for otherwise only direct exchange is possible. There must be varying degrees of marketability for these goods, or some physical feature of other goods that makes them less suitable for shopping with; otherwise, there is no advantage to indirect exchange. These features are

---

[8] John Maynard Keynes (1935, pp. 4–5), even while asserting the relevance to the modern world of "the doctrine that money is peculiarly a creation of the State," recognized that the original establishment of a conventional unit of account preceded government involvement: "Thus the Age of Money had succeeded to the Age of Barter as soon as men had adopted a money-of-account. And the Age of . . . State Money was reached when the State claimed the right to declare what thing should answer as money to the current money-of-account – when it claimed the right not only to enforce the dictionary but also to write the dictionary."

not always present in abstract economic models purported to be models of monetary economies. In a world where all goods are perfectly and costlessly marketable (so that there are no economic barriers to barter), there is no rationale for a distinctive money. Barter with interest-bearing financial assets would dominate the use of any non-interest-bearing money.

From Simple Commodity Money to Coins

An evolutionary or neo-Mengerian perspective can help to explain the emergence of gold and silver as the predominant commodity monies in the world, and the later emergence of such monetary institutions as coinage and bank-issued paper money.

The earliest form of money, following Menger's account, must have been a useful commodity. A good must have acceptability in barter before it can acquire wider acceptability as a medium of exchange. It must have some usefulness as a commodity to be accepted in barter. Anthropological evidence indicates that the goods that became monies in several cultures originally had ornamental uses (Melitz 1974).[9] This was true of Pacific and African shell monies, North American wampum, and, also, gold and silver. Other primitive monies have been foodstuffs, like grain or salt.

The eventual predominance of gold and silver as money, over other commodities which early on would have had equally wide acceptability, can be explained by at least four (partly physical) characteristics that promoted their ready marketability and convenience (low usage costs) as media of exchange. These characteristics were a staple subject of discussion in money-and-banking texts during the era of metallic monetary standards.

1 Goods like livestock or tobacco, whose quality is variable and difficult to assess, are more troublesome to exchange than goods of *uniform* and *easily recognized quality*.[10] Pure gold and silver, as chemical elements, are absolutely uniform. The purity (fineness) of a particular piece of gold or silver can be tested at low cost by biting it, sounding it, or (with a bit more trouble) by assaying it. Traders were commonly experienced in these assessment methods in the past. As

---

[9] I used to add "or ceremonial uses," until I discovered that "ceremonial use" is the anthropologist's shorthand for "we have no idea what it was used for."

[10] Armen Alchian's account (1977) of "Why Money?" relies exclusively on low authentication costs for selecting which commodity will become money. See also King and Plosser (1986). Other things equal, this characteristic can be decisive but, more generally, it is only one characteristic among several that can play a part in promoting a commodity's use as a medium of exchange.

will be discussed below, coinage arose to relieve the difficulties created by the non-uniformity of gold and silver in rawer forms (nuggets or dust or ingots).

2   Gold and silver are *durable*, so that there are no extra carrying costs due to spoilage. The deterioration of goods like grain and olive oil makes them costly to hold in inventory. The possibility of deterioration also creates the above-mentioned problem of exchange being encumbered by the need for costly verification of the goods' current quality.

3   The precious metals are easily *divisible and fusible*, so that payment can be tailored to purchase size. Large pieces can easily be split into small pieces, and small pieces can be united to form larger pieces. This is not true of jewels or, certainly, of livestock.

4   Finally, gold and silver are *portable*, that is, have high ratios of value to bulk. Portability means a low cost of taking the medium of exchange from the site where it is acquired to the site where it is spent. Commodities like salt lost their suitability as media of exchange when their value per pound became too low. The copper money of seventeenth-century Sweden, a non-precious metallic money, was notoriously cumbersome. Individual pieces of copper "plate money" eventually weighed up to 20 kilograms (44 pounds). Strong young men had to be employed to carry the copper necessary to make an ordinary-sized commercial purchase. Finally, Swedes stopped using copper, except in the smallest transactions. A similar process may have promoted the historical dominance of gold over silver in international payments of large sums: it was less costly to send one boat laden with gold than to send fifteen laden with silver.[11]

The displacement of one money by another can follow the general Mengerian logic of a self-reinforcing convergence process. As individuals from two regions with different commodity monies come into contact and begin to trade, an entryway is created for the better of the two monies to spread to the other region. Traders on the margin, not only those physically adjacent to the border but also merchants who do a large fraction of their trade with users of the foreign money, will favor the foreign money, if it is markedly better in some of the four areas listed above. Merchants and border-dwellers will accept the favored money on somewhat better terms, and

---

[11] Fleming (1994) finds, however, that the general historical switch from silver to gold standards was not market-driven. It was, in fact, mainly due to the legal overvaluation of gold relative to silver by the governments of Britain and the US, which set Gresham's Law in motion (the legally overvalued or "bad" money drove out the legally undervalued or "good" money). Other nations deliberately followed suit in a sort of bandwagon effect.

can use it among themselves where, before, they used the local money. The margin can then spread: those who deal substantially with these merchants, and those who live adjacent to the areas adjacent to the border, can find it advantageous to be paid in the foreign money. Its sphere of acceptance can snowball, following the Mengerian logic, until a single money unites the two regions.

Coinage, the practice of fashioning monetary metal into standardized marked discs, though it involves technical advances and not merely the formation of a social convention, also developed in step-by-step fashion. Where nuggets or gold dust served as money, merchants had to assess weight and quality when accepting payment. It made sense for a merchant to mark a piece of assessed gold, so as to avoid the costs of re-assessment when paying the piece out later. Other traders who trusted this merchant could then also rely on his mark. To prevent the possibility of shaving off gold around the marked area, the piece could be covered with marks. Punching, stamping, and finally modern methods of minting developed as low-cost methods of fashioning reliably marked pieces of gold. Historical examples of these stages can be observed in the money of ancient Lydia (Burns 1927; Cribb 1986).

Mints arose spontaneously, then, to meet the demand for authentication services. With the development of coinage, the marketability of coined metal became discontinuously greater than that of uncoined metal (in this context, branded bars of bullion may be thought of as large coins). Gold miners found it much easier to spend coined than uncoined gold, and, therefore, were willing to pay for the service of minting their raw gold into coins. Numismatic publications indicate that more than twenty private gold and silver mints operated during the gold and silver rushes in nineteenth-century America (Kagin 1981), and one in Australia (McDonald 1987, p. 122).

In practice, governments have typically monopolized the coinage industry, but there are no signs that coinage is a natural monopoly. There are ample signs that governments have wanted to exercise monopoly over money production so as to reap the monopoly profits known as *seigniorage* (Selgin and White 1999). In a later chapter, we will consider in more detail both seigniorage in its medieval form, and seigniorage in its modern form of the profit from monopoly issue of fiat money.

Bank-issued Money

The next step to consider, in the evolution of monetary institutions, is the emergence of money issued by commercial banks. Full-bodied coins (and other types of full-bodied commodity money, like shells) originate outside of any commercial banking system. We may call them "outside" money, whereas bank-issued money is "inside" money. Outside money is an asset for its holder but not a liability of, or financial claim against, anyone else. The media of exchange produced by a commercial bank, by contrast, are claims against it. A large literature attempts to explain why banks exist as intermediaries between savers and borrowers (Santomero 1984).[12] Our object here is, rather, to explain why banks participate in the payments system, by offering a logical evolutionary account of why and how claims against banks came to be used as money.

The earliest bank liabilities were claims to outside money deposited with bankers. Historical records indicate that bankers in medieval Italy began as money-changers, but by AD1200 had moved into accepting time and demand deposits (de Roover 1974a, 1974b). In a region of numerous city-states, each with its own distinct coinage, money-changers provided the service of trading local coins for the less spendable foreign coins brought by inbound merchants and other travelers, and of trading the reverse way with outbound travelers. A simple explanation of why money-changers became deposit-takers is that merchants found it easier to leave money with them "on account," to be called for when needed, rather than to take away domestic coin equal in value to the foreign coin tendered (or vice versa) on every occasion. Essentially, this means that the money-changers' vaults were being used for temporary safekeeping of coin. In this respect, the development of deposit banking in Italy was similar to its development in England where, according to numerous accounts, early deposits were taken by goldsmiths whose vaults provided safekeeping.

Bank deposits began to play a monetary role when they became a medium of exchange, that is, when transfer of deposit balances became an accepted method of payment among bank customers. The practice of deposit transfer evolved by steps. Where a bank provided safekeeping services, depositors no doubt discovered cases in which party Alice planned to withdraw coins from the vault and laboriously transfer them to party Bob, who in turn planned to lug them back to the same vault and redeposit them. At the end of the day, the coins were back where they started, Alice's deposit balance had been reduced, and Bob's balance had been enlarged by the same amount. Only a little imagination was needed for Alice and Bob to recognize that an easier method of accomplishing this result would be for them to meet in the banker's office (in the coin-lugging method, both had to

---

[12] An intermediary is an institution that issues financial claims (debt or equity) against itself, and uses the proceeds to acquire financial claims on other agents. Because it is irredeemable and not a financial claim, fiat money is outside rather than inside money, and an institution that issues it (typically a central "bank") is not, in that respect, acting as an intermediary. The text's distinction between outside and inside money is different from the one used by Gurley and Shaw (1960).

go to there anyway) and there persuade the banker simply to transfer the desired amount of deposit balances *on his books*. Alice and Bob thereby avoid physical lugging around of coins, which simply stay in the vault. Early banking documents, studied by de Roover (1974a; 1974b), record such three-way meetings among payer, payee, and banker to authorize deposit transfers.

Later developments made transfers still easier to accomplish. Written slips for authorizing transfers made it unnecessary for both parties to travel to the banker's office. (In a checking system, Alice hands Bob a check, and only Bob goes to the bank, to deposit it; in a "giro" system, only Alice goes to the bank, to authorize the transfer into Bob's account.) Today, we see the growing use of *electronic* funds transfer, that is, methods of authorizing deposit transfers using electronic messages (sent using a telephone, home computer, automatic teller machine, or debit card and point-of-sale terminal) in place of slips of paper. These methods do not change the nature of the payment system as one of deposit transfer. The "front end" of the deposit transfer is different from writing a check, but not the "back end" (what happens on the bank's balance sheet). Nor – despite excited predictions that the future holds "a world without money" – do they threaten the definition, or real existence, of money. The depositor's bank balance, not the transfer-authorization device (e.g. the check), is money.

In addition to deposits, bank-issued claims in currency form were important historically, and may soon become important again. *Banknotes* are bank-issued claims to outside money that are not in any customer's name, but are payable to (redeemable by) whoever happens to be the bearer. Such bearer claims are transferable without the bank's knowledge or involvement – Alice simply hands them over to Bob – and can change hands repeatedly before being redeemed. Today some versions of "smart card" payments, namely those like Mondex which allow transfer of balances directly from card to card without the bank's knowledge or involvement, amount to the reintroduction of banknotes in digital form.

Banknotes may have evolved from the practice of making payment by signing over a deposit receipt or cashier's check. When such payments are foreseen, depositors could ask for deposit receipts in round denominations for convenience, and in bearer form, to streamline and certify the payment. Payment was streamlined because signing over is no longer necessary. It was certified in the sense that the bearer note is a claim against the bank only, and not against any account that might have insufficient funds, nor against any subsequent endorser. No one who accepts a banknote – unlike a deposit receipt that is successively signed over – needs to worry that the goodness of the claim depends on the funds of those who have previously held it, or that he or she might be called upon to make good on it for those who hold it subsequently. A banker is happy to comply with requests to issue such claims, as a way of increasing his circulation and profits. According to several accounts, this was the path by which goldsmith's deposit receipts historically evolved into banknotes (Usher 1943, Richards 1965).

The widespread use of banknotes historically preceded the widespread use of checking accounts (Bagehot 1873). For most British banks, note circulation exceeded deposits up to 1850. For banks in other countries, the date at which deposits began to exceed notes in circulation came even later. If banknotes evolved from deposit receipts, however, deposits on some scale must have preceded the use of banknotes.

Banknotes historically have paid no interest, even in competitive settings where deposits have, because there seems to be no easy way to pay interest on a bearer instrument whose convenience rests on its circulating at face value. In smart card payment systems thus far test-marketed, card balances similarly do not bear interest. The view that bank-issued bearer claims should be expected to bear interest in a competitive banking system will concern us in the last chapter of this book.

Regular Par Acceptance

Suppose a payments system has a common standard money, arrived at in the Mengerian way, with many banks issuing redeemable currency and deposit liabilities, but each bank refuses to accept any other bank's liabilities at par (face value). Bank-issued money then has limited marketability. This section argues that the profit motive, without legal compulsion, will move the banks toward par acceptance of one another's currency and deposits. An important side effect is the formation of an institution for interbank clearing and settlement of currency and deposit claims. The exposition refers explicitly to banknotes, both for convenience and for historical applicability to systems dominated by notes early on, but the argument applies just as well to par acceptance of deposit claims and digital currency.

An individual who has come into possession of a sum of notes issued by Bank X, and who wishes to deposit the sum into her account at Bank Y, has two options when Bank Y does not accept X-notes. She may bear the expense of taking the notes back to Bank X for redemption in outside money, or pay a fee to a note-changer (in the form of a discount on the X-notes and possibly a commission) who purchases the X-notes for outside money or Y-notes. Either option is naturally more expensive, the farther the noteholder is from a redemption site for the notes in question. Given these costs, X-notes are likely to circulate readily only in the vicinity of Bank X offices. Coin or other brands of notes will be preferred for transactions elsewhere.

In this situation, there are at least three logical scenarios whereby the pursuit of profit leads toward widespread par acceptance; Selgin and White (1987, pp. 225–33) discuss these scenarios and offer historical illustrations:

1 Banks as note-changers
2 Note dueling
3 Mutual par-acceptance packs

Banks as note-changers: Banks can out-compete non-bank note-changers because they have the advantage of being able to issue their own notes (or deposit balances) to purchase other banks' notes. Where a non-issuing note-changer must hold costly till money on the asset side of its balance sheet, an issuing bank can hold interest-earning assets, giving it a profit from "float" for as long as the notes issued remain in circulation. (The Suffolk Bank of Boston in the 1830s succeeded famously at this business.) By swapping Y-notes for X-notes, Bank Y can maintain a larger stock of its own notes in circulation. Where the transactions and redemption costs of note changing are low enough to be covered by the float profit from additional circulation, competition will bring the issuing banks' note-changing fee down to zero. That is, competition will bring the banks to practice par acceptance. (Bank Y would never offer to buy X-notes at a price above par, because the note-changing customer could make arbitrage profits by turning around and immediately redeeming the Y-notes issued.) If all banks are thus drawn into zero-fee note-changing, mutual par acceptance develops de facto.

Note dueling: Bank Y may accept, or even aggressively purchase, X-notes, and then, suddenly, return a large quantity to Bank X for redemption in reserve money, hoping to gain a greater share of the banking market by embarrassing its rival. The trouble with this tactic is that two can play it. Bank X can collect and redeem Y-notes, both to return the damage, and to replenish its own reserves. Vigorous pursuit of the tactic on both sides (known historically as "note dueling," and practiced for example by the first and second chartered banks in Scotland upon the entry of the second) may drive note-changing commissions to zero. In a repeated game of this sort, however, a non-aggressive "tit for tat" strategy (return an opponent's blows in kind, but meet cooperation with cooperation) should evolve (Axelrod 1984). When both sides practice note dueling, both find it ineffectual and expensive. Greater non-earning reserves must be held at all times to meet a rival's large redemption demands that may arrive at any time. If neither party can win the duel, both should eventually recognize that a regular, and amicable, exchange of collected notes would benefit both by allowing them to economize on reserves. Fees will nonetheless remain zero as a defensive measure, allowing each to collect enough rival notes to safeguard its reserves.

Mutual par-acceptance pacts: As the fee for buying Y-notes with X-notes falls, and *a fortiori* as it reaches zero (Bank *Y* offers commission-free par acceptance of *X*-notes), the cost of accepting *X*-notes falls and thus the circulation of *X*-notes grows relative to the circulation of outside money. This result is no part of the intention of Bank *Y* in the above scenarios, and may not be anticipated before the fact. (The Suffolk Bank was evidently surprised to find that by purchasing country bank notes at par, it was not vacuuming them from circulation but, in fact, encouraging their wider acceptance and use.) Bank *Y* aims only at an expanded circulation of its own notes, which indeed is also a result. Banks that accept other banks' notes at par improve the circulation both of their own notes, and of the notes they accept. If two banks both recognize *ex ante* the availability of these circulation gains from mutual par acceptance, they may explicitly enter a pact to accept one another's notes at par. Par-acceptance pacts among pairs of provincial Scottish banks provide historical examples of such agreements. Acceptance at par in a wider area increases the marketability of each brand of notes, and thereby the quantity willingly held by the public. The same logic explains the recent spread in the USA and elsewhere, of agreements among banks to form networks of mutual acceptance for cards giving access to automatic teller machine services. By participating in an ATM network, a bank improves the accessibility of its own deposits, and thereby attracts more depositors.

Par acceptance, developed through any of these routes, is generally more profitable, the wider its scope. The potential gains are not exhausted until all reputable banks practice par acceptance toward all others. Thus every bank's liabilities come to circulate at par throughout an economic region. The boundaries of the region will lie where the circulation-enhancing benefits of membership (presumably declining at the geographic margin as distance from the financial center increases) become equal to the transaction, transportation, and administrative costs of membership (presumably rising at the margin). As transaction and transportation costs secularly fall, the par-acceptance region expands. Par circulation of notes became nationwide with the spread of railroads in the nineteenth century. ATM networks are rapidly becoming global today.

Clearing Arrangements

Following any of these scenarios, Bank *Y* will be collecting *X*-notes, and Bank *X* will be collecting *Y*-notes, during the course of the business week. Each bank will want to redeem the collected notes, rather than to pay them back out again (as the whole profitability of the arrangement comes from placing and maintaining more of its *own* notes into circulation) or to accumulate them indefinitely (reserve money is more useful, and no more costly to hold). A regular meeting for bilateral redemption, where X-notes are traded for Y-notes and the difference settled in reserve money, or some agreed substitute, will be arranged when the banks find that it is cheaper than unilateral or irregular redemption.

The practice of regular bilateral redemption may emerge without the banks' management planning it. If note-porters are sent from each bank to redeem at the other bank's counter, and they happen to meet, it should readily occur to them that an exchange of notes would save them time and the effort of lugging a great deal of gold (all but the difference) back home. They will arrange to meet regularly at a specified time and place to exchange notes. Bank management will endorse the arrangement not only because it saves transportation costs, but also because bilateral netting (using Bank Y's claims against Bank X to offset Bank X's claims against Bank Y) allows smaller reserves to be held.

The gains in going from unilateral to bilateral note-exchange are further extended in going to multi-lateral exchange in a system of more than a few issuers. Time and transportation costs are further economized by having one all-encompassing meeting rather than numerous pairwise meetings, and the holding of reserves can be further reduced with multilateral netting of claims that in pairwise clearing would have to be settled in reserve money. Multilateral exchange may evolve from bilateral exchange in the same way that bilateral exchange evolves from unilateral exchange. The note-exchange agent for Bank X, having concluded his or her regular exchange session at Bank Y, may happen to meet the agent for Bank Z arriving for his or her meeting at Bank Y. There are the economies just mentioned in combining the two meetings, and absorbing as well the regular pairwise meeting between X and Z agents. (The London note-exchange reportedly grew out of such note-porters' meetings in pubs.) Unified computation, and settlement of combined net clearing balances, can economically replace three bilateral exchanges.

Other banks may be invited to join the clearing sessions subsequently, either individually or through combination with a similar multi-sided clearing group. Eventually, all reputable banks within the par-acceptance region will be linked through a single clearinghouse, or through a small number of subregional clearinghouses that regularly clear against one another. The development of clearing arrangements in Edinburgh, London, and New York all conform to this general pattern. The final outcome – a unified clearing system encompassing all banks – is not part of any bank's initial design. Each aims only at increasing the market for its own liabilities, and at economizing on redemption and reserve-holding costs. Systemwide par acceptance, and its embodiment in the clearinghouse, in this sense, represent a spontaneous institutional order.

The simplest and initial way of settling interbank clearing balances is through the physical transfer of outside money at the end of the clearing session. Echoing the original development of deposit-transfer banks to provide payments more cheaply between bank customers like Alice and Bob, the banks may find it economical to make interbank payments by means of a banker's bank. They can settle up by transferring claims to outside money held in the clearinghouse vault rather than by physically carting outside money around. Clearinghouse association (CHA) banks in US cities in the nineteenth century issued claims in the form of paper certificates to be used for interbank settlements. Other CHAs have used clearinghouse deposits for the same purpose.

Historically, CHAs have been known to take on functions additional to their core function of economically clearing and settling claims among banks. One is the sharing of information on loan defaulters, passers of bad checks, and the like. More significant are certain "hierarchical" functions associated with policing the soundness of member banks. Chapter 4 discusses the possible connection between such functions and the emergence of central banking.

The Path to Fiat Money

At this point, we can take stock of the spontaneously or "naturally" developed monetary system so far described. The definitive money is specie. Except in interbank settlements, transactors commonly make payments using bank-issued currency and transferable deposits. A specie unit is the unit of account. Bank-issued money is denominated in the specie unit, and is widely accepted at par. All banks are linked into a unified system by one or more clearinghouses. These outcomes are not purely theoretical, but could be seen historically in banking systems that were free of significant legal restrictions.[13]

Is there a spontaneous or market-driven path from this system to the non-commodity, or fiat, standards that prevails today? No. If any single bank in the system were unilaterally to stop redeeming, it would have breached its contracts with its customers. If it were to announce in advance that it would stop redeeming next month, holders of its notes and deposits would redeem them all before next month, and would take their business elsewhere. (Alternatively, if the bank tried to replace ordinary open-ended notes and deposits with new liabilities whose redeemability was scheduled to expire on a specified date, nobody would take the liabilities as the date approached.) The other banks and the public would reject the irredeemable liabilities because without redeemability at par for specie, there would be no assurance of continued par value in terms of the specie unit of account. (Chapter 12 considers the question of private irredeemable money in more detail.)

---

[13] See Dowd (1992b) for case studies.

The forces that lead to convergence on a common monetary standard, as in Menger's account, continue to operate once a standard is reached. Nobody wants to make trading harder by offering or accepting only a non-standard money, different from that routinely accepted and offered by others. Consequently, nobody would want to go first in switching to a completely novel monetary standard, even if he were persuaded that, in theory, it would work better supposing that *everyone* switched. (The policy implications of this phenomenon are discussed in chapter 5). If nobody goes first, the switch never occurs.

If all the banks, together, could coordinate a simultaneous switchover to a fiat standard (a very big "if," but banks did coordinate the beginnings and ends of temporary systemwide suspensions of payments during a few of the nineteenth-century US banking panics) the new standard might stick. However, it is not clear what market forces would compel banks to want to make such a move. Also, if it meant breaching pre-existing redemption contracts (as suspensions of payments historically did), it would not be a voluntary switch by the users of money.

In historical practice, a nation's switch to fiat money was typically made by the central government first granting a legal monopoly of note-issue to a single institution, a central bank, whose liabilities became as widely accepted as specie, and displaced specie as the reserves for other banks. The government then suspended, permanently, the redemption of the central bank's liabilities. With their permanent suspension, central bank notes and deposits became a fiat base money. The fiat-money unit correspondingly became the unit of account. Typically, the central bank for continuity's sake retained the old specie unit name (e.g. "dollar"), which was printed on the notes in circulation at the moment of suspension, while severing its specie definition. The now-irredeemable notes can continue to circulate because they are familiar, and the practice of continuing to accept them is self-reinforcing: it is not in any one trader's self-interest to refuse them if she expects others to continue accepting them.[14]

Thus, fiat money is possible where paper banknotes had previously gained

---

[14] In addition, the government can reinforce their continued acceptance by making the now-irredeemable central bank liabilities

   1 *publicly receivable* – taking them for tax payments and for purchases from state enterprises;

   2 *legal tender* for payment of old debts contracted in the unit of account;

   3 *forced tender* in all domestic exchanges, including spot transactions that traders would rather conduct in another currency and repayment of old debts specifically denominated in metallic units.

As a final step, the government can, as the US government did, require the public to turn in its specie.

common acceptance as redeemable notes.[15] Likewise, to launch a new fiat money today (for example, in former Soviet republics), it must at first be made redeemable for the prevailing money (the ruble). Selgin (1994a) likens initial redeemability to a "launching vehicle" that can fall away once the new currency gets into orbit.

Spontaneous Separation between the Media of Redemption and Account?

A few authors, in recent years, have argued that the story of market monetary evolution should not end with banks operating on a silver or gold standard. Absent legal restrictions, Kevin Dowd (1996, pp. 14–18) argues that the next logical market-driven steps would be:

1 a discontinuation of direct redemption for precious metal, and
2 a switching over of the medium of account to a multi-commodity standard.[16]

Dowd's scenario for the discontinuation of direct redemption runs as follows. Once the stage is reached where gold coins no longer commonly circulate, because everyone prefers to use bank-issued money for all transactions, the public will no longer care about having the option to redeem for gold as such. Because a bank can pay its depositors a higher return by replacing all its non-interest-bearing gold reserves with interest-bearing assets, competition would compel banks to make the switch, and, correspondingly, to offer redemption in equivalent financial assets rather than gold itself (call this "indirect redemption"). At this juncture, a weight of gold would still define the unit of account, but gold would no longer serve as the medium of redemption. If, for example, one "dollar" is one-twentieth of a Troy ounce of gold, the holder of a $100 banknote could redeem it for financial assets (perhaps blue-chip bonds or equity shares) equivalent at market prices to five ounces of gold. Ounces-worth or "indirect" redeemability,

[15] Two historical cases are instructive here. When the Bank of England suspended payments from 1797 to 1819, Northern Ireland remained on a specie standard because banknotes did not yet commonly circulate there. For the same reason, California remained on a specie standard while the rest of the Union went on to an irredeemable "greenback" dollar standard during the American Civil War.
[16] Cowen and Kroszner (1994, pp. 38–44), using quite a different argument, imagine evolution toward a variety of parallel standards. Greenfield and Yeager (1983) propose a multi-commodity standard, but do not claim that spontaneous market forces are enough to ensure its adoption.

like direct redeemability, satisfies the customer's demand for contractual assurance of the value of bank-issued money. Though the typical retail customer might never exercise the new redemption option, just as he or she had come never to exercise the old, the option maintains an avenue for arbitrage. It keeps the market price of gold, quoted in any particular brand of dollar-denominated banknotes and deposits, tied to the definitional gold content of the dollar.

Is this scenario convincing? There is historical evidence that, in a gold-standard country with a sophisticated banking system, the use of gold coins as a hand-to-hand medium of exchange has indeed tended to diminish substantially. There is certainly evidence that banks take steps to economize on their holdings of non-interest-bearing reserves. Dowd (1989, p. 155) cites the case of the nineteenth-century Scottish banks whose customers were often (which is not the same as *always*) satisfied to redeem their liabilities for drafts on London correspondent banks (presumably because they had payments to make in London) rather than gold. Those Scottish banks could hold much (which is not the same as *all*) of their reserves in the form of interest-bearing accounts in London. The case suggests that, if customers and their banks sometimes mutually prefer redemption in something other than gold coins, then a competitive bank would offer its customers that option *in addition* to gold redemption.

There are, however, no known historical cases where competition led banks to reduce their gold reserves literally to *zero,* and to remove entirely the option of direct redemption in the medium of account from their banknote and deposit contracts. Thus, we have little reason to be confident that the public would, in fact, welcome the elimination of direct redemption. At the gold reserve ratios observed historically in the most sophisticated banking systems (2 percent and less), only *very* small increases in deposit yields are available by reducing reserves the rest of the way to zero. Unless the option of demanding gold rather than financial assets were completely valueless, it is doubtful that the public would welcome the final reduction of reserves to zero, and the complete elimination of the direct redemption option from bank liabilities.

The heaviest users of the redemption option are not retail bank customers, but the banks themselves: every day, banks redeem huge volumes of claims on one another at the clearinghouse. Whether direct redemption would spontaneously disappear thus depends on whether banks themselves would welcome the switch by their clearing partners, and would agree to accept settlement in financial assets (bonds or equity shares) rather than in the medium of account (e.g. gold or clearinghouse claims directly redeemable at par for gold). As noted above, banks historically found it convenient to settle net clearing balances by transferring claims to precious metal, kept in the clearinghouse vault, rather than by physically carting bullion, or bags of coins, to and fro. However, there are no known historical cases where member banks agreed to reduce the clearinghouse's vault cash to zero, and to settle in clearinghouse claims that were not directly redeemable for outside money.[17] A straightforward explanation is that no historical clearinghouse in a gold-standard banking system could do without gold reserves because its members had to be prepared to pay gold to the rest of the world. No clearinghouse embraced all the banks in the world, and gold remained the medium of settlement between banking systems.[18] A move to indirect redemption is conceivable only for the clearinghouse of a closed economy, which in the world of an international gold standard means a global clearinghouse.

Members of a clearinghouse might agree to have it hold fractional reserves, so that their clearing account balances could bear interest. (The New York Clearinghouse in the nineteenth century, however, typically held 100 percent reserves.) This does not imply an end to direct redeemability, or settlement with financial assets. The convention of settling in one of the two traditional ways, either by transferring physical units of outside money, or by transferring directly redeemable (and hence par-valued) clearin house claims to outside money, reduces transaction costs because it transfers a single homogenous asset with an unambiguous unit-of-account value. All parties can agree that a $10,000 clearing balance is settled with $10,000 in full-bodied coins or a claim redeemable at the clearinghouse for $10,000 in coins. An imagined system of settling with financial assets, by contrast, appears to face banks with the problem of continually negotiating agreements about *which specific assets* are acceptable, and for each asset *at what price* within the interval bounded by the asset's current bid and ask prices (which prices would have to be continuous tracked in a system of continuous settlement). It does not appear that these agreements could simply be reached once for all time, because the set of financial assets available is continually changing. Even items within the set change in their characteristics. In the bond market, for example, new bonds are being issued, old bonds are being retired, extant bonds are shrinking in duration and, hence, in interest-rate risk as they approach maturity, the default

---

[17] Dowd (1989, p. 96) wishes to attribute the non-realization of his scenario to state intervention, but it is not clear that private clearinghouse associations were everywhere prohibited from taking such a step.

[18] Describing the international payments system in the early part of the twentieth century, Ludwig von Mises (1980, pp. 325–6) observed that although "the clearing system has without difficulty transcursed political boundaries and created for itself a world-embracing organization in the international bill and check system," there were still no bank-issued payment media "that are recognized internationally and consequently able to take the place of [metallic] money in international trade for settling the balances that remain over after the clearing process." The absence of global branch banking and globally accepted bank liabilities was, of course, at least partly due to legal restrictions.

risk associated with particular issuers is varying, and the liquidity of particular securities (as indicated by the size of their bid-ask spreads) is changing.[19]

Dowd's scenario for the spontaneous mutation of the medium of account runs as follows. So long as the unit of account is defined as a fixed weight of gold, the price level is subject to disturbance by supply and demand shocks in the market for gold. (This feature of a gold standard is analyzed in chapter 2). "A time would therefore come when the banks would decide to reduce price-level instability" by replacing gold with a medium of account "with a more stable relative price," most likely consisting of "a basket of goods and services" (Dowd 1996, p. 16).[20] The banks would arrange to act in unison. The public would go along because they prefer greater price level stability.

The question poses itself in this case as well: if this unit-of-account switch is a move worth making, why have banks and clearinghouses historically avoided it? One explanation, parallel to the previous discussion, is that no historical clearinghouse found it advantageous to switch its medium of account while the rest of the world stayed on gold. If no single clearinghouse (or its members' customers) would wish to "float" against the rest of the world, then a move to the new regime – from the status quo of an international gold standard – is again conceivable only for a global clearinghouse. Chapter 5 below discusses in more detail the idea that no one finds it worthwhile to switch the unit of account unless everyone switches together.

It is not necessary to switch the unit of account, however, for a bank or clearinghouse to insulate the value of its liabilities from changes in the relative price of gold: it could index its redemption rate. To allow continuous adjustment of the redemption rate, the indexation could be to the price of a basket of standardized commodities continuously traded on organized exchanges.[21] The question becomes, then, why did banks and clearinghouses on the gold standard avoid indexation of their liabilities? (White 1990, p.

---

[19] Why wouldn't it be enough for the banks simply to agree once-for-all to accept settlement only in *default-risk-free* securities, like present-day US Treasury bills? First, default risk is not the only relevant risk for banks holding bonds. Second, under a commodity standard, there simply are no default-risk-free bonds. Under a gold standard, for example, no government can print up gold to repay its gold-denominated bonds. In this respect, the euro standard acts like a commodity standard: no participating national government can issue default-risk-free bonds denominated in euros, because no nation can print euros to redeem its bonds. (Only the European Central Bank can print euros.)

[20] This switch in the medium of account could, in principle, be made whether the banks practiced direct or indirect redemption. With the banks practicing direct redemption in gold, it amounts to switching from an unindexed to an indexed redemption rate. With indirect redemption, the banks would already be indexing the redemption rate in financial assets to the gold price of the assets; now they would switch to indexing in the basket price.

[21] This sort of indexation is discussed at greater length in chapter 12, in connection with the reform proposal of Greenfield and Yeager (1983).

197) Perhaps the theory of indexation and the organization of commodity exchanges were simply not developed enough by the time the gold standard was ended by other means. Or, perhaps indexation would not have been worth the bother because the instability of the relative price of gold (when gold is money) is not much greater than that of any feasible index basket that allows for continuous tracking.

Questions

1   Once traders begin using indirect exchange, why do they tend to converge on a single good as the commonly accepted medium of exchange? Could they converge on two or three goods?

2   If all goods were equally salable, would money still emerge out of barter?

3   Why did commodity monies, rather than fiat monies, historically emerge out of barter economies?

4   Consider a system where gold coins are the commonly accepted medium of exchange. Absent legal restrictions, would private issuers have incentives enough to establish a *uniform* monetary standard? Or, would a variety of coins, of different weights and finesses, circulate?

5   Why have traders, historically, often preferred to use claims on banks (like banknotes and checks) even though the claims might be dishonored, rather than precious-metal coins?

6   Why has the unit of account typically been some quantity of the commonly accepted medium of exchange?

7   J. Huston McCulloch (1982, pp. 6–7) has argued that "the development of money is very similar to the development of language." There is a tendency, in any society, for *one* verbal utterance to be singled out as *the* spoken word for "fire," but it is "fundamentally arbitrary which grunt or series of noises" people adopt for that purpose. Likewise, there is a tendency for one commodity to be singled out as *the* common medium of exchange, but "which commodity is singled out is largely a historical accident." In what respects do you agree, in what respects do you disagree, and why? Cite theoretical, and historical, support for your position.

8   "As the supply of metals in the world has repeatedly been insufficient to meet the increasing need for money, the use of paper [currency] has spread." (Cribb 1986) Do you agree or disagree with Cribb's explanation for the historical shift from coins to banknotes? Explain why.

9   John Browning and Spencer Reiss (1998) define "feedback, positive" as "success that breeds success" and elaborate:

Positive-feedback loops create a winner-take-all world: whoever or whatever starts ahead gets further and further ahead. . . . Incumbents literally own their markets. . . . Once a positive-feedback loop does kick in, the result can be awesome concentrations of economic power. Bill Gates once explained it this way, talking about Windows: "Momentum creates momentum. If you have volume, then people write apps. If people write apps, you have momentum." And if it goes on long enough, you have $40 billion.

(a)   Is Menger's theory of the origin of commodity money a story about a positive-feedback loop? How or how not?

(b)   Does convergence to a common commodity money standard lead to an incumbent owning the market, or to a concentration of economic power? How or how not?

2

Commodity Money

Chapter 1 noted that the earliest money must have been a useful commodity. It ascribed the historical predominance of gold and silver over other commodity monies to their being both widely salable and having characteristics that made them particularly convenient (especially after the development of coinage) for use as hand-to-hand media of exchange. Even after the development of bank-issued money, and its displacement of coinage in most retail transactions, gold or silver remained the medium of redemption: the basic money in terms of which bank-issued money is denominated and redeemable.

This chapter considers the operating characteristics of a commodity standard (or commodity money regime), in particular how it determines the quantity and value of money. We generically define a commodity standard as a system in which money is meaningfully denominated in units of a useful good (or set of goods). A piece of money may be "full-bodied" and materially contain the money commodity, as a silver coin does under a silver standard. Or, it may be a claim denominated in, and redeemable for, a specified quantity and form of the commodity, for example a banknote or deposit redeemable for silver coin. A "useful good" (or "commodity") here means a good that is scarce, and in demand for non-monetary uses. Silver, to continue the example, has a positive market value even in economies where it plays no monetary role. A fiat money, by contrast, is useless outside its monetary role.

Note that, under the generic definition, a commodity standard does not require that the public actually carry full-bodied commodity money in their pockets and purses. The public might hold all its money in the form of redeemable claims (token coins, banknotes, and transferable deposits), with all full-bodied commodity money residing in bank vaults. Note also that nothing in the definition, contrary to some alternative suggestions, refers particularly to what a central bank or any other government agency is prepared to do. It is not *generically* true that "a gold standard means that the central bank is prepared to buy and sell gold at a fixed price" (Schwartz 1986) or that "the pledge [of 'the monetary authorities'] to fix the price of a country's currency in terms of gold represents the basic rule of the gold standard" (Bordo 1993, p. 160). Gold standards in the generic sense – monetary systems using gold and gold-denominated claims – antedated central banking by centuries. A central bank (whose roles are discussed in chapter 4) is thus not necessary for a gold standard to exist. (And if a central bank *does* happen to be part of a gold standard, its transactions are better described as redeeming its own gold-denominated currency, than as "fixing the price of gold" or "fixing the price of domestic currency.")

For the sake of concreteness, the remainder of this chapter will speak in terms of a particular type of commodity money regime, namely a gold coin standard. (The same analysis would apply exactly to a silver coin standard, and would apply in most respects to a non-metallic commodity standard.) For analytical simplicity, we assume that the principle of unrestricted coinage applies, and that the coinage process is zero-priced. Anyone can bring as much gold as he likes to the mint (which may be a zero-cost competitive firm, or a state-owned institution) to be coined without charge. Existing coins may be melted down without cost or restriction. Under these conditions, gold can flow between monetary and non-monetary use unhindered, exactly equalizing its purchasing power in the two sectors.

Determining the Price Level

If money were denominated and prices quoted in troy ounces of gold, the unit in which gold is today ordinarily measured, the "price level", would simply be the price of a representative basket of goods in troy ounces of gold. In practice, there is usually a small complication. The monetary unit (or unit of account) has a distinct name, defined in terms of the money commodity (the "medium of account"). For example, the US economy, before 1933, used a unit of account called "the dollar," defined as .04838 troy oz. (or equivalently 23.22 grains) of gold, 90 percent fine.

With prices denominated in dollars, and dollars defined in terms of gold, the price level P in dollars is the product of two factors:

1   the gold content of the dollar, and
2   the purchasing power of gold in terms of the goods in the price index basket, or, equivalently, the relative price of the index-basket goods in terms of gold.

Where P denotes the number of dollars it takes to buy a representative basket of goods, we can decompose P into the product of two ratios as follows:

$$\frac{\$P}{\text{basket of goods}} = \left(\frac{\$Q}{\text{oz Au}}\right) \times \left(\frac{R \text{ oz Au}}{\text{basket of goods}}\right)$$

where $P = QR$.

In this expression, the ratio $\$Q$ / oz Au is the definition of the dollar in terms of gold (chemical symbol, Au). To return to the example cited above, the pre-1933 definition of the dollar, \$1 per .04838 troy oz Au, was equivalent to \$20.67 per troy oz Au (so $Q = 20.67$). A figure like .04838 oz of gold (per dollar) can be called "the gold content of the dollar." A figure like \$20.67 (per oz Au) is sometimes called the "official price of gold," a potentially misleading expression. The figure in question isn't a market price ratio between two distinct goods, but simply follows mathematically from defining one "dollar" as a certain weight of gold. Unlike a price, the figure does not vary with supply and demand conditions.[1]

The ratio R oz Au/basket of goods is the inverse of the *purchasing power of gold*, hereafter abbreviated ppg. (The ppg is measured in baskets of goods per ounce of gold.) This *is* a market price ratio, the relative price of gold in terms of goods-baskets. It *is* a figure that changes with supply and demand conditions in the market for gold.

We assume for the rest of this chapter that the definition of the monetary unit in terms of gold (Q) does not change. It remains fixed by convention or law.[2] Our analysis accordingly focuses on the determination of the purchasing power of gold ($1/R$) by supply and demand. Events that increase the ppg must lower P in the same proportion; events that reduce the ppg, raise P in the same proportion.

The Simple Stock-flow Analytics of Gold Supply and Demand

For now we begin (and end) our thought-experiments in the benchmark position of *stationary equilibrium*, defined as an equilibrium in which the

---

[1] Nor need it be "official" in the sense of being sanctioned by any authority other than common usage or convention.

[2] Nothing of consequence depends on the specific definition; i.e. on the particular metallic weight of the unit of account ("the dollar") provided it does not change. Changes in the weight can have important transitional effects. A unilateral reduction of the dollar's weight (a devaluation of the dollar), combined with a legal rule that old debts can be discharged in an unchanged number of dollars, would cause a redistribution of wealth from creditors to debtors.

relative price and stock of gold are both constant over time, with neither demand nor supply curves shifting. Later, we consider non-stationary equilibrium growth paths. We focus on the gold standard economy as a whole, which may comprise many countries or the entire world, rather than on any small country taken by itself. For the world as a whole, additions to the total stock of gold (monetary plus non-monetary) can only come from gold mining.

We need to distinguish between the market for gold *flows* and the market for gold *stocks*. Flows of gold, such as the current rate of production of the gold mining industry, are measured in ounces per year. Gold stocks, like the quantity of monetary gold existing on a given date, are measured in ounces without a per-time-period dimension. In this chapter, lower-case italic letters are used to denote flow variables, upper-case italic letters to denote stock variables.

Flow equilibrium, e, is shown in figure. 2.1(a) by the intersection of flow demand and supply curves. The flow demand for gold is the total of *consumptive* demands for gold, i.e. demands that "use up" gold, or fix it permanently in non-monetary forms. The flow quantity of gold demanded, g^d, is a decreasing function of the relative price (or purchasing power) of gold, and the demand curve is thus downward sloping, for the standard reasons that demand curves are generally downward sloping. The higher is the ppg, the greater the incentive to substitute into alternative materials, and, so, the fewer the ounces of gold demanded each year for consumptive purposes.

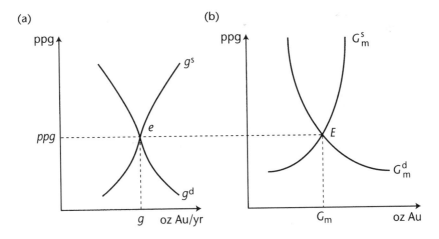

Figure 2.1   Stationary equilibrium in the markets for gold: (a) the market for gold flows is in equilibrium; (b) the market for monetary gold stocks is in equilibrium

For simplicity, we initially assume that the stationary flow demand for gold is entirely *non-monetary*. That is, we neglect wear-and-tear on gold bullion and coins. This is reasonable enough if all gold bars and coins reside in bank vaults, with bank-issued money forming the common circulating media.

The flow quantity supplied, g^s, is an increasing function of the ppg, and thus the supply curve is upward sloping, for the standard reasons supply curves are generally upward sloping. At a higher ppg, more ounces will be mined each year, as mine-owners find it profitable to dig deeper into gold veins, and to schedule longer working days.

Stock equilibrium, E, is shown in figure 2.1(b) by the intersection of monetary stock demand and supply curves. The monetary stock demand for gold represents demands by banks and the public to hold gold in monetary forms (coins or bullion). The stock quantity of monetary gold demanded, G_m^d, is a decreasing function of the ppg because (proportionately) fewer ounces are needed to accomplish transactions when ppg is higher.[3]

The stock quantity of monetary gold supplied, G_m^s, is assumed to be an increasing function of ppg, and thus the stock monetary supply curve is upward sloping (not vertical). The stock quantity supplied for monetary holdings is simply the difference between the total stock of gold (which is fixed at any moment), and the stock quantity demanded for non-monetary purposes. A downward-sloping demand curve for non-monetary gold items (such as candlesticks and jewelry) implies an upward-sloping supply curve for monetary gold. An increasing number of candlesticks and bracelets will be melted down and coined as the opportunity cost of holding them – the purchasing power of gold – rises.

Two peculiar features of our stationary equilibrium benchmark should be noted.

1   Under the assumption of zero wear-and-tear on monetary gold, the flow of gold into the mints must also be zero in stationary equilibrium. Otherwise, the stock of monetary gold would be increasing. The mints must be standing by idly, waiting for the next occasion of a temporary disequilibrium in which there is an excess flow supply to be coined.

---

[3] Proportionality is shown by drawing the monetary stock demand for gold curve as a rectangular hyperbola. The demand curve thus drawn is a compensated demand curve, or per Patinkin (1965, pp. 48–50) a "market-equilibrium curve," which assumes that an individual hypothetically confronted with higher prices is simultaneously given an equiproportional increase in nominal money balances. No result in this chapter rests on proportionality, however.

2   If there are *no* consumptive uses of gold – if every industrial use merely augments the total stock of non-monetary gold that is available to be melted down at negligible cost and coined – then any volume of gold mining increases the total stock of gold, and shifts the monetary stock supply curve to the right. In that case, no stationary equilibrium is possible, except where the gold mines also shut down. While it may be chemically true that gold atoms are preserved and not lost in every industrial use of gold, what matters here is whether the cost of conversion of gold from industrial uses to coins is negligible. If some gold is fixed into forms (e.g. fillings or circuit boards) from which it can be recovered only at a cost that will never in practice be worth bearing, that is economically equivalent to consumption. Additions to that part of the total gold stock shift only that part of the monetary stock supply curve that lies above the relevant range.

Let us now consider how the system responds, in the short run and in the long run, to simple supply and demand shocks.

Shifts in the monetary gold stock demand and supply curves

Beginning from a stationary stock-flow equilibrium, suppose that the monetary stock demand for gold increases. A large and sudden increase of this sort would occur when a large country joins the international gold standard, and goes about acquiring an inventory of monetary gold. A smaller, or more gradual, shift would occur with an increase in the real income of the gold-standard countries.

Graphically (see figure 2.2), the monetary stock demand curve shifts out from $G^d_{m_0}$ to $G^d_{m_1}$. Assuming that the ppg is proximately determined in the monetary stock market (rather than in the flow market), short-run equilibrium moves from E_0 to E_1, and the ppg rises immediately from ppg_0 to ppg_1. The only immediate response in monetary stock quantity supplied comes from converting non-monetary stocks of gold (melting down candlesticks and coining them). However, the monetary stock market is not in stationary equilibrium at E_1, because increased mining and reduced consumption of gold will lead, over time, to an accumulation of additional monetary gold stocks.

Over in the flow market, the higher value of gold at ppg_1 increases the flow quantity of gold supplied by the mines. The mining industry moves up the flow supply curve (g^s), from flow equilibrium point e_0 to the new short-run supply point e^s_1. Meanwhile, with the ppg higher, the flow quantity demanded for non-monetary (consumptive) purposes retreats up the g^d curve

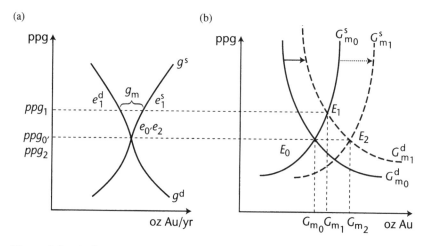

Figure 2.2   An increase in the monetary demand for gold: first, the stock demand for monetary gold increases – shown by the solid arrow in (b) – raising the ppg in the short run; then, – see (a) – the rise in the ppg increases the flow quantity supplied of gold from the mines, and reduces consumptive flow quantity demanded and the difference, g_m, flows into coinage each period; the accumulation of new coins over time gradually increases the stock of monetary gold – shown by the dashed arrow in (b) – so that, in the long run, stationary equilibrium is restored at the original ppg – as shown in both (a) and (b)

to e_1^d. The flow quantity supplied at ppg_1 exceeds the flow quantity demanded for consumptive purposes.

Where does the excess gold flow go? Assuming unrestricted coinage, mine-owners will take it to the mints to be coined, converting it directly into money. Mine-owners can obtain the value ppg_1 for their gold by coining and spending it, whereas additional sales to consumptive demanders are no longer possible except at a lower price. Gold flows into the mints at the rate shown graphically as g_m.

As a result of the new mint activity, the stock of monetary gold, G_m, begins to grow over time. As new coins accumulate, the monetary stock supply curve shifts gradually rightward, as shown in the shift from $G_{m_0}^s$ to $G_{m_1}^s$ in figure 2.2 (b). (The *gradual* shift is indicated by the *dotted* arrow.) As the monetary stock supply curve shifts rightward, monetary stock equilibrium moves from E_1 toward E_2. The ppg falls, from ppg_1 toward ppg_2. The stock of monetary gold G_m grows from G_{m_1} toward G_{m_2}. Where does the accumulation process end? Stationary equilibrium is restored only when the ppg reaches a level (call it ppg_2) that once again shuts off the flow of gold to the mints. Under the *ceteris paribus* assumption that there have been no shifts in the flow supply or demand curves, the purchasing power and annual volume of gold flow must return exactly to where they started: equilibrium points e_2 and e_0 coincide, and $ppg_2 = ppg_0$.

In this scenario, because the flow and stock quantities of gold supplied respond to the increase in the purchasing power of gold, the short-run change in the ppg (from ppg_0 to ppg_1) is fully reversed in the long run. A price-elastic supply of gold thus dampens changes in the ppg (and thus in the price level) due to monetary demand shifts. Ultimately, the demand shift is met entirely by an adjustment in the quantity and not in the purchasing power of gold. This result illustrates the *price-level-stabilizing property* of a gold standard that is often cited as a virtue by its proponents.

There are at least two ways of modifying the assumptions of the case just illustrated that would interfere with the exact restoration of the original ppg_0.

1   If we allow for an annual flow demand to replace wear-and-tear on monetary gold, equal to some percentage (say 2 percent) of the stock of monetary gold, then the starting and ending flow equilibria and will no longer exactly coincide ppg_0 ppg_2. Because the monetary gold stock is larger at stock equilibrium E_2, the flow demand curve g^d would be shifted somewhat to the right, and the new stationary equilibrium would imply a ppg_2 somewhat higher than ppg_0.

2   If gold mining is subject to a depletion effect, then the cost of gold mining rises with the total number of ounces previously mined. Mine-owners first dig up the gold deposits that are easier to reach, and leave for later those that are harder to reach. A depletion effect by itself pulls the flow supply curve leftward a bit each period, putting the ppg on an upward secular path. We can imagine a stationary equilibrium economy in which the net movement in the flow supply curve for gold is zero, because the depletion effect is just offset each period by technical advances in gold mining and extraction, or by a series of new prospecting discoveries. In such an economy, a monetary demand shock that increases the volume of mining would accelerate depletion, and shift the flow supply curve g^s to the left on net. Again, ppg_2 would be somewhat higher than ppg_0.[4]

In arriving at his well-known estimate of the resource cost of a commodity standard, Milton Friedman (1953 and 1960) considers a case in which neither of these complications obtains. Thus the long-run path of the ppg remains flat in the face of ongoing steady growth in the monetary demand for gold. As G_m^d shifts out, annual gold mining shifts G_m^s out just enough to

---

[4] For numerical simulations of the impact of a depletion effect, see Bordo and Ellson (1985).

maintain a constant ppg. The constant ppg continues to generate the same
amount of mining every period. This case is further discussed and illustrated below.

A *decrease* in the monetary stock demand for gold – due for example to a
large country leaving the gold standard and shedding its monetary gold
stocks, or banks switching to lower reserve ratios – sets an exactly contrary
chain of events in motion. The purchasing power of gold falls. Graphically,
the monetary stock demand curve shifts to the left, moving the equilibrium
point down the monetary stock supply curve. (In figure 2.2b, letting E_2 represent the initial stationary equilibrium, and assuming the demand curve
shifts from $G^d_{m_1}$ to $G^d_{m_0}$, the new short-run equilibrium is at the unlabelled
intersection of $G^d_{m_0}$ and supply curve $G^s_{m_1}$.) The stock of monetary gold
immediately shrinks somewhat, because the lower relative price of gold
increases the stock demand for non-monetary gold. Money-holders melt
down some of their existing coins because they can now own gold jewelry
and candlesticks at a lower cost.

In the flow market, the lower ppg causes an increase in the volume of
consumptive demand for gold, and a fall in the output of the mines, such
that a *negative* flow of gold into coinage arises. That is, while the ppg is
depressed, each year the flow demand for gold will consume not only the
entire output of the mines but also some portion of the existing stock of
coins and monetary bullion, further shrinking the stock of monetary gold.
The monetary stock supply curve gradually shifts to the *left* over time, as
monetary gold *de*cumulates. The shrinkage helps to bring the purchasing
power of gold back up, and continues (absent wear-and-tear and depletion
effects) until the original ppg is restored. (In figure 2.2b, long-run equilibrium would be reached at E_0.)

In these scenarios, the movement of the monetary stock supply curve is
gradual, and is the endogenous result of the flow-market effects of movement in the ppg. A sudden and exogenous shift in the stock supply curve is
somewhat harder to imagine. The plot of the film *Goldfinger* provides one
fanciful example: Goldfinger plans to set off a thermonuclear device in Fort
Knox to render the gold there useless by radioactive contamination. If we
assume that nuking the gold is the equivalent of making it disappear, we can
treat the event as a sudden leftward shift in the stock supply curve, and
proceed as we did in analyzing demand shifts. (The graphics are left as an
exercise to the reader.) As Goldfinger intends, the nuking would indeed
drive up the value of his own gold stocks. In the long run, however, the
higher ppg would encourage extra gold mining, and discourage gold consumption, enough to eventually re-accumulate the lost gold and reverse the
effect on the ppg. The final stationary equilibrium position would coincide
exactly with the initial position. Absent depletion effects, Goldfinger's plan
is pointless in the long run.

Precisely the opposite effects would be produced by an event from classical mythology: a sudden one-time shower of gold coins from heaven. The ppg would drop in the short run, and return again to its original level in the long run as mining was discouraged and gold consumption was encouraged. From the point of view of Old World, the looting of gold from the Aztecs and Incas by the Spanish conquistadors had the same effect.

A less fanciful source of shifts in the monetary stock supply curve follows from the fact that the curve reflects the given total stock of gold minus the demand for non-monetary stocks of gold. A sudden craze for genuine gold jewelry, by shifting rightward the (not shown) *non-monetary* stock demand curve for gold, would shift leftward the monetary stock supply curve. A drop in the popularity of gold jewelry would, conversely, shift the monetary stock supply curve to the right. The short-run and long-run adjustments described above would follow.

Shifts in gold flow supply and demand curves

Suppose that a significant new lode of gold ore is discovered, completely by accident, or, suppose that an inexpensive new technique is accidentally discovered for extracting gold from ore previously not worth mining. New gold mines open. Graphically (as shown in figure 2.3), g_0^s shifts out to g_1^s, and the flow

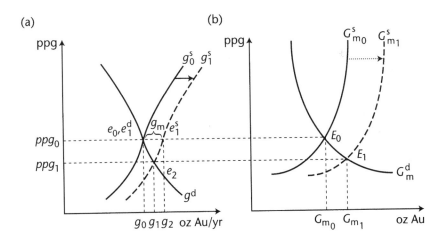

Figure 2.3   An increase in the flow supply of gold: following the discovery of a new gold lode, new mines open, shifting the flow supply curve for gold – in (a) – to the right and opening a flow of gold into coinage, g_m; then, in (b), the accumulation of new coins gradually increases the monetary gold stock over time and permanently reduces the ppg

supply of gold increases. We continue to assume that the ppg is proximately determined in the monetary gold stock market, so there is no *immediate* change in the ppg with the shift in flow supply. Change in the ppg will occur gradually as the accumulating new gold increases the monetary gold stock.

At ppg_0, production shifts from e_0 to e_1 on the new flow supply curve g_1^s. A larger flow, g_1, begins to come from the mining industry. There being no immediate change in the quantity demanded for non-monetary uses, the new flow quantity supplied exceeds the quantity demanded for non-monetary uses. As in the earlier case (figure 2.2(a)) the excess, denoted g_m, goes to the mints to be coined. Over time, as the newly minted coins accumulate, the stock supply curve of monetary gold, G_m, gradually shifts from G_{m_0} to G_{m_1} in figure 2.3(b). As G_m gradually rises, the ppg falls, moving along the unchanged monetary stock demand curve G_m^d.

The adjustment process eventually reaches its limit, and a new stationary equilibrium is established, at e_2 and E_2, with the new market-clearing value of gold equal to ppg_1. The height of ppg_1 is determined by the intersection of g_1^s with g^d, the point at which the flow of new gold into the mints, g_m, returns to zero. At any ppg above ppg_1, g_m remains positive, so coined gold continues to accumulate, shifting G_m further to the right and pushing the ppg further down. Once ppg_1 has been reached, the flow into the mints stops and stationary equilibrium has been re-established.

The opposite case of a *decrease* in the flow supply of gold could be similarly traced. We have noted that a depletion effect would gradually push the flow supply curve to the left. A nuclear accident in a major mining region would have the same effect more suddenly. An exogenous event that caused a sharp increase in the wage rates of miners (such as a rise in their productivity in other industries) would also do the trick of pushing the flow supply curve to the left. The result would be a permanent *increase* in the purchasing power of gold.

Unlike in the cases of monetary demand shocks, the change in the purchasing power of gold caused by a flow supply shock is permanent. The ppg does not return to its original starting point. This result illustrates the potential vulnerability of the price level to gold supply shocks under a gold standard, a feature often cited as a drawback by the gold standard's critics.

The size of the movement in the purchasing power of gold depends on the size of the supply shock, obviously. It also depends on the slopes of the flow supply and demand curves. At a lower ppg, the flow quantity demanded for consumptive uses rises, and this dampens the drop in the ppg. The flatter (more price-elastic) is the non-monetary flow demand curve, the smaller is the change in ppg. (This could be shown graphically be redrawing figure 2.3 with a flatter flow demand curve, an exercise left for the reader.) Likewise, the flow quantity supplied by mine-owners falls as the ppg falls; we move down along g_1^s from e_1 to e_2. The flatter (more price-elastic) is the flow supply curve, the smaller is the change in ppg before e_2 is reached. Thus, the greater the elasticity of flow demand and supply for gold, the more dampened are potential price-level movements.

The Historical Sources of Gold Supply Disturbances

Analyzing the stock supply and demand for gold in a similar fashion (while leaving the flow market implicit), Hugh Rockoff (1984) emphasizes that an observed change in the monetary gold stock is not always the result of a supply shock. It is often (as in figure 2.2 above) an endogenous adjustment to a situation in which, perhaps due to a previous demand shock, the gold market is temporarily out of long-run stock equilibrium.

A similar point can be made about shifts in the flow supply curve. If the flow supply curve in figure 2.3(a) is a *short-run* supply curve, showing the supply response from existing mines *only*, a shift in its position may speed the system's return to, rather than disturb, the long-run equilibrium value of the purchasing power of gold. For example, suppose that an increase in monetary stock demand for gold raises the ppg temporarily above its long-run level. The high ppg creates excess profits in mining. The rise in the profitability not only prompts mine-owners to work existing mines more intensively (the effect shown by moving up the existing short-run flow supply curve), but it also stimulates increased *prospecting* for new sources of gold. When new sources are found, the short-run flow supply curve rotates or shifts such that an even greater flow quantity is supplied at the high ppg. The increased flow of gold from the mines brings the ppg back to its long-run normal value more quickly than if there had been no discovery.[5]

Thus we need to distinguish between

1   gold discoveries that are endogenous (movements along the long-run flow supply curve) and that stabilize the purchasing power of gold in the long run, and
2   discoveries that are exogenous (shifts of the entire flow supply curve) and destabilize the ppg.

---

[5] Thus, as is generally the case, the long-run supply curve is more elastic than the short-run supply curve. If, in the transition from short run to long run, the supply curve were to make a parallel shift to the right (rather that rotating on the original flow equilibrium point), the long-run equilibrium ppg would be reduced. This would obtain if the fixed costs of operating a mine were entirely sunk costs once a mine is opened, so that existing mines will produce less but none will shut down (from inability to cover its average cost even while covering its marginal cost) at a lower ppg.

Which picture fits the major historical gold strikes? Rockoff (1984, pp. 625–7) understandably judges the California discovery of 1848, which was purely fortuitous, to have been an exogenous supply shock. The initial discoveries in Australia and New Zealand a few years later were by prospectors, but those prospectors were inspired by the California discovery rather than responding to a high purchasing power of gold, so these may also be counted as exogenous and destabilizing supply shocks.[6] Later discoveries in western Australia, however, and other major discoveries of the nineteenth century, namely South Africa (1874–86), Colorado (1890s), and Alaska (1890s) followed years of intense prospecting due to a high ppg, and may be counted as endogenous and stabilizing.

Like the discovery of a new gold field, technological progress in gold mining can also shift out the flow supply curve. But again, such a shift helps to stabilize the purchasing power of gold if it offsets a shift in the monetary demand for gold that would otherwise raise the ppg. An increase in money demand normally accompanies economic growth, and an important source of economic growth is technological progress in industry and agriculture generally. Technical progress in the gold mining industry thus helps to stabilize the ppg when it proceeds at roughly the same rate as technical progress generally. Historically, probably the only technological innovation big enough to have been potentially a significant source of supply disturbance was the invention of the cyanide process for extracting pure gold from ore, a breakthrough that greatly expanded the profitable exploitation of the South African gold deposits. However, Rockoff (1984, p. 830) notes that the research that led to a commercially useful version of the cyanide process (introduced in 1899) "was the product of the high price of gold prevailing in the mid-1880s." Thus, like many gold field discoveries, the development of the cyanide process may be viewed as part of an endogenous movement along an elastic long-run supply curve.

How long did it take to reach the long run? In the event of a sizable increase in the stock demand for gold, how many years would elapse (absent other shocks) before the increase in the ppg was at least half reversed by the supply response? (If the adjustment process slows down as the distance from long-run equilibrium shrinks, complete reversal might take place only in the limit.) No precise estimate is available in the literature, but deviations of the ppg above, or below, its long-run trend did last for decades. So, the adjustment process probably required a decade or more on average, particularly if we factor in prospecting as part of the process. Long and

---

[6] Rockoff (1984, p. 621, table 14.1) reports that the world monetary gold stock grew at an average annual rate of 6.39 percent during the period 1849–1859. In no other reported decade (1839–1929) was the growth rate above 3.79 percent.

variable lags could separate the emergence of a high ppg from the discovery of new gold fields, the bringing of additional gold mines on line, and, finally, the accumulation new gold output sufficient to restore the normal purchasing power of gold. Bordo (1984, p. 217, n. 36) reports statistical evidence that the lagged response of gold output to a deviation in the purchasing power of gold was strongest at a lag of 25 years.

The Benefits of a Gold Standard

A commodity standard like gold provides a credible "anchor" for the price level. The money stock automatically adjusts to counteract shocks to money demand, at least in the long run, as discussed above. The money supply cannot be *arbitrarily* increased: shocks to the quantity of money only occur when there are shocks to the profitability of producing gold. These properties limit movement in the price level, and anchor the expected price level. The expected inflation rate has a zero mean (or a negative mean, if a depletion effect operates), at least over long time horizons, in a system where the gold standard prevails and is expected to be left alone. Rolnick and Weber (1994) find that the average rate of inflation in historical commodity money (silver and gold standard) episodes has been approximately −.5 percent per year. This suggests that the "long-run stock supply curve" for monetary gold is almost, but not quite, flat. A mild depletion effect, or a wear-and-tear effect with secularly growing monetary gold stocks, appears to have operated.

Fiat money systems have typically behaved differently. Though economists have imagined and proposed firmly anchored fiat systems, and some fiat systems have behaved better than others, actual fiat money systems have exhibited much higher inflation on average. Rolnick and Weber (1994) reckon an average fiat inflation rate of approximately 6.5 percent per year when cases of fiat hyperinflation are omitted. (The number is closer to 18 percent when hyperinflations are included).

In addition to the *average* rate of inflation, investors worry about the *unpredictability* of the price level or the inflation rate. Clear and meaningful measurements of unpredictability, allowing a reliable historical comparison of commodity with fiat regimes, are hard to make, basically because expectations cannot be directly observed. One important piece of evidence strongly suggests, however, that investors had greater confidence of their ability to predict the price level, at least at long horizons, under the historical gold standard: the long-maturity end of the bond market has sharply contracted with the switch to fiat standards. Risk-averse investors naturally shy away from (unindexed) securities that promise payoffs of nominal dollars 25 years in the future, if they cannot confidently forecast the purchasing power of the dollar 25 years ahead. Under the gold standard in the nineteenth century, some railroad companies found ready buyers for 50- and 100-year bonds. Today, corporate bonds of 25 or more years in maturity are uncommon. As calculated by Benjamin Klein (1975, p. 480), the weighted average maturity of new corporate debt issued by US firms during the 1900–1915 period was 29.2 years; during the 1956–1972 period it was 20.9 years. One would expect that the figure has shrunk even more since 1972.

The main utilitarian arguments for adhering to a gold standard rest on the proposition that it more reliably preserves the purchasing power of money (gold is said to be more "trustworthy" and "honest") than a fiat standard.[7]

1   A more reliable unit of account lowers the risk of long-term nominal contracts, as we have just noted with respect to bonds. Lower risk on long-term bonds encourages more long-horizon investment. When savers are more willing (do not demand so large a purchasing-power risk premium) to buy long-term bonds, a firm with a long-payback project, like a railroad company, can more cheaply sell bonds long enough to match the duration of its expected payoff stream from the real assets being financed. Such duration-matching eliminates the significant refinancing risk involved in relying on short-term debt, which is the risk that interest rates will be higher when the firm goes to roll over its debt. High-payoff long-horizon investment projects are therefore not shelved simply because of inflation risk, which undoubtedly aids economic growth, though the size of the effect would be hard to estimate.

2   The gold standard's automatic mechanism for determining the quantity of money arguably reduces the burden of tracking the current, and likely future, money supply (the "fed-watching" costs in the current US monetary regime). This benefit relates to *how* the gold standard provides a reliable nominal anchor: market forces determine the money stock, rather than a committee of central bank officials who are subject to changes in outlook and possibly to political pressures. In later chapters, we discuss a variety of models for predicting the actions of a discretionary monetary authority. For now, the point is that investors may feel compelled to spend more on obtaining up-to-date information on the system's probable direction under a fiat standard. As Meltzer (1986, p. 124) puts it, "the flexibility that permits govern-

---

[7] Commentators sometimes speak of the gold standard's "mystique". Presumably, this means that the commentator is not persuaded by history (or by such figures as those in the text) that a gold standard is more reliable than a fiat standard, and does not understand why others are.

ment to change [monetary] policy . . . has a cost: anticipations about the future conduct of policy are altered, and uncertainty about the future conduct of policy increases."[8]

3 Classical defenders of the gold standard emphasized the importance of preserving "the ancient and honorable parity." So long as convertibility and other gold-denominated contracts are enforced as written, and the gold content of the monetary unit is not reduced, currency-holders under a gold standard are free from the government tax on currency-holding ("seigniorage" or "the inflation tax") imposed – often unexpectedly – by an arbitrary monetary expansion or debasement that makes the path of the price level jump.[9] The tax is particularly severe in a hyperinflationary expansion or an extreme debasement. The absence of seigniorage eliminates not only the standard welfare cost of the inflation tax (resources used up in keeping real balances low, e.g., by making additional trips to the bank), but also eliminates wasteful rent-seeking struggles over the spending of the proceeds.

Historically, it is of course true that governments sometimes (or chronically, under some regimes) reduced the gold content of the monetary unit, the ratio Q oz Au/\$. What does such a policy accomplish? In the *long run*, in terms of our price-level equation above, the policy has no impact on the ppg or its inverse R oz Au/basket of goods). It does not affect the real determinants of the flow supply or demand for gold, or alter real gold stocks (measured in ounces). It does not shift the curves in any of our gold-market diagrams (note that the vertical axis is in baskets/oz Au, not in nominal terms). Rather, the long-run effect of the policy is merely to raise the price level P in proportion to the increase in $1/Q$. Why bother, then? First, because there is a one-shot scaling-down of the government's real debts if those are denominated in units of account rather than in bullion weight of gold. Second, where the government has a mint monopoly, combining a debasement with a recoinage reaps seigniorage. When existing coins are called in, and their gold content is reduced, the gold extracted from each existing coin constitutes tax revenue to the government.

---

[8] Rockoff's evidence (1984, p. 62, table 14.1) indicates that the standard deviation of annual percentage rates of change (around decade-average rates of change) has usually been larger for the US monetary base, 1949–1979, than it was for the world's stock of monetary gold, 1839–1929. Meltzer's (1986) risk and uncertainty estimates (produced by multistate Kalman filter techniques) run mostly in the opposite direction, but are based on a shorter gold standard sample period.

[9] A detailed account of seigniorage is provided in chapter 7. The absence of surprise tax levies on currency holding is presumably an important part of what is meant by those who speak of gold as "honest money."

Barring seigniorage is a benefit to coin-holding members of the public, but a sacrifice to the government. For that reason, an unalterable gold standard was historically viewed as an important constraint on those activities of governments, particularly war-making, that were commonly financed by the burst of revenue available through a large seigniorage levy.

The Resource Costs of a Gold Standard

The leading objection economists have made to commodity standards are the resource costs involved: paper money is much cheaper to produce than gold coins.

The resource costs of an ongoing gold standard (meaning, the opportunity cost of the resources tied up) have both stock and flow components. The *stock* resource cost is the cost of *holding existing* monetary gold. Its magnitude is the value of all the "inherited" gold coins and bullion, if that gold were given over to non-monetary uses like tooth fillings, jewelry, and electronics. The *flow* resource cost is the cost of *acquiring additional* gold (and of replacing worn coins, if wear-and-tear is non-zero). Its magnitude is the value in alternative employment of all the labor, capital, and land devoted each period to mining gold for monetary purposes, or to producing net exports to be traded for monetary gold.[10] To avoid double counting, the alternative-use (stock) and production (flow) costs should not be added together for the same ounce of gold.

Acquiring additional gold is ordinarily called for to meet growth in money demand. A country switching from a fiat to a gold standard would incur a one-time (stock) resource cost of acquiring the gold needed for coinage and bank reserves, and, in subsequent years, would incur the (flow) resource costs of acquiring additional gold as money demand grew. Stock resource costs would be zero under a gold standard only if gold (like fiat money) had no value in non-monetary uses. Flow resource costs would be zero only if the monetary gold stock could not grow (all gold mines and other sources had already been exhausted) or no flow of gold into the mints was called for (demand for monetary gold did not grow, and wear-and-tear on existing gold coins was zero).

---

[10] Because the reward necessary to secure the services of a factor in a competitive market is at least what others are willing to pay for it, which equals their estimate of the value it would contribute to their production, the standard measure of the alternative value of any input is the rate of pay (wage or rental) it currently receives. Some factors may be specific to the gold-mining industry – for example, specialized machines or skills of experienced gold-miners – and not as valuable outside of the industry, but an end to the mining of gold *for monetary purposes* is not an end to the industry as a whole.

Switching to a fiat money regime does not *automatically* escape these resource costs. First, to eliminate the stock resource cost, banks and central banks that are holding gold when the transition to fiat money is made must sell off their gold stocks to release the gold for alternative uses. For whatever reason, the world has not in fact seen a meltdown of more than a small fraction of central banks' gold stocks since the end of the classical gold standard or even since the end of Bretton Woods. (Central banks have at least stopped accumulating gold, so that the system no longer incurs flow resource costs to meet increased money demand.) Second, if the public is uncertain about the reliability of a fiat money, and buys newly minted gold coins and bullion as an inflation hedge, flow resource costs of a (quasi-) monetary kind *are still* incurred.

For these two reasons, it is an empirical question under which regime the resource costs are actually lower in a particular country's, or the world's, case. Sufficient data on gold quantities – ounces mined and held – are not available to answer the question. Privately held stocks of quasi-monetary gold have most likely risen since the 1971 end of Bretton Woods. Certainly they have risen in the US, where private gold ownership was illegal between 1933 and 1975. However, precise quantities are unknown because individuals do not (or do not reliably) report the sizes of their holdings (for obvious reasons). Another way to address the question, though, is to look at data on the real price of gold. Assuming that the switch in regime has altered only the world monetary stock demand for gold (leaving unshifted the monetary stock supply curve and the flow supply and demand curves), the question of whether world resource costs are lower under fiat regimes reduces to the question of whether the monetary stock demand for gold has fallen. The answer is "yes" if, and only if, the purchasing power of gold has fallen. A lower ppg implies that more of the existing stock and flow have been freed to non-monetary use, and less mining activity is being undertaken. A higher ppg implies the opposite.

In point of fact, the purchasing power or real price of gold is higher today than it was in the gold standard era. $300 per ounce in 1998 is equivalent to more than $60 at 1967 prices, whereas gold was $35 per ounce in 1967. It is equivalent to more than $31 at 1929 prices, whereas gold was $20.67 per ounce in 1929.[11] The implication is that the switch to fiat standards has *increased* rather than decreased the (quasi-) monetary stock demand for gold, and has ironically *increased* the resource costs of the monetary system.

A well-known, and still-cited, estimate of the flow resource cost of a gold standard is Milton Friedman's (1953; 1960) theoretically derived estimate that the costs of acquiring new gold would annually consume 2.5 percent of

---

[11] Using 1967 = 100 as the base year, the CPI for 1928 and 1929 was 51.3; for November 1998, it was 492.

national income. If this estimate were accurate, a gold standard would be very expensive indeed. Friedman assumes that wear-and-tear is zero, and focuses entirely on the annual amount of gold mining or importation called for by growing real money demand. (A constant stock of monetary gold cannot be an equilibrium in growing economy, in a world with non-exhausted mines, because, with growing money demand, the ppg would continually rise, making mining increasingly profitable.)

To estimate the size of the ratio $\Delta G/Y$, where ΔG is the dollar value of the annual change in the stock of monetary gold and Y is annual national income, Friedman decomposes it into other ratios for which, given further assumptions, empirical values can be found and plugged in:

$$\frac{\Delta G}{Y} = \left(\frac{\Delta G}{\Delta M}\right)\left(\frac{\Delta M}{M}\right)\left(\frac{M}{Y}\right)$$

where M is the size of the M2 money stock and ΔM is the annual change in M2. It will be easiest to consider the ratios in reverse order. To plug in a value for (M/Y), Friedman (1960) took the most recent ratio of M2 to net national product (NNP), namely M2/NNP = .625. More recent figures are very similar in magnitude,[12] so there is no problem here. Plugging in a value for the second ratio, the annual growth rate in the money stock $(\Delta M/M)$ requires an assumption about the behavior of gold stock. Assume (just as we did in figure 2.2 above) that all long-run equilibrium points lie along a flat "long-run supply curve" such that the purchasing power of gold always remains at the same level as monetary demand grows.[13] Then the stock of monetary gold must adjust to keep the quantity of money equal to the quantity demanded at a constant ppg. In other words, the money stock must grow at the rate just sufficient to maintain a constant price level or zero inflation rate. Such an economy is pictured in figure 2.4.

We can find the implied money growth rate using the dynamic equation of exchange

---

[12] In other words, the velocity of M2 is back in the same neighborhood, though it has drifted a bit in the interim.

[13] I put "long run supply curve" in quotes because normally a long-run Marshallian supply curve describes a long-run relationship between price and *flow* quantity supplied, not the long-run stock results of the accumulation of flows. (A stock supply curve is normally drawn on the assumption of a *fixed* total stock being allocated among competing uses). A sufficient condition for the long-run value of the ppg to be constant is that the long-run flow supply curve is flat. The same result obtains without a flat flow supply curve if the flow supply and demand curves simply continue to intersect at the same ppg, either because neither shifts or because they always happen to shift in parallel.

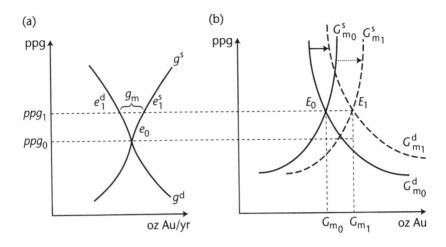

Figure 2.4 Ongoing steady growth in the monetary demand for gold: as shown in (b), the monetary stock demand for gold increases steadily each period; the ppg is continually kept at ppg_1, above its stationary equilibrium value ppg_0; in (a) the high ppg generates a flow of gold into coinage each period g_m; in (b), the accumulation of new coins shifts the monetary gold stock to the right each period, balancing the increased stock quantity demand at ppg_1

$$\frac{\Delta M}{M} + \frac{\Delta V}{V} = \frac{\Delta P}{P} + \frac{\Delta y}{y}$$

where $\Delta V/V$ is the rate of growth of velocity, $\Delta P/P$ is the inflation rate, and $\Delta y/y$ is the rate of growth of real income. We plug in empirically derived figures for the real income growth and velocity growth terms (whose difference is the rate of growth of real money demand), plug in zero for the inflation rate, and solve for money stock growth. Historical evidence on secular trends at the time of Friedman's estimate suggested that $\Delta V/V$ as –1 percent and $\Delta y/y$ as 3 percent were appropriate per annum figures. Thus, the implied $\Delta M/M$ equals 4 percent. The money stock would have to grow at 4 percent per annum under a gold standard to keep the ppg constant given the assumed rates of real income and velocity growth.

Finally, we need a value for $(\Delta G/\Delta M)$, the ratio of additional gold to the additional M2 money stock. In other words, how many dollars' worth of gold has to be mined to support $100 worth of new M2? Friedman assumed, remarkably, that the stock of gold equals *100 percent* of M2, so that $G/M = 1$ and $\Delta G/\Delta M = 1$. That is, he assumed that banks hold 100 percent reserves of gold, not only against demand liabilities, but even against time deposits.

His rationale was that he wanted to estimate the resource costs of a "pure" gold monetary system, a system in which all forms of money (and even all time deposits) are literally gold or warehouse receipts for gold.

Plugging in all these figures,

$$\frac{\Delta G}{Y} = \left(\frac{\Delta G}{M}\right)\left(\frac{\Delta M}{M}\right)\left(\frac{M}{Y}\right)$$

$$= (1)(.04)(.625)$$

$$= .025$$

Thus the value of newly acquired gold each year would equal 2.5 percent of GNP. Put another way, 2.5 percent of GNP would be the economy's annual cost of acquiring gold, given that, in equilibrium, the cost of extracting or importing new gold equals the value of the gold extracted or imported.

Whatever its value as an estimate of the resource cost of a 100 percent-reserve gold standard,[14] Friedman's calculation gives a huge overestimate of the resource costs of a gold standard with an advanced banking system in the absence of legal reserve requirements. A gold standard, as noted early in this chapter, generically means a system in which money is *meaningfully denominated* in gold. It need not be the case that every piece of money *consists of* gold or is backed 100 percent by gold in a vault. Historically, most payments in gold-standard systems were made with fractional-reserve banknotes, and demand deposits, that were denominated and re-deemable in gold coin. Reserve ratios were nowhere near 100 percent against these demand liabilities, let alone against banks' total liabilities including time deposits.

To reach a more reasonable estimate of the resource cost of a generic gold standard, we need to plug in a more reasonable figure for the ratio of gold to money in the broader sense, G/M. The stock of monetary gold equals bank reserves plus gold coins. Together, these have historically been a small fraction, not 100 percent, of M2. Continuing to work with M2 as the measure of the money stock, we can estimate the ratio by figuring

$$\frac{G}{M} = R + \frac{C_p}{M} = \left(\frac{R}{N} + D\right)\left(N + \frac{D}{M}\right) + \frac{C_p}{M}$$

---

[14] It is hard to understand why Friedman used M2 rather than M1 as the relevant measure of the money stock, since the time deposits included in M2 are clearly not media of exchange. Even the advocates of a 100 percent-reserve gold standard (e.g. Rothbard 1995) limit the application of their reserve requirement to demand liabilities. (For a critique of the 100-percent reserve position, see Selgin and White 1996).

where R is bank reserves, C_p is gold coins held by the public, and M is M2. $R/(N + D)$ is the ratio banks maintain between their gold reserves and their demand liabilities (bank-issued currency notes and deposits), $(N + D)/M$ is the ratio of currency notes and deposits (i.e. M1 minus coins) to the M2 money stock, and C_p/M is the ratio of coins to M2. In sophisticated gold-based banking systems without legal restrictions on reserve ratios, like Scotland's in the nineteenth century, the stock of bank reserves equaled about 2 percent of demand liabilities.[15] Coins in the present-day USA are about 8 percent of currency, currency is about 51 percent of M1, and M1 is about 32 percent of M2. Currency notes and demand deposits are thus about 30.7 percent of M2, and coins about 1.3 percent of M2. (Note that treating all coins as full-bodied gold coins errs on the side of overestimating the amount of gold in use, because small change under a gold standard can and often did consist of redeemable token coins.) Multiplying the reserve ratio of 2 percent by the currency note and demand deposit portion of M2 (.288), and adding the coin portion:

$$\frac{G}{M} = .02(.307) + .013 = .00614 + .013 = .01914$$

Assuming that the marginal reserve ratio $\Delta G/\Delta M$ is the same as the average reserve ratio G/M, the marginal ratio of gold to the broad money stock thus equals approximately 2 percent. Plugging in 2 percent where Friedman plugged in 100 percent obviously reduces our estimate of the resource cost of a gold standard to *one-fiftieth* of Friedman's figure:

$$\frac{\Delta G}{Y} = \left(\frac{\Delta G}{M}\right)\left(\frac{\Delta M}{M}\right)\left(\frac{M}{Y}\right)$$
$$= (.02)(.04)(.625)$$
$$= .0005$$

Taking fractional reserve banking into account thus reduces the estimated resource cost of a gold standard down to 0.05 percent, or five hundredths of 1 percent, of national income.

An adjustment might also be made to the second ratio. Recall that Friedman's 1960 figure of $\Delta M/M = 4$ percent assumed annual real income growth of 3 percent and velocity growth of -1 percent. Since 1960 in the USA, the 3 percent figure for annual real income growth has held up fairly well. Annual velocity growth was actually about $+3$ percent during 1960–1980 (as inflation rose), but has been approximately 0 percent since 1980 (as infla-

---

[15] Some Scottish banks held reserve ratios as low as .5 percent.

tion fell). Plugging in velocity growth of 1 percent in place of Friedman's −1 percent would reduce the implied money growth figure to 2 percent, cutting the resource cost estimate in half, resulting in a revised figure of .00025 (or .025 percent) two-and-a-half hundredths of 1 percent of national income. By this benchmark, Friedman's estimate is *100 times too high* for a system with fractional reserves..

The estimate might be further tweaked, in either the upward or the downward direction. The estimate would rise if we add in an allowance for wear-and-tear depletion of the existing monetary gold stock, which would require additional mining to offset it, but such depletion is most likely trivial in a sophisticated monetary system. Gold bars held in clearinghouse vaults are seldom handled and thus do not wear away. Gold coins in circulation do suffer wear, but, for that very reason, a token coinage is likely is likely to replace them. Because two-thirds of the monetary gold stock consists of coins in our estimates above, assuming the replacement of full-bodied coins with fractionally backed tokens would reduce our estimates by another factor of three, making our most optimistic estimate less than .01 percent of national income.

Is a Gold Standard Worth the Resource Cost?

Suppose it is agreed that a reasonable range of estimates of the resource cost of a gold standard is .01 to .05 percent of national income. Assume, ideally, that these resource costs could be entirely avoided under a fiat regime. Does a gold standard provide enough advantages, in comparison to a fiat standard, to make the resource cost worth bearing from the perspective of enhancing net national income? One advantage, comparing actual gold and silver standards with actual fiat standards, is lower inflation. Rolnick and Weber (1994) find that the average annual rate of inflation under commodity money has been approximately 7 percentage points lower (−.5 percent versus 6.5 percent per year, excluding episodes of fiat hyperinflation). The public bears a lower deadweight loss from the distortions associated with a 7 percent tax on holding money. How large an advantage is that as a percentage of national income? A standard approach to estimating the welfare cost of inflation is to plot a money demand curve against the inflation rate, and then to measure the size of the deadweight loss triangle under the curve (the amount by which the dollar value of lost consumer surplus exceeds the gained government revenue from monetary expansion) at specified rates of inflation. Two commonly cited estimates of the cost of a 10 percent inflation rate, arrived at this way, put it respectively at .3 or .45 percent of national income (see Cooley and Hansen 1989, p. 744). If the welfare cost of a 7 percent inflation rate differential (going from −.5 percent to 6.5 percent) can conservatively be put at one-half of the lower figure (the area of the deadweight loss triangle varies as the square of its leg, and $.7^2 \approx .5$), it is still three times our upper-bound estimate of the resource cost of a gold standard. A gold standard's resource cost is worth bearing if the alternative is a fiat standard with 6.5 percent inflation.

To put the same idea the other way around, a *fiat* standard is not worth having where its deadweight burden exceeds .05 percent of national income, which (following the above interpolation method) implies that it is not worth having where it produces an inflation rate of about 4 percent or more. A country where fiat money is managed so as to keep inflation below 4 percent can do without a gold standard; but a high-inflation country would be better off with gold.

As an alternative approach to the sizes of costs and benefits we are talking about, note that Robert Lucas (1987) has tried to put a price tag on the risk caused by instability (variation) of real consumption in the post-war economy. Assuming a reasonable degree of risk aversion on the part of a representative consumer, Lucas conservatively estimates that bearing the risk is equivalent to a loss of one-tenth of 1 percent of income. This figure is two to ten times our estimate of the resource cost of a gold standard. If monetary instability is an important source of income instability, a gold standard would only have to relieve a fraction of monetary instability to cover its resource costs.

But would a gold standard even contribute in the right direction to relieving monetary or consumption instability? "Countercyclical" or "activist" monetary policies are not possible with a system in which the gold standard automatically, rather than a central bank with discretion, regulates the quantity of money. That may be a blessing or a curse, depending on whether activist monetary policies actually relieve instability, or instead they (inadvertently) contribute to it. The effectiveness of activist policy is a familiar theme in the Keynesian–Monetarist debate in macroeconomics. We defer discussion of that debate to later chapters, but simply note that a gold standard is more likely to appeal to those who, like Monetarists, find that central bank activism tends to be destabilizing in practice.

Attempts to measure real income instability under the classical gold standard, to contrast it with instability in the post-war era, often conclude that real income was *less* stable under the gold standard. These measurements may not be reliable as indicators of the degree that would be experienced under a modern gold standard, however, for two reasons. The first reason relates to the data: real and nominal national income statistics for the pre-World-War-I period are not based on as broad an array of industry data as are post-war statistics, making cross-regime comparison problematic (Romer 1986). Second, the banking system in the USA, and other nations, was regulated in ways that almost surely contributed to monetary instability. It would be necessary to disentangle these regulatory effects from any instability due to the gold standard as such.

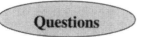

1 If, under a gold standard, banks are required by law to hold 100 percent reserves of gold against demand liabilities, what does that imply for the purchasing power of gold, monetary stock of gold, and annual production of gold? How does it affect the resource costs of the monetary system, compared to leaving reserve ratios legally unrestricted?

2 Is the opportunity cost of holding currency higher for individuals in a gold standard regime, or in a fiat money regime?

3 Did the gold rushes of the nineteenth century stabilize, or destabilize, the purchasing power of gold?

4 Under a gold standard, does technological progress produce a tendency toward a rising, or a falling, price level?

5 "The development of the clearing system and of fiduciary media [fractionally backed bank-issued money] has [historically] at least kept pace with the potential increase of the demand for [metallic] money brought about by the extension of the money economy, so that the tremendous increase in the exchange value of money, which otherwise would have occurred as a consequence of the extension of the use of money, has been completely avoided . . . If it had not been for this, the increase in the exchange value of . . . the monetary metal, would have given an increased impetus to the production of the metal." (Ludwig von Mises, 1980, p. 333)

(a) Use flow and stock supply-and-demand diagrams to illustrate the impact of an increase in the demand for metallic money, ceteris paribus. How do your diagrams show an "increase in the exchange value of the monetary metal" (purchasing power of gold), and an "increased impetus to the production of the metal"?

(b) Assume that Mises's first sentence is historically accurate. Illustrate the *joint* impact of the increase in the demand for money (as shown in (a)) together with the development of clearing and fractional-reserve banking.

6 Assume a closed gold-standard economy in which
(a) all potential gold-extraction sites have already been discovered,
(b) the marginal cost of extracting gold rises as existing sites are depleted, and
(c) the real demand for money is a constant fraction of annual real income. What do these conditions imply for the long-run path of

the price level as real income grows? (Assume that wear-and-tear on monetary gold is zero.)

7   Using flow and stock supply-and-demand diagrams for gold, show short-run and long-run responses of the ppg, stock of monetary gold, and flow production of gold, to each of the following events. Assume that flow and stock markets begin and end in stationary equilibria.

   (a)   An economical process is accidentally discovered for extracting gold from seawater.
   (b)   A huge treasure of gold is discovered in a fleet of wrecked ships on the floor of the Caribbean.
   (c)   Banks develop inventory-management techniques that reduce their demand for gold reserves.
   (d)   "Audiophile" gold DVDs become popular, using discs that bond gold to plastic in a way that makes the gold unrecoverable at any relevant price.
   (e)   Goldfinger vaporizes the gold in Fort Knox.
   (f)   Solid gold jewelry becomes suddenly more popular.

8   Joseph T. Salerno (1987) writes: "Under a genuine gold standard, then, the growth in real output tends to naturally call forth additions to the money supply." Explain how one might reach this conclusion. That is, why and how does growth in real output of non-money goods and services in an economy (real GDP) lead to growth in the stock of monetary gold?

9   "Proponents of the gold standard cite its low-inflation record. These days, money's stable value during the gold standard has come to be associated with gold per se. However, the gold standard ultimately worked because of restraint, the restraint to hold gold's dollar price constant rather than make periodic revaluations. In short, it is the commitment, not the commodity, that makes paper money hold its value – then and now. The real [guarantee of stable-valued money] is honesty, not gold." (Haslag 1996)

   (a)   Explain how periodically changing "gold's dollar price" (the defined gold content of the dollar) would change the inflation rate under a gold standard. That is, spell out the role the gold content of the dollar plays in determining the price level in dollars, and how changing the former changes the latter.
   (b)   Suppose the gold content of the dollar is "honestly" held constant. Is that enough to make the dollar "hold its value" – i.e. does it imply a constant purchasing power for the dollar? If so, explain why. If something more is required for stable purchasing power, identify what it is and explain why.

10 In the spirit of Friedman's general approach to calculating the resource cost of a commodity standard, what would go into a compa-

rable calculation of the resource cost of a fiat standard? Are there any important difference between the costs of an *ideal* fiat regime and the costs of *actual* regimes seen today?

3
Money Issue by Unrestricted Banks

Chapter 2 examined how a gold standard determines the quantity of monetary gold and the purchasing power of the monetary unit. In a world where all money consisted of full-bodied gold coin, such a theory of the supply and demand for monetary gold would be enough to explain the quantity of money in general. In a sophisticated and freely evolved monetary system (as described in chapter 1), however, the public can be expected to use bank-issued money in the form of redeemable currency and transferable deposits, rather than full-bodied coin, for most payments. This chapter therefore examines how the value and quantity of bank-issued money are determined under free competition. In particular, if banks are subject to no legal ceiling on currency issues, or floor on reserve ratios, what economic forces, if any, compel banks to limit their issues and to hold positive reserves?

Historically, such questions arose where "free banking" was debated as an alternative to "central banking".[1] "Free banking" in that context meant a regime in which private banks could competitively issue paper currency notes (and transferable deposits, but the debates focused on note-issue), without significant legal restrictions, rather than a state-sponsored institution (the central bank) having a monopoly on the issue of notes. Today, the same questions arise where commercial banks, and other firms, are poised to re-enter the currency market by offering "cash cards," "pre-paid cards," or "smart cards." Like banknotes, the balances on these cards are (at least under some technologies) anonymously transferable bearer claims on

---

[1] Smith (1990) provides a classic survey of these debates in several nations. On the British debates, see White (1995).

banks, and can circulate from bearer to bearer without bank involvement. The claims are carried not as ink engraved on paper but as digital information encoded on a readable and writable microchip within a credit-card-sized piece of plastic. We explore, in this chapter, how a competitive issuing system – using paper or chip media – would work. We will use the term "currency" to refer both to traditional banknotes and circulating smart-card balances.

In the historical debates, given the evolved institutional setting, theorists assumed that bank-issued currency would be redeemable for full-bodied gold or silver coin (specie). Here, to be more general, it is convenient to speak of the medium of redemption as "reserves." Today, it is clear that a specie standard is not logically required for competitive currency issue, or even for the absence of a central bank. Allowing competing banks to issue currency does not, by itself, select any particular monetary standard. Competitive currency issue is possible under a fiat standard, with fiat money (residing in bank vaults, or on the balance sheet of the central bank if it remains open) serving as the unit of account and medium of redemption.[2] We briefly discuss below the determination of the purchasing power of money in such a system, but a fuller discussion of fiat money is left for chapter 5.

Other possible regimes for competitive money issue by unrestricted banks include a system with indirect redemption and a multi-commodity unit of account, and a system of competing *private* fiat-type (irredeemable) monies; see Selgin and White (1994a). We defer discussion of these possibilities to the last two chapters of this book.

We assume, based on historical experience, that a banking system with free entry would support active competition among a plurality of issuing banks. There is no apparent natural monopoly in the market for bank-issued money. Consistent with the limiting case of perfect competition, we treat each bank as a price-taker in deposit and loan markets. For reasons argued in chapter 1, we assume that all bank currencies and deposit transfers are accepted at par.

The Purchasing Power of Money

If we assume that bank-issued money is redeemable for full-bodied gold coin, so that gold is the basic money that both defines the medium of account and serves as the medium of redemption, the purchasing power of

---

[2] Friedman (1987) and Selgin (1988) suggest that the quantity of fiat central bank liabilities be frozen. Retiring the central bank from monetary policy in this way, or any other way, and retiring it from currency issue, are distinct propositions.

money is the purchasing power of gold (ppg). The supply and demand for gold determine the ppg, as analyzed in chapter 2. The monetary stock demand for gold is the sum of the banks' demand for reserves and, if bank-issued money has not completely displaced their use, the public's demand for full-bodied coins. The demand for bank reserves, in the absence of reserve requirements, derives from each bank solving a reserve-holding optimization problem we examine below.

Chapter 2 analyzed the determination of the purchasing power of gold for a closed economy, the world as a whole. Here, it is convenient to treat the banking system as an open economy that is such a small subset of the international gold standard that its fraction of global demand for gold is negligible. The banking system then faces a flat long-run stock supply curve for gold, and the ppg is exogenous in the long run, given to the system as the ppg determined on the world market. In the event of a local money supply or demand shock, the stock quantities supplied and demanded for gold, G_m^s and G_m^d, are brought back into long-run equilibrium. Equilibration occurs not by accumulations or decumulations of coin that involve the mining industry, and may take decades, but by international flows of gold that operate much more quickly.

David Hume's (1970) classic treatment of the equilibrating process – the "price-specie-flow mechanism" – assumed that the flows are not instantaneous, in which case the short-run supply curve is still upward sloping. If the flows are instantaneous, then the short-run curve collapses into the long-run curve. In either case, the banking system's stock of monetary gold is endogenous. In long-run equilibrium, with the ppg identical everywhere, the ith country's share of the world gold stock (G_i / G_w) corresponds to that country's share of world gold-holding demand:

$$\frac{G_i}{G_w} = \frac{G_i^d}{G_w^d}$$

at the equilibrium ppg, because in equilibrium $G_i = G_i^d$ and $G_w = G_w^d$.

In a closed economy, such as a gold-based global banking system or a frozen-fiat-base national system, by contrast, the purchasing power of money (ppm) cannot be taken as exogenous, but is determined by the interaction of the supply of reserve money and the demand for bank reserves. The ppm will respond to shifts in the demand for bank reserves. *Ceteris paribus*, greater economization of bank reserves (due to technological advance in clearing) will lower the ppm. In a system with fiat base money, complete economization of non-interest-bearing bank reserves would make the demand for fiat base money vanish, and with it any positive ppm. This limiting case is not a problem in a gold standard, because the ppg would still be positive due to non-monetary demand. In what follows, we consider both the open and closed economy cases.

Bank Optimization and the Equilibrium Quantity of Bank-issued Money

To capture the essential tradeoffs facing an issuing bank, we consider the simplified balance sheet shown in Table 3.1.

Table 3.1   A simplified balance sheet

Assets	Liabilities + Equity
R reserves	N notes or currency-card balances in circulation
L loans and securities	D deposits
	K equity capital

These balance sheet items are choice variables for the bank, which seeks the optimal total size and mix on each side of the balance sheet. To simplify, we assume K is given parametrically.[3] With K fixed, the balance sheet identity imposes the constraint

$$R + L = N + D + K$$

The objective function to be maximized is the profit function, given by

$$\pi = i_L L - i_D D - C - Q$$

where

π = expected profit
i_L = interest yield on loans and securities
i_D = interest rate on deposits
C = operating cost
Q = liquidity cost (see below).

We assume that i_L and i_D are not choice variables but given (the bank is a price-taker in loan and deposit markets). Operating costs are a continuous (and positive) function of each of the balance sheet items:

$$C = f(R, L, N, D); \; C_R > 0, \; C_L > 0, \; C_N > 0, \; C_D > 0$$

[3] In a more general treatment, K would be determined endogenously by maximizing the rate of return on equity, adjusted by insolvency risk (Baltensperger 1972).

where C_R is the marginal cost of holding greater reserves, and so on.

The bank's incentive to hold adequate reserves is to enhance its profit by reducing its liquidity cost, Q, which is the expected value of costs incurred in the event the bank runs out of reserves. The value of Q is found by multiplying the cost of reserves going negative by a certain amount by the probability of that happening, for each possible amount, and summing up all the products.[4] Graphically, the probability of illiquidity (negative reserves) is shown in figure 3.1 as the shaded area of the probability distribution. The cost of negative reserves may be a legal penalty, a penalty imposed by the clearinghouse which has to cover the shortfall, or the bank's cost of scrambling to liquidate assets on short notice to cover its position. The bank's choices of its reserve level R, and its currency and deposit circulation volumes N and D, depend on how the choices of N, D, and R influence Q. It is natural to assume that $Q_N > 0$ and likewise $Q_D > 0$. Having a greater volume of either currency or deposits in circulation increases the volume of claims against the bank that might be redeemed and thus naturally increases the probability of adverse clearings large enough to deplete reserves. Holding a larger reserve clearly reduces the probability of reserve depletion, so $Q_R < 0$.

Static profit maximization implies a set of six equi-marginal conditions:[5]

---

[4] More formally, we can assume a continuous probability density function for reserve losses, and integrate over the left tail for reserve losses greater than initial reserves. The liquidity cost function may be written

$$Q = p(X - R) \, \phi \, (X \mid N, D) \, dX$$

where

X = outflow of reserves
$\phi(X \mid N, D)$ = probability density function over X, conditional on N and D
p = penalty cost as a percentage of of realized illiquidity, $p = 0$ for $X - R \, 0$, $p > 0$ for $X - R > 0$.

Note that to motivate the holding of positive reserves, when the cost of a reserve shortfall is thus proportional to the size of the shortfall, and the mean of ϕ is zero (so that the probability of an adverse clearing is .5), the penalty cost p must exceed twice the opportunity cost of holding reserves.

[5] Formally, to derive the first-order conditions for profit maximization we write out the Langragean

$$\pi(R, L, N, D) = i_L L - i_D D - C - Q + \lambda (K - R - L + N + D)$$

from which we derive the first-order conditions

$\pi_R = -C_R - Q_R - \lambda = 0$
$\pi_L = i_L - C_L - \lambda = 0$ (we assume $Q_L = 0$)
$\pi_N = -C_N - Q_N + \lambda = 0$
$\pi_D = -i_D - C_D - Q_D + \lambda = 0.$

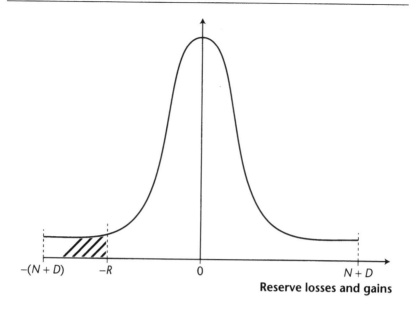

Figure 3.1   The probability of illiquidity: probability of reserve losses exceed starting reserves is represented by the shaded area to the left of $-R$ (area under the curve = 1)

$$i_L - C_L = -C_R - Q_R \qquad (3.1)$$

The left-hand side of the equation is the marginal net revenue from making loans or holding securities (their interest yield minus the marginal operating costs of making loans). The right-hand side is the marginal net benefit from holding reserves (the reduction in liquidity cost minus the marginal operating costs of reserve holding). The profit-maximizing bank must be indifferent at the margin between holding extra loans or securities and holding extra reserves of the same market value, because it can trade one for the other.

$$i_L - C_L = C_N + Q_N \qquad (3.2)$$

The marginal net revenue from making loans equals the marginal cost of maintaining currency in circulation, which is the sum of the marginal operating cost and marginal liquidity cost of currency circulation. An economic limit to the bank's extending loans or purchasing securities with its currency is set by the rising marginal costs associated with keeping a growing volume of currency outstanding.

$$i_L - C_L = i_D + C_D + Q_D \tag{3.3}$$

The marginal net revenue from making loans is equal to the total marginal cost of maintaining and servicing deposits, which includes interest payments, marginal operating cost, and marginal liquidity cost. The rising marginal cost of acquiring funds via deposits sets a limit to the amount of loans purchases profitably funded that way.

$$-C_R - Q_R = C_N + Q_N \tag{3.4}$$

$$-C_R - Q_R = i_D + C_D + Q_D \tag{3.5}$$

Equation (3.4), which is implied by equations (3.1) and (3.2), says that the bank's marginal net benefit from holding reserves is equal to the total marginal cost of maintaining currency in circulation. The rising marginal cost of maintaining currency in circulation limits the extent to which the bank can profitably increase its reserve holdings by issuing currency. A bank cannot just print up currency to buy reserves without limit, because it has to keep the currency in circulation. The costs of keeping currency in circulation are discussed in more detail below. Equation (3.5), which is implied by equations (3.1) and (3.3), similarly says that the marginal net benefit from holding reserves is equal to the total marginal cost of maintaining deposits. The rising marginal cost of expanding the deposit base limits the profitability of acquiring reserves by attracting additional deposits.

$$C_N + Q_N = i_D + C_D + Q_D \tag{3.6}$$

Finally, the marginal cost of expanding the currency circulation (in order to enlarge the bank's assets) is equal to the marginal cost of expanding the bank's deposit base. At the margin, the two sources of funds are equally costly in profit-maximizing equilibrium; otherwise, it would pay the bank to rely more heavily on the lower-cost source, and less heavily on the other.

From the equi-marginal conditions, we see that the desired currency circulation for an issuing bank is limited by the rising marginal cost of keeping currency in circulation. While it is cheap to print up notes, or load smart cards with digital balances, and to put them into circulation, a bank can use currency issue to expand its portfolio of earning assets only if the currency *stays* in circulation. To keep a volume of redeemable currency in circulation in a competitive environment, the issuing bank must have a clientele which in the aggregate will *hold* that currency, rather than exercise the option to redeem it for reserves or exchange it for deposits or the currency of another bank. Given a rising marginal cost of cultivating such a clientele, legally unrestricted currency-issuers will not issue without limit nor earn unlimited profits.

The costs of cultivating a larger clientele for a particular bank's brand of currency include the costs of

1   enhancing its spendability by recruiting more retailers to accept the brand;
2   making redemption easier by opening more branch offices, hiring more tellers, staying open more hours;
3   boosting public awareness of, and confidence in, the brand through advertising;
4   reducing the public's risk of holding the brand by anti-counterfeiting measures; and
5   making the currency devices (notes or cards) more physically attractive.

These forms of non-price competition are similar to the forms used in competition for checking account customers. Historical experience suggests that currency competition took place *exclusively* along non-price dimensions because there was no cost-effective means to pay interest on paper currency. In chapter 6, we will discuss whether an exclusive focus on non-price competition is consistent with efficiency, or is instead wasteful. In chapter 14, we will discuss the view of the "legal restrictions theory" that all currency should be expected to bear interest under laissez faire.

Correcting Over-issue by an Individual Bank

For any particular bank, there is an equilibrium size of its currency circulation that satisfies the above equi-marginal conditions. (The same is true for its deposits, but, for convenience, we focus on currency.) This size is the value of the public's desired holdings of currency issued by bank i, given the bank's optimizing expenditures on non-price competition (which we categorize as operating costs). We denote this value N_p^{i*}, where the subscript p indicates the public for whom the currency is an asset, the superscript i denotes the issuing bank for whom it is a liability, and * means that it is a desired value. What happens if the bank's actual circulation exceeds the desired level, $N_p^i > N_p^{i*}$? Nineteenth-century writers, in their various attempts to answer this question, spoke of the return of excess currency to the over-issuing bank as a process of "reflux".[6] (They paid more attention to the potential for over-issue than to under-issue, presumably because the incentive not to under-issue is more obvious.) We aim to explain here how N_p^i converges on

---

[6] John Fullarton's (1845) "law of the reflux" is probably the most famous attempt. Unfortunately, it is not the most cogent. For a critique, see White (1995, pp. 127–8).

$N_p^{i}*$ as the public adjusts toward its desired portfolio of assets.

Suppose that excess currency is introduced by means of loans. The borrowers spend the currency. The recipients of the spending now have balances of bank i currency in excess of their desired levels. A recipient individual q for whom $N_q^{i} > N_q^{i}*$ can respond in any of three ways. *Direct redemption* for reserves at the issuer's counter is the least likely way, especially in a mature system where little or no reserve money is held by the public, but it clearly would directly reduce N^{i} and simultaneously reduce the bank's reserves R_i. *Deposit of the excess currency* into another bank (the bank where q keeps his demand deposit account) is presumably more common. It brings the currency-exchange mechanism into play, generating adverse clearings for the over-issuer as the recipient bank presents the deposited currency claims for redemption at the clearinghouse. Settling the clearing balances entails a loss of reserves R_i just as direct redemption does. The volume of currency in circulation N^{i} is reduced by the return of the excess currency to bank i, unless the bank immediately re-issues it. However, the reserve loss signals to bank i that reissuing the currency would lead to further hemorrhaging of reserves, so it should accept the reduction in its circulation. Deposit of the excess currency into bank i itself, an event that is less likely the smaller is bank i's share of the deposit market, does not generate adverse clearings. However, it does mean a higher marginal interest cost of liabilities, and a higher liquidity cost, than before the expansion. An issuer that was maximizing profit before will thus find the expansion now unprofitable.[7] *Spending* the excess currency transfers the excess to a new individual who also has the same three options. With some probability, this new individual will directly redeem or deposit the currency, leading again (with a slightly longer lag) to a reserve loss for bank i and a contraction of N^{i}.

As a consequence of reserve losses, bank i finds its reserves lower than it desires ($R_i < R_i*$). The marginal net benefit of holding reserves now exceeds the marginal net revenue from making loans or holding securities, prompting the bank to sell securities (or not roll over maturing loans) in order to increase its reserves. Reserves return to bank i from the rest of the banking system.

Correcting Over-issue by the System as a Whole

If there is some spending and respending of excess currency, might this not have system-wide or macroeconomic effects? In a price-specie-flow model,

---

[7] Glasner (1997, p. 22) emphasizes the role played in Fullarton's (1845, pp. 92–93) theory of the reflux by the public's conversion of unwanted currency into interest-bearing deposits. Fullarton did not, however, lay much stress on the adverse clearings that result when notes issued by bank i are deposited into bank j.

the answer is yes. The effects presumably vary in magnitude with the size of the overissue, and the length of time before it is corrected.

There are two routes for the transmission of the overissue into system-wide reserve losses (traditionally known as an "external drain"). The *direct* effect is that some of the extra spending, prompted by the excess stock of currency, will be on imports. The imports will be paid for (the trade deficit settled) by exporting specie, which comes out of bank reserves. The *indirect* effect operates via the domestic price level. If the domestic and world ppm can temporarily diverge, and if all currency brands continue to trade at par, then the extra spending on domestic goods raises prices and reduces the domestic purchasing power of money generally, not just the value of the currency brand overissued. Exports will be depressed and imports stimulated by the high price of domestic goods. Again, the resulting balance of payments deficit will be settled by exporting reserve money from bank vaults. The outflow of reserves is driven by, but also corrects, the excess supply of money and the price level divergence, returning the domestic price level to equality with the world price level. The direct effect impinges only on the over-issuing bank, as only its currency is in excess supply. The indirect effect, acting through the price level, draws reserves from all banks, not just the over-issuer, and thus raises the possibility of that innocent banks may suffer reserve losses. Simultaneously, however, the innocent banks are enjoying positive clearings as the domestically spent excess currency is received and deposited by their customers.

Where the overissuing bank is small, the price level effect, and thus in-directly prompted spending on imports, will be small relative to the adverse clearings resulting from interbank deposits and directly prompted import spending, so that the effects of over-issue will not be significantly shifted onto other banks.[8] The larger the overissue as a percentage of domestic currency, the greater will be the adjustment through external drain rather than adverse clearing. The size of the overissue is the product of the percentage of overissue by bank i times bank i's initial share of total circulation. For example, if a bank that has 10 percent of the total circulation overissues by 20 percent, then the aggregate overissue is only 2 percent of the total currency circulation. Because plurality in currency issue reduces any one issuer's share of the circulation, it limits the danger of a large-scale overissue. Provided that banks act independently (do not expand in concert), random money-supply errors will tend to offset one another in the aggregate. When a single issuer has a 100 percent share of the circulation,

---

[8] If international goods arbitrage is so strong that domestic prices cannot rise relative to world prices, even in the short run, then the indirect spending effect is completely absent, and the spillover effect on other banks is zero.

on the other hand, the likelihood of a random large-scale overissue is greatest.

A currency monopolist's overissue, or an error by plural issuers hypothetically acting in concert, will not be corrected in the usual way by domestic adverse clearings. In an open economy – i.e. where the banks acting in concert are a subset of the entire world's banks – it will be corrected by external drain.[9]

But what if, going beyond the open-economy assumption, *all* the banks in the world over-issue? In this limiting case, which is of more theoretical interest than practical relevance, neither interbank adverse clearings in the usual fashion, nor external drain, limit the expansion. That is, there is no *systematic* tendency for any bank or set of banks to lose reserves to another set. Stochastic reserve losses, however, do remain a concern for every bank. Each bank continues to have a determinate demand for reserves related to the threat of reserve depletion arising from random adverse clearings. As George Selgin (1988) has shown, the desire to maintain a certain level of safety against reserve depletion thus establishes a definite limit to bank expansion. An in-concert expansion will increase the threat to every bank by increasing the volume of payments made in its liabilities. (We hold constant the banks' real expenditures on non-price competition, and, so, the public's demand to hold bank liabilities relative to its spending.) The mean of net clearings (the mean of the $\phi(X|N, D)$ distribution mentioned in footnote 4 above) can remain zero for each bank. Yet the risk of reserve depletion increases because the increase in *gross* clearings widens the reserve-loss probability distribution and thus enlarges the area of the left tail beyond any given level of reserves. (See figure 3.2.) Each bank will feel its risk of running out of reserves too great. Because the closed system has a limited quantity of total reserves available, relief from the excess demand for reserves requires the banks to contract their liabilities (N and/or D) in order to re-establish their desired levels of illiquidity risk. Given the marginal cost functions the individual banks face for expanding mean demand to hold their liabilities, the volume of system reserves, the stochastic process generating adverse clearings, and the level of safety each bank desires against reserve depletion, there exists a unique equilibrium volume of system liabilities. Beginning from such an equilibrium, with no change in any of these

---

[9] This point is sometimes considered an objection to competitive currency issue, because it indicates that the domestic adverse clearing mechanism *as such* is not enough to pin down the system as a whole. It is hardly a point in favor of monopoly currency issue, however, to argue that, in the limiting case of in-concert over-expansion, a system of plural issuers is no more constrained by adverse clearings than is a single issuer. (We will see below that this argument is not even correct.) It provides no reason to believe that a single issuer is constrained more effectively.

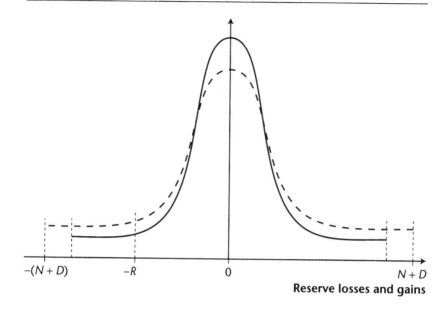

$-(N + D)$ $-R$ 0 $N + D$

Reserve losses and gains

Figure 3.2   An in-concert expansion by all banks broadens the probability distribution over reserve losses and, thereby, increases a representative bank's probability of illiquidity with a given level of starting reserves

fundamentals, an in-concert expansion is inconsistent with sustaining an equilibrium in which all banks are optimizing.[10]

Responding to Shifts in Demand

An overissue need not come about because a bank has increased the supply of its liabilities. It can equally well come about as a result of a drop in

---

[10] Suppose, for the sake of argument, that as the proponents of in-concert-expansion scenarios sometimes suggest, any aggregate volume of bank liabilities is potentially an equilibrium, provided only that the movement to it is concerted among the banks. (We hold constant the banks' expenditures on demand-enhancing non-price competition.) By implication, a continuum of reserve ratios are consistent with equilibrium. If so, why couldn't the banks acting in concert, holding their liabilities constant, equally well reduce the quantity of reserves they hold to an arbitrarily low figure? If there is a unique optimizing volume of reserves for a bank, given its mean liability volume and the distribution of clearing gains and losses around that mean, then there is an optimizing volume of liabilities, given that distribution and the bank's reserves. If arbitrary in-concert reserve reduction is non-optimizing, so too is arbitrary in-concert liability expansion.

demand. Beginning with a drop in demand, the same processes discussed above come into motion to correct the excess of liabilities in circulation.

Now consider the opposite case of an individual bank i experiencing a rise in demand to hold its currency (for simplicity we will continue to speak in terms of currency, but the analysis again applies equally to deposits). An increase in the demand to hold bank i's currency, unmatched by an increase in the supply, creates the reverse of an overexpansion. The actual circulation *falls short* of the desired circulation:

$$N_p^i < N_p^i*$$

A simple (and unrealistic) way to see that the bank's profit motive compels it to remedy the under-issue is to imagine that customers come to the bank to borrow the precise quantity of additional currency they wish to hold, and credibly promise to keep their currency balances permanently higher.[11] Making the loans increases N and L on bank i's balance sheet, increasing the bank's marginal revenue $(i_L - C_L)$ more than its marginal cost $(C_N + Q_N)$. By hypothesis, the demand to hold i-currency has risen without additional selling costs by bank i, so its marginal operating cost (C_N) is no higher, and because the currency will not be spent the marginal liquidity cost (Q_N) is likewise no higher than before, despite the larger volume.

In a more realistic scenario, the bank customers, whose demand for i-currency has risen, hold on to more i-currency instead of spending it. Less i-currency enters the clearing system, and bank i enjoys positive clearings. As a result, bank i finds its reserves greater than desired $(R_i > R_i*)$, and is prompted by the profit motive to expand its loans and securities holdings, increasing its interest income and ridding itself of undesired reserves. In the new equilibrium reserves R_i are returned to (or nearly to) their old level, with a larger volume of i-currency in circulation and a larger portfolio of earning assets. In this way, the supply of money by an individual bank is *demand-elastic*: bank i finds it profitable to respond to a rise in N_p^i* by raising N_p^i, and the reverse for a fall.

Now consider a *general* rise in the public's desired holdings of currency (across all brands). A simultaneous rise in demand for several banks – which might be due to a general rise in an economy's real income – creates the reverse of an in-concert over-issue. We can again imagine a simple and unrealistic scenario, in this case *all* banks facing customers who apply to borrow more currency, and promise to hold larger average currency

---

[11] An individual's currency balances are, of course, an inventory that fluctuates. "Holding additional currency" or "keeping currency balances higher" means holding a larger inventory *on average* over time.

balances permanently. Although no bank systematically gains reserves, each bank can safely and profitably expand: because the public is not spending more, but only *holding* more of its currency, its risk of reserve depletion is no greater despite its lower reserve ratio. In the more realistic scenario, customers seek to accumulate a greater stock of currency in proportion to their spending by temporarily spending less or trying to earn more. Spending flows fall relative to the stocks of bank-issued money and reserves. Again, in contrast to the single-bank case, no bank enjoys systematically positive clearings from the others.

In the open-economy case, the banks do enjoy net positive clearings against the rest of the banks in the world. As net spending on imports is curtailed by the public's attempt to build up its money balances, reserves flow in from abroad to settle the balance of payments. The banks thereby gain additional reserves.

In the closed-economy case, a *general* rise in the public's desired holdings of currency, shared by *all* the banks in the world, creates the reverse of a global in-concert over-issue. The banks' reserves are made more than sufficient by the reduction in liquidity costs from reduced spending per unit of currency. The reduction in *gross* clearings reduces desired reserves R_i^* by reducing the chance of reserve depletion for any given starting level of reserves. In response, the banking system will expand its liabilities, raising banks' desired reserves, until desired reserves again match the given stock of reserves. In these ways, the supply of money by *the banking system as a whole* is demand-elastic: the banks as a group find it profitable to respond to a general rise in N_p^* by raising N_p.

In the new equilibrium, real intermediation through the banking system has increased: the banking system has a larger volume of currency liabilities and a larger portfolio of assets. This indicates that the voluntary holding of bank-issued money is one component of the supply of loanable funds. To hold a bank's currency or deposit liabilities is to lend it funds which it can then intermediate (re-lend). Whether an increase in the holding of bank-issued currency is associated with a *net* increase in the supply of loanable funds depends on whether it is matched by a fall in the public's savings in other forms. The spending that the public sacrifices to build up its money balances need not be consumption spending; it might, instead, be spending on acquisition of alternative financial assets.

A general *fall* in the demand to hold currency or deposits sets in motion the adjustments to an overissue, which correspond to the adjustments just described but take the opposite signs. Spending rises relative to the stock of bank-issued money, as holders try to spend off excess balances. In an open economy, reserves are lost to the rest of the world via the price-specie-flow mechanism, and the money stock declines. In a closed economy, the probability of reserve depletion increases, and the volume of desired reserves

R_b* rises above the given stock of available reserves. The volume of currency and deposits must fall to restore reserve-holding equilibrium.

The demand-elasticity of the currency supply N_p in a closed economy can be described another way: a fall or rise in the "velocity" of bank-issued money leads to an offsetting change in the stock of bank-issued money by changing the money multiplier. A rise in the demand to hold bank-issued money relative to spending implies a fall in velocity (the ratio of spending to money balances). By reducing spending flows, and thus the "turnover" of bank-issued money, the shift reduces the probability of large adverse clearings. Liquidity cost thus falls, and the banks can safely keep more liabilities in circulation, and correspondingly can make more loans. The rise in its liabilities $(N + D)$ restores equilibrium by pushing back up the marginal benefit of holding reserves (Q_R) for the representative bank.

The supply of bank-issued money is thus endogenous even in a closed economy, in contrast with the usual thought experiments involving fiat money. Holding real income constant, a 10 percent rise in the demand for (fall in the velocity of) bank-issued money, unlike a similar rise in the demand for fiat money, is *not* equilibrated by a 10 percent fall in the price level P. If P were to fall 10 percent, nominal income and spending would also fall 10 percent, rendering the unchanged nominal stock of reserves R_b excessive, prompting banks to expand.

Because M moves to offset changes in V in the closed-economy case, the system acts automatically to stabilize MV, nominal aggregate demand for goods, or Py, nominal income (Selgin 1994b).[12] A number of monetary theorists have argued that nominal income stabilization has desirable macroeconomic properties, and have advocated that central banks should pursue it as a policy. Our analysis, here, suggests that a competitive issuing system tends to stabilize nominal income automatically in the face of velocity shocks.

Shifts between Deposits and Currency

Where a competitive bank issues both deposits and currency as liabilities, the bank can meet shifts by the public from deposits into currency, or vice versa, with a simple change in the liability mix. The change has no impact on the actual stock of the bank reserves, R_i. If marginal liquidity costs are

---

[12] The equivalence of MV stabilization to Py stabilization follows from the income version of the equation of exchange, $MV = Py$, so far as changes in income velocity match changes in total transactions velocity. The turnover of its liabilities a bank must worry about is not only from spending on final goods and services, but from all transactions. Thus, the theory really applies better to transactions velocity, and indicates a stabilization not of nominal income (Py or nominal GDP) but of total nominal transactions volume (PT).

equal for the two liabilities, $Q_N = Q_D$, then the change in the liability mix does not affect the bank's desired reserves, R_i^*, either.[13] The bank remains at its reserve-holding optimum, and has no reason to change total quantity of its liabilities. Shifts between currency and deposits thus have no impact on the quantity of money.

In contrast, in a system where the public holds "high-powered" currency that banks also use as reserves, a shift from deposits to currency draws reserves out of the banks, prompting a multiple contraction of the money stock. Contractions of this sort were historically a problem in the banking panics of the late 1800s in the USA. When the public wanted to switch at the margin from deposits to currency, e.g. to pay farmworkers during "crop-moving" season, banks were prevented by the National Banking laws from issuing more notes; for more details, see chapter 4. The banks could offer depositors only reserve currency (specie or greenbacks). A shift toward currency thus led to a liquidity crisis and monetary contraction as banks' reserves were depleted. Where banks can issue currency on the same basis as deposits, a multiple contraction can happen only if the public desires to hold more reserve money in particular rather than currency in general, which was not the case in these historical panics. In a fiat money system, where the public's currency is (as today) a liability of the central bank that also serves as bank reserves, changes in the currency–deposit ratio will (ceteris paribus) alter the money stock. To prevent such alterations, the central bank must expand, or contract, the monetary base in timely fashion, and in the right magnitude. Its monopoly of currency issue thus makes the central bank's job more difficult. A return to competitive currency issue would simplify the conduct of monetary policy (Selgin 1997a).

Questions

1 Assume that Georgia is one state within a larger dollar-standard continent, banks are state-specific, and dollar-denominated currency is entirely bank-issued. If all the banks in Georgia were to overissue currency in concert, what, if anything, returns the system to its initial equilibrium?

2 Nineteenth-century "free banking school" authors, like Henry Parnell, concluded that over-issues of money are likely to be more serious under central banking (a single currency issuer) than under free bank-

---

[13] If liquidity costs are identical for the two liabilities at every circulation volume, then only their sum matters to the bank. Formally, the probability-of-reserve-loss function $\phi(X \mid N, D)$ could be written $\phi(X \mid N + D)$.

ing (competitive currency issue). What case might they have made?

3   Discussing the competitive issue of redeemable currency, Kevin Dowd (1988) writes: "A bank can put as many notes into circulation as it likes, but the public will determine how many of them actually stay there." Assuming that the public commonly accepts payment in Bank X's notes, is Dowd correct? Does anything actually limit the willingness of the public to hold more Bank X notes?

4   In the absence of government guarantees, Morris J. Markowitz (1993, p. 76) writes, notes issued by fractional-reserve banks would take the form of interest-bearing commercial paper and "never would achieve the status of money." Instead "100-percent backed notes . . . will circulate as money, by the natural workings of the market." Do you agree or disagree with this prediction? Provide relevant theoretical or historical support for your position.

5   "A banknote promising $10 to the bearer on demand, issued by a bank with a one-fifth reserve, is the equivalent of a lottery ticket with a one-fifth chance of winning $10, and will therefore trade for about one-fifth of its face value ($2)." Is this correct or incorrect? Why?

6   "The United States had no central bank until 1913, so every bank issued its own dollar bills. In the early days these bills were different colors and sizes, and some of them weren't worth the paper they were printed on. The same thing is happening with smartcards. 7-Eleven [a chain of convenience stores] is issuing smartcards." (Wriston 1996, p. 142)

(a)   Why were the notes issued by most banks worth *more* than the paper they were printed on?

(b)   What restrained those banks from issuing an unlimited amount of notes?

(c)   Assume that 7-Eleven really does get into the business of issuing currency smart cards (as far as I can ascertain, the chain to date has only issued *phone* cards). What would restrain 7-Eleven from issuing an unlimited amount of smartcard balances?

4

The Evolution and Rationales
of Central Banking

Chapter 1 logically reconstructed the evolution of market monetary institutions into a sophisticated and integrated monetary system. The institution of a central bank played no role in the story. However, central banks do play major roles in virtually all real-world monetary systems today. It is obviously important to account for them.

Can we account for the emergence of central banking by extending the invisible-hand story of market evolution? The answer depends on just what is meant by the term "central banking." If government sponsorship[1] is among the defining characteristics of a central bank, then the answer is no. In that case, the story of a central bank's emergence obviously cannot rely entirely on market processes. At some point, deliberate state action must enter the story. If government sponsorship is not essential, then the answer might be yes, depending on what functions are considered to constitute central banking.

If we decide that a certain sort of private institution without government sponsorship qualifies as a central bank, we need to keep in mind that an account of *its* evolution says nothing immediately about the rationale for establishing, or the subsequent development of, a government-sponsored central bank. It remains to be seen how the two sorts of institutions are related. For this reason, it is important to keep the broader concept of central banking distinct from the narrower concept of the functions undertaken by a government-sponsored monetary authority.

---

[1] Government "sponsorship" rather than "ownership" is the operative term inasmuch as the Bank of England became a central bank long before it was officially nationalized until 1946. Private member banks even today nominally own the regional Federal Reserve banks.

Central Banking Roles and CHAs

What makes an institution a central bank? The literature shows a surprising lack of consensus on the question. Economists have identified central banking with at least five major roles:

1 serving as a bankers' bank,
2 having a monopoly of note issue,
3 acting as a lender of last resort,
4 regulating commercial banks, and
5 conducting monetary policy.

An institution can play one or more of these roles without playing all five. The question of whether "a central bank" is a market-evolved institution is thus more usefully reformulated as the question of *which* of these central banking roles are likely to be played by private institutions, and which are peculiar to government-sponsored monetary authorities.

A bankers' bank

The minimal role commonly cited as defining a central bank is that of acting as "a bankers' bank," an institution whose liabilities are held by commercial banks as part of their reserves.[2] (A bank that provides correspondent banking services to other banks is not generally called a "bankers' bank" except insofar as its correspondents hold its liabilities as reserves.) A private clearinghouse association (CHA) bank of the sort discussed at the end of chapter 1, whose liabilities are held by member banks, and transferred among them as a medium of settlement, certainly qualifies as a central bank in this minimal sense. We have seen that such a bankers' bank can emerge spontaneously as an economical device for interbank money transfers.

Is there any reason for a government-sponsored bank to absorb the role of bankers' bank? Walter Bagehot, the pre-eminent Victorian banking authority, persuasively argued in his classic work *Lombard Street* (1873, pp. 92–100) that the government-granted privileges of the Bank of England – its exclusive possession of the government's balances, its monopoly of note-issue in London, its effective monopoly of joint-stock banking in England up to 1826, and its implicit guarantee against failure – had played a crucial part in its gaining the deposits of other banks. Bagehot concluded:

---

[2] The *Penguin Dictionary of Economics* (Bannock et al.1974, p. 63) defines a central bank as "a banker's bank and lender of last resort."

With so many advantages over all competitors, it is quite natural that the Bank of England should have far outstripped them all. Inevitably it became *the* bank in London; all the other bankers grouped themselves round it, and lodged their [gold] reserve with it. Thus our *one*-reserve system was not deliberately founded upon definite reasons; it was the gradual consequence of many singular events, and of an accumulation of legal privileges on a single bank which has not been altered, and which no one would now defend.

In a more recent account, drawing on historical experiences in several nations, Charles Goodhart (1988, p. 5) confirms that the typical central bank gained its role of being a bankers' bank in the way Bagehot described:

[Its] privileged legal position, as banker to the government and in note issue, then brought about consequently, and naturally, a degree of centralization of reserves within the banking system in the Central Bank, so it became a bankers' bank.

Thus, *if* the central government grants legal privileges to a particular commercial bank, sufficient to make that bank distinctly larger and more secure than any other in the financial center, it is understandable that the privileged bank will become a banker to the lesser banks in the system, even though that development may have been no part of anyone's original intention. From the granting of privileges onward, one might call the development of a government-favored bank into a central bank "natural" as Bagehot and Goodhart do.[3] This path of development, as a whole, crucially depends on the granting of special privileges to a particular bank, however, and such privileges are neither inevitable nor compelled by market forces. In other historical cases, where large commercial banks have acquired sizable interbank reserve deposits, for example in New York in the last century, the reason has been laws against branch banking that excluded outside banks from opening their own offices in the financial center.[4]

As Bagehot (1873, pp. 66–8) explained, "the natural system – that which would have sprung up if Government had let banking alone – is that of

---

[3] The development is then "natural" in the same sense that comedian Steven Wright suggests that it counts as "dying a natural death" when one is hit by a train: "You get hit by a train, *naturally* you die." The standard meaning of "natural" in economics – as in the phrase "natural monopoly" – is, however, "brought about by market forces rather than by government intervention."

[4] For a contrary view, see Goodhart (1988, pp. 34–5), who believes that purely market forces account for "a concentration of such interbank balances among a few, central, well-established commercial banks." Congdon (1981) believes that a national government cannot avoid sponsoring a central bank, because it supposedly must give its own banking business to a single commercial bank, which then inevitably becomes the bankers' bank.

many banks of equal or not altogether unequal size." In such a system, no commercial bank "gets so much before the others that the others voluntarily place their reserves in its keeping." A clearinghouse bank that serves as the bankers' bank in such a "natural system" is not a commercial rival, but a jointly owned institution that specializes in clearing and settlement.[5]

Monopoly of currency issue

For Bagehot and Goodhart, a legal monopoly in the issue of banknotes contributes importantly to turning the institution possessing it into a central bank. Vera Smith, whose *The Rationale of Central Banking* offered the most thorough discussion of the topic in the century following Bagehot, argued emphatically that the other central banking functions followed from the monopoly of notes. In her view, it is therefore the monopoly of note-issue, and not any of the "secondary" other functions, that is the essential or defining attribute of a central bank. Wrote Smith (1990, p. 168):

> The primary definition of central banking is a banking system in which a single bank has either a complete or a residuary monopoly in the note issue. A residuary monopoly denotes the case where there are a number of note issuers, but all of these except one are working under narrow limitation, and this one authority is responsible for the bulk of the circulation, and is the sole bank possessing that measure of elasticity in its note issue which gives it the power to exercise control over the total amount of currency and credit available.
>
> It was out of monopolies in the note issue that were derived the secondary functions and characteristics of our modern central banks.

Smith identified these "secondary functions" as the holding of the bulk of the banking system's outside-money reserves (serving as the bankers' bank), and the power to exercise control over the credit market (a form of monetary policy).

Smith found that a monopoly of note issue is not a natural monopoly, the product of economies of scale, but is rather the product of legislation. Thus she concluded: "A central bank is not a natural product of banking development. It is imposed from outside or comes into being as the result of Government favours." There is no reason to believe that a single commercial

---

[5] The Suffolk Bank clearing system of New England, 1819–1858, was an exception, being administered by a single commercial bank that charged other banks for its services. Most of the Suffolk's clearing business was eventually taken, however, by the Bank for Mutual Redemption, which was organized as a cooperative among member banks, to whom it offered better terms than the Suffolk had (Mullineaux 1987).

bank, or a clearinghouse bank of the sort discussed above, would acquire a monopoly of note issue absent government intervention. According to a survey of the historical record by Kurt Schuler (1992), every banking system that has allowed competitive note-issue – even that of the tiny island of Malta – has supported a plurality of issuing banks.

Lender of last resort

For Goodhart (1989a) and others, a key characteristic of a modern central bank is that it supports the banking system by acting as a lender of last resort. A lender of last resort stands ready to inject high-powered money into the system in the event of an internal drain. An "internal drain" occurs when the public's increased preference for holding high-powered money prompts redemption of bank-issued money on a scale that threatens to deplete a fractional-reserve banking system of reserves, and so force a sharp contraction in the quantity of bank-issued money. "High-powered money" is money that currently or potentially serves as bank reserves.[6]

Humphrey and Keleher (1984, p. 277) thus speak of the lender of last resort acting as a "backstop or guarantor to prevent a panic-induced collapse of a fractional-reserve banking system." An injection of high-powered money can be made through loans to troubled banks, as it traditionally was, and as the term "lender of last resort" suggests. However, in modern banking systems, the injection can instead be made – and there are strong arguments (Goodfriend and King 1988) for preferring that it be made – through open-market purchases. In such cases, the term "lender of last resort" is something of a misnomer.

Bagehot (1873, pp. 57–71) provided the now-classic argument that "whatever bank or banks keep the ultimate banking reserve of the country must lend that reserve most freely in time of apprehension." His argument was directed at the contemporary management of the Bank of England, which through "privileges and monopolies" had acquired the "very anomalous"

---

[6] A dictionary (Pearce 1986, pp. 182–3) notes: "The reserve assets which form the base on which the banking system creates bank deposits [or bank-issued currency] . . . are collectively termed 'high-powered money' since . . . a change in the quantity of these assets will produce a multiplied change in the bank deposit component of the money stock" in a fractional-reserve system. Two details should be mentioned.

1 The stock of high-powered money is not coextensive with the actual stock of bank reserves, as it also includes any currency in the hands of the public that could *potentially* serve as bank reserves.

2 High-powered money need not be the system's most basic money. In a banking system where central bank liabilities are held as commercial bank reserve assets, but are themselves redeemable for commodity money, they are high-powered money but not outside or definitive money.

and "very dangerous" position of being the sole holder of ultimate (gold) reserves: "Whether rightly or wrongly, at present and in fact the Bank of England keeps our ultimate bank reserve, and therefore it must use it in this manner." A bank in that position is "the only place where at such a moment new [high-powered] money is to be had." It therefore has the duty of providing new high-powered money to the market when an internal drain threatens to contract the banking system and commercial credit. Further, it should assure the market, in advance, that it will pursue such a policy, to allay depositors' apprehension that if they don't withdraw now their banks will be out of reserves, and unable to pay when they do seek to withdraw.[7]

It is clear in Bagehot's work, and in the subsequent literature, that to undertake a lender of last resort role is to fulfill a *prescription* for central bank behavior, rather than a part of the *definition* of what constitutes a central bank. A central bank may fail to act as a lender of last resort (the Federal Reserve System in 1931–3 is often cited as an example), but it does not in that event stop being a central bank. The attribute that helps define a central bank is rather the *ability* to act as a lender of last resort, and that means: the ability to expand the stock of high-powered money at the appropriate time.

An institution is *capable* of playing a lender of last resort role if it can, when the occasion arises, expand the available stock of the assets that commercial banks hold as reserves. A bankers' bank will normally have the capability. Unless barred by some legal restriction, a bankers' bank can expand the volume of its own liabilities, which ordinary banks hold as reserves, by expanding its own balance sheet.[8] As already noted, one source of the bankers' bank role is a legal note monopoly. An institution with a monopoly of note-issue, whose notes serve as a reserve asset for ordinary banks, can expand the stock of high-powered money (at least in the short run, which is the time-frame within which a lender of last resort operates), again provided that there are no legal barriers to expansion.[9]

A government may be able to expand the stock of high-powered money, and thereby to act as a lender of last resort, even without employing an agency that engages in banking (in the normal sense of deposit-taking). The US Treasury occasionally did so between 1850 and 1907. It deposited its

---

[7] To reduce moral hazard, Bagehot advised that the lender of last resort should lend at a "penalty" rate (high enough to make the borrowing bank regret being in the position of needing the loan), and should lend only to solvent (but illiquid) banks. The Bank of England at that time not having audited balance sheet information on other commercial banks, Bagehot's proposed test for solvency was whether the borrowing bank could offer good collateral.

[8] A strict currency board, because it is not allowed to go below 100 percent reserves, is not able to act as a lender of last resort.

[9] Peel's Act of 1844 restricted the Bank of England from expanding its note circulation at its discretion, but not from expanding its deposits.

own gold into the banking system, and made open-market purchases of securities, to expand the stock of bank reserves in timely fashion (Timberlake 1978, pp. 176–80). The Government of Canada acted to supplement bank reserves in 1907 and 1914, and provided a lender-of-last-resort rediscounting facility between 1914 and 1934 (Bordo 1990, p. 26). Thus, the ability to play a lender of last resort role is not by itself *sufficient* to make an institution a central bank. At a minimum, the institution must also be a bank.

A private clearinghouse association (hereafter CHA) bank, whose members hold its liabilities as reserves, also has the potential to expand the sum of high-powered money in an active fashion, and thereby to act as a lender of last resort, provided that its members authorize it to do so. Where a CHA bank's liabilities are high-powered money to its member banks, but not to the banking system generally, an expansion in the stock of high-powered money is more effectively achieved through advances to member banks than through open-market operations.[10] The banks receiving advances can use them in trying to meet the public's unusually high demand for high-powered money.

Each CHA member is exposed to a risk of loss on CHA loans. This risk may deter members from agreeing to a CHA policy of making loans in ordinary periods. When there is no extraordinary demand for high-powered money by the public, an individual bank that is illiquid, but solvent, should be able at reasonable rates to borrow from, or sell assets to, holders of existing high-powered money. In a panic, such loans and asset sales are extraordinarily costly. A bank that would be solvent at normal asset prices may become insolvent if forced to sell off assets at panic prices. A CHA policy of making loans in panics serves as coinsurance scheme (Gorton 1985a, p. 281) against an individual member bank's risk of finding itself in such a bind.

The CHA can offer loans at an interest rate below the market rate prevailing in a panic, thus providing the burden-sharing of insurance, but above the normal market rate, thus reducing the potential moral hazard of a bank responding to the insurance by taking insufficient care to keep adequate reserves. (By meeting a temporary peak in the real demand for high-powered money with a temporary increase in supply, the lender-of-last-resort policy can be expected to help to moderate the peak in interest rates, and the valley in asset prices that occurs.) Although a bank that finds itself in a strong reserve position when a panic occurs might, at that moment, prefer the CHA *not* to lend to weaker banks, the same bank may agree before the fact to a lender-of-last-resort policy because it recognizes the chance that it might find itself in need of aid.

---

[10] An open-market purchase of securities might simply result in a drain of reserves in favor of non-member banks.

Richard H. Timberlake (1984) and Gary Gorton (1985a) have recounted how the CHAs in various US cities came to recognize, and use, their potential to expand the stock of high-powered money during the banking panics of 1857–1907. These CHAs provide examples of the spontaneous development of private lenders of last resort.

During normal times the New York Clearing House Association (NYCHA) held a 100 per cent cash reserve against its liabilities which were used to settle interbank clearings.[11] The NYCHA liabilities took the form of large-denomination bearer certificates rather than book-entry deposits. In the panic of 1857, the Association agreed to issue certificates against member bank "deposits" of temporarily irredeemable country bank notes, in effect loaning new certificates into existence. (The country banks agreed to pay interest to the Association for the implicit loan of holding their suspended notes, and the interest was passed on to the holders of the "loan certificates.") As Timberlake (1984, p. 4) points out, "the issue of clearinghouse loan certificates temporarily made the clearinghouse itself into a fractional reserve institution," and it thereby expanded the stock of high-powered money. This successful experiment became the precedent for an established CHA policy in later panics, in New York and other cities, of issuing extra certificates through loans to member banks against collateral securities. After a panic had passed the loans were repaid and the extra certificates retired.

CHAs also developed the policy, in later panics, of issuing small-denomination notes that member banks could borrow, and pay out, to satisfy the extra currency-holding demands of the public. The CHAs took on the role of issuing currency only because the National Banking Acts in force legally prevented commercial banks from supplying additional banknotes at their discretion. The clearinghouse notes also violated the laws, but their obvious usefulness prevented any federal prosecution.

Regulation of commercial banks

Modern government central banks devote much of their manpower to regulating commercial banks. Regulation of the banking industry need not come from an external source, however. Member banks are impelled by self-interest to delegate a certain amount of regulatory authority to a private CHA even though they initially form the association simply to handle clearing and settlement. CHAs have, historically, been an important vehicle for "self-policing" by commercial banks, and, in fact, pioneered external bank examination, and several other practices now used by government regulators.

---

[11] Evidently the use of CHA bank liabilities, rather than specie, in settlement was motivated by the desire for easy physical transfer rather than for interest on reserves.

Each bank wants to be assured that its fellow members, whose notes and checks it accepts every day, will not default at the next clearing session. For this reason, the banks have good reason to welcome CHA monitoring of every member's solvency and liquidity. Private CHAs have historically required, as a condition for membership, that member banks meet a minimum capital requirement, furnish regular financial statements, and submit to auditing by CHA examiners.

The history of the Chicago Clearing House Association, as chronicled in the work of F. Cyril James (1938, pp. 372–3, 499, 515–16), illustrates this motive at work in the development of CHA regulation. The Association was founded as a partnership of the member banks in 1865. Within two years, "it had begun to insist that all members, even the private and unincorporated banks, should furnish periodical statements of financial condition as a demonstration of their solvency." After the panic of 1873, it required "an unimpaired paid-up capital of $250,000" as a condition for new members, and "it was agreed that member banks which cleared checks for [non-member] institutions should assume responsibility for the ultimate payment of cashier's checks and certificates of deposit issued by the non-members." In 1876, the Association authorized the governing Clearing House Committee "to make an examination of any bank connected with the Clearing House whenever the Committee thought such action desirable." A particular bank, whose examination showed problems in 1881, was required to furnish "a bond of $500,000 to guarantee its clearing debts until such time as its condition should improve." In other cases, the Committee called for capital infusions. The ultimate penalty for non-compliance with CHA regulations was expulsion from the Association, which would deal a serious blow to a bank's reputation, as well as raising its costs of clearing and settlement.

Each of these regulations[12] reflects the desire of each member bank to eliminate the danger of others defaulting. The CHA certifies the soundness of banks, primarily for the sake of other banks, their clearing partners.

Gary Gorton and Donald J. Mullineaux (1987) have proposed a second possible motive for "endogenous regulation," namely the "joint production" of *public* confidence in bank liabilities through CHA certification. Maintaining the public's confidence in any given bank is in the interest of all the others, they argue, because one bank's failure might set off runs on the others. Consistent with the public-confidence motive, the New York City Clearing House Association would audit a bank rumored publicly to

---

[12] Some other CHAs (New York, Philadelphia) also employed reserve requirements against deposits, and monitored the borrowing, and purchasing, of specie from outside to meet obligations (Gorton and Mullineaux 1987, p. 462).

be in trouble, and would publish the results (not merely report them to its members). Gorton and Mullineaux also argue that the motive of reassuring the public explains why CHA regulation became more intensive during panics.

It is important to note, however, that contagion effects were negligible in nineteenth-century banking systems that were relatively free of destabilizing legal restrictions (e.g. Canada and Scotland). Banking in the US suffered under restrictions that blocked branch banking, compelled banks to hold similar sets of assets, encouraged pyramiding of reserves, and in other ways fostered underdiversification, homogeneity, and interdependence among banks. Such regulations provided a rational reason for contagion, i.e. for the failure of one bank to raise the public's estimate of the probability (given all the other information at hand) that another bank was insolvent. As noted by Dowd (1992a), CHAs in freer systems had less need to worry about default by their members, did much less in the way of regulation than the US CHAs examined by Gorton and Mullineaux, and did little or no last-resort lending. In a free banking system, then, banks may simply have no need for a lender of last resort or for the "joint production of confidence" through clearinghouses.

In any case, a member-controlled CHA will regulate banks only in ways that the banks themselves consider beneficial. Regulation hostile to banks, for example the restriction of interest rates on loans, or the geographic restriction of lending, is exclusively the province of central banks or other government agencies. *Official* regulation, which some have suggested as an essential function of a central bank, must by definition be the job of a government-sponsored agency.[13]

Conduct of monetary policy

Likewise, only an official central bank can be expected to execute an *official* monetary policy, i.e. pursue the government's macroeconomic goals through control of a monetary aggregate. But is there any sense in which a private CHA in a spontaneously evolved monetary system would conduct its own monetary policy? Even if a CHA does conduct a lender-of-last-resort policy, which involves a commitment to make deliberate changes in the stock of high-powered money on rare occasions, it conducts at most an *occasional* monetary policy. In normal times, and in the long run, a CHA bank does not control the quantity of high-powered money.

---

[13] Thus the definition of "central bank" offered by *The MIT Dictionary of Modern Economics* (Pearce 1986, p. 59), "the institution charged primarily with controlling a country's money and banking system," implies a government regulatory agency.

In a system without an official central bank, as studied in chapter 3, the public, in choosing the quantities of basic and bank-issued monies it desires to hold (in light of the purchasing power of the monetary unit and the competitive behavior of the banks), and the banks, in choosing the quantities in which they desire to hold basic money reserves (in light of the behavior of the public), jointly determine the quantities of basic and bank-issued monies. In a commodity-money system, as studied in chapter 2, the market for the commodity that serves as outside money determines the purchasing power of the monetary unit. There is no agency with the mission, or the power, to vary the quantity of high-powered money in pursuit of any goal like price stability or full employment.

The Origins of Government Central Banks

A private CHA bank can (and some historical examples of such institutions did) play three central banking roles: acting as a bankers' bank, acting as a lender of last resort when one is necessary, and regulating commercial banks in ways useful for enhancing safety and soundness. These three roles can be (and were) effectively filled without governmental action. Where a government central bank has been legislatively superimposed on a mature banking system, as in the US, these three roles have typically been nationalized.[14] The government's motives for nationalizing these clearinghouse functions may therefore offer at least a partial explanation for government sponsorship of an official central bank in such a country. It is not obvious, without investigating a specific historical case, what those motives might be.

Only a government-sponsored institution, on the other hand, can play the remaining two central-banking roles: monopolizing the provision of banknotes, and conducting a monetary policy involving continuous control over the stock of high-powered money. Here, one motive for government intervention is fairly obvious: the desire for revenue. The government's revenue motives may therefore offer at least a partial explanation for government sponsorship of an official central bank that takes on these two roles.

The creation of a note-issue monopoly, like the creation of any statutory monopoly, can be an important source of revenue through a sale of the exclusive privilege to a private firm. The sale can be implicit, as when monopoly privileges are awarded in return for loans at below-market rates, or the government can operate the sole bank of issue itself to collect a stream

---

[14] An exception: the Bank of Canada, established in 1935, did not absorb the bankers' bank function, which continued to be provided by a private CHA. In the 1980s, the clearinghouse was nationalized, but it is still administered separately from the Bank of Canada.

of monopoly profits. Monopoly profits are collected in the form of a zero-interest loan from the public's holding of non-interest-bearing banknotes. In a competitive system, banks that issue non-interest-bearing notes return the "float" to their customers via the in-kind benefits they must provide to compete along non-price dimensions. A statutory monopoly issuer, by contrast, need not compete along non-price dimensions and thus can keep the float. (Chapter 6 gives an analysis of which arrangement is more efficient.)

The conduct of a monetary policy can also yield fiscal benefits to government. The benefits are most obvious when, under a fiat money regime, the central bank expands stock of high-powered money as a direct source of revenue (see chapter 7). The leading government central banks were founded during an era of commodity money regimes, however, and it is unlikely that inflationary finance of this sort was envisioned at the time. The monopoly of note issue did pave the way for the later establishment fiat money by giving central bank notes a special status that made it possible for them to continue circulating even after redeemability had been removed. Under a commodity money regime, a government may see monetary policy as a means to influence credit market conditions and thereby to cheapen the terms on which it borrows, or, it may see monetary policy as a means to influence business cycles.

Historical Cases

England

The Bank of England, which became the prototype for many government-sponsored central banks around the world, acquired its government's sponsorship for fiscal reasons. The government of William III in 1694, together with a Parliament controlled by the Whig party, wanted to finance a war with France, but their credit was exhausted.[15] The government agreed to William Patterson's plan to induce a group of subscribers to fund new government debt in exchange for a charter of incorporation as the Bank of England. In Bagehot's (1873, p. 94) words, the Bank was a "Whig finance company . . . founded by a Whig government . . . in desperate want of money." The charter gave the Bank limited liability and exclusive possession of the government's deposits. The Bank subsequently gained greater

---

[15] Note that under a commodity standard, government bonds are denominated in commodity money that the government cannot manufacture ad lib, and are therefore always subject to default risk (unlike US government debt denominated in fiat dollars today). Classical liberals who opposed empire-building therefore favored continuous, and strict, adherence to the prevailing commodity standard as a fiscal constraint on their governments.

privileges in return for taking up more debt. In 1697, Parliament made the corporate charter exclusive, so that other banks in England could only be partnerships with unlimited liability. In 1708, the right of note-issue was denied to any other bank with more than six partners. As a result, the Bank of England was the sole bank of issue in the greater London area, had one-half to two-thirds the note circulation in England as a whole, and was by far the most important deposit bank.

Literally hundreds of issuing banks with six or fewer partners did business in the cities and towns outside London, where the Bank of England did not open branches until the nineteenth century, but these "country" banks were undercapitalized and notoriously weak. Writers referred to the "mushroom" banks that sprang up by the dozens overnight, and disappeared as quickly. The weakness of the country banks served the agenda of the Bank of England's partisans, who argued that the supplying of money could not be left safely to competition, but must be centralized in the Bank of England. The push for centralization eventually prevailed, though not without opposition. The Bank of England's charter came under criticism in the 1820s, and, in 1826, there was a tangible move toward freer banking with the legalization of issuing banks with unlimited numbers of partners, though only outside the London area. The threat to the Bank's London monopoly of issue was turned back in 1833, when the Bank's charter was renewed and its notes were made a legal redemption medium for other banks.

Prime Minister Robert Peel's Bank Charter Act of 1844 cemented the Bank's privileged position. New entry into note-issue was sealed off, and the circulations allowed to existing issuers were frozen. Provision was made for the Bank to absorb, over time, the authorized circulations of banks outside London, as they failed or merged, or as the Bank purchased their authorizations. In this way, the Bank of England would eventually gain a complete monopoly of the note-issue in England and Wales, but existing issuers would not protest (in fact, they were naturally pleased with the provisions that barred new entry and cartelized the industry).[16] As Bagehot argued, the Bank of England's roles as a bankers' bank, and lender of last resort, grew out of this whole series of artificial legislated advantages.[17]

---

[16] Not surprisingly, the Governor and Deputy Governor of the Bank proposed the Act to Peel, early in 1844. Accounts of the Peel Act often overlook its monopolizing features, however, and emphasize instead the provisions that fastened on the Bank of England a 100 per cent marginal specie reserve requirement for note issues in excess of its own authorized circulation, and that separated the Bank's Issuing Department from its Banking Department as a way to enforce this rule. I view these provisions as the Bank's attempt to insulate its policy (and hence its monopoly) from public criticism (White 1995).

[17] For a more detailed account of these developments, see Dowd (1991).

Other banks lodged their gold reserves with the Bank, making it the sole holder of gold for the entire banking system, with the powers and (he argued) duties that implied.

Scotland

The sharp contrast of Scotland's banking evolution to England's underscores the point that legislation, and not market forces, was responsible for the development of the Bank of England into a central bank. By a quirk of political fate, the Bank of Scotland could not become attached to its national government. The Scots Parliament that chartered the bank in 1695, and granted it a 21-year monopoly, was dissolved in 1707 with the union of the Parliaments. The British Parliament in London would not renew the Bank of Scotland's monopoly, and, in fact, deliberately chartered a rival bank, the Royal Bank of Scotland in 1727, over the Old Bank's protests.

The six-partner rule that restricted English banks did not extend to Scotland, so non-chartered banks could have any number of partners. Their entry expanded the number of Scottish banks decade by decade. A third chartered firm, the British Linen Company, moved into banking, and initiated the trend toward nationwide branch banking. There was a shakeout with the failure of the Ayr Bank in 1772 (described by Adam Smith in *The Wealth of Nations*), but the industry quickly recovered. The period 1810–1844 might be identified as the "heyday" of competitive note-issue, as many large banks, capitalized by several hundreds of shareholder-partners and equal in balance-sheet size to the three chartered banks, began entering after 1810. There were 29 banks of issue by 1826. Mergers and consolidations brought the number down to 19 in 1845. Peel's Act of 1844, and a supplementary act for Scotland the following year, closed off free entry.

In its heyday, the Scottish system combined vigorous competition with safe non-failure-prone banking. England, by contrast, had safety but little competition in London, and vigorous competition, but little safety, in the countryside. Striking evidence of the Scottish system's competitiveness is seen in the spread between loan and deposit interest rates, which was typically only one to two percentage points. No single bank was disproportionately large: the largest share of the note circulation in 1844 was about 14 percent, and five other banks had 9–12 percent each. All but a few banks were extensively branched, giving Scotland more bank offices per capita than England or the US. Most banks' notes circulated easily throughout the country at par, as all issuing banks belonged to the Edinburgh clearinghouse. The clearinghouse did not become a bankers' bank. Each bank held its own reserves, though they commonly had correspondent relationships with London deposit banks, and commonly settled among themselves with drafts on London. No central banking institution emerged in Edinburgh, nor did the Bank of England provide central banking services to the Scottish banks.[18]

The United States of America

The Federal Reserve Act of 1913, establishing a central bank for the US, incorporated many competing ideas, but its principal rationale was to prevent the recurrent banking panics (the Panic of 1907 was the worst of them) that were being fostered by the existing regulatory regime. The "National Banking" system, instituted for fiscal reasons during the Civil War, required banks to hold federal bonds as collateral for all notes they issued. As a result, the banking system could not expand the stock of currency to meet peak demands that arose seasonally and cyclically. The public, when it wanted but could not get more banknote currency, drained the banks of reserve currency. Severe cases of reserve shortage touched off the scrambles for liquidity (distress borrowing at high interest rates, and sometimes bank runs) characteristic of the panics.[19]

As discussed above, private CHAs had developed methods for coping with the panics. The Federal Reserve was supposed to do, officially and legally, what the CHAs had done privately and illegally. Thus, the Federal Reserve was to take over the central banking roles (serving as a bankers' bank, providing lender-of-last-resort facilities, regulating member banks for safety and soundness) that the CHA banks had developed. As Gary Gorton (1985a, p. 277) comments: "In fact, it is almost literally true that the Federal Reserve System, as originally conceived, was simply the nationalization of the private clearinghouse system." The Federal Reserve (Fed) soon began to conduct monetary policy continuously, rather than waiting for occasions of panic. When the Fed was founded the national banks continued to issue their own notes, but the course was set for the Fed to acquire a monopoly of note issue through the Treasury's eventual retirement of the bonds that national banks were required to hold as collateral backing for their banknotes.[20]

The motives behind the nationalization of clearinghouse functions were several. Some backers of the Federal Reserve Act merely wanted a legal,

---

[18] For more detail, see White (1995, chs. 2–3).

[19] For this diagnosis of the problems with the National Banking system, see Noyes (1910), Smith (1990), and Selgin and White (1994b; 1995).

[20] Thus Gorton's qualifiers "almost" and "as originally conceived" are important. Private CHA banks did not have a monopoly of the note issue (or even normally issue notes at all), nor continuously regulate the stock of high-powered money, roles the Federal Reserve would come to acquire.

and official, version of the CHAs, to make more currency and more reserves available at seasonal and crisis times of peak demand. Others, in the
spirit of the Progressive Era, wanted a more actively hands-on government
monetary policy institution that would emulate European central banks.[21] A
revenue motive may also have been indirectly at work. An alternative remedy for "inelasticity", proposed at the time, was deregulation of note-issue,
in particular an end to the bond-collateral requirement. Thus Vera Smith
wrote: "A retrospective consideration of the background and circumstances
of the foundation of the Federal Reserve System would seem to suggest that
many, perhaps most, of the defects of American banking could, in principle,
have been more naturally remedied otherwise than by the establishment of
a central bank." The bond-collateral requirement, dating from the Civil War
banking legislation, had been imposed as a way of force-feeding federal
government debt to the banking system. Its elimination would have been
fiscally disadvantageous to the government, as it would have meant an increase in the interest rate the federal government would have to pay in refinancing its debt.

Canada

The Bank of Canada was not founded until 1935, evidently because there
was little felt economic need for an official central bank in Canada. As
Bordo and Redish (1987) relate, the national clearinghouse maintained in
Montreal by the Canadian Bankers Association filled the bankers' bank role.[22]
Solvency and liquidity regulation was provided partly by the CHA and partly
by statutory chartering requirements. The Treasury monopolized the issue
of small notes ($5 and less), and also issued $10,000 notes used as bank
reserves, but the competing private banks supplied the intervening denominations. The Treasury stood ready to advance its Dominion notes to banks,
and had played a lender-of-last-resort role in 1907 and 1914. There had,
otherwise, been no panics or seasonal liquidity crises, in contrast to the US,
because branch banking and the elasticity of private banknote issue were
unrestricted. Bordo and Redish (1987) attribute the passage of the Bank of
Canada Act in 1935 not to any inefficiency in the status quo, and not to an
intention to overthrow the gold standard, but to a combination of "political
imperatives." To satisfy domestic public opinion, the government had to be
seen as doing something to combat the Great Depression, and, to achieve

---

[21] On the debate over the Federal Reserve Act, see West (1974), Timberlake (1978), and
Livingston (1986).
[22] The Bank of Montreal was banker to the national government, but lacking a note
monopoly, and the other privileges enjoyed by the Bank of England, did not become a bankers' bank.

international prestige, Canada had to join the club of nations sending official central bank governors to participate in international conferences of central bankers. The establishment of the Bank of Canada – like the establishment at about the same time of a state-owned airline and a state-owned radio broadcasting network – also appealed to the Canadian nationalism that prevailed in wake of Canada's receiving Dominion status in 1931.

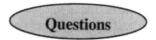

Questions

1   "Most of us would trust GM, IBM, or AT&T currency more readily than that of many developing nations because the 'currency' represented by these companies is more likely to remain convertible. After all, a guarantee is only as good as the guarantor." (Negroponte 1996) Why then are central banks, today, the sole issuers of paper currency?

2   "Competition does little to keep banks safe, because the public is not expert enough to evaluate a bank's claim that it is safe. Without government regulation, the public would have no credible assurance of bank solvency and liquidity." True or false? Explain.

3   Charles Goodhart argues that "as a lender of last resort, a central bank *has* to be involved in supervisory matters," i.e. monitoring individual commercial banks to see that they stay solvent and liquid. Is this true for the classical conception of the lender-of-last-resort role? Is it true for the modern conception of the role?

4   Walter Bagehot argued that in a "natural" banking system under laissez faire, "none of [the banks] gets so much before the others that the others voluntarily place their reserves in its keeping."

   (a)   Does the Bank of England in the nineteenth century, a dominant private commercial bank that did receive interbank deposits, provide a counter-example to Bagehot's argument? Why, or why not?

   (b)   Do the CHAs in the late nineteenth-century US, in whose keeping commercial banks did voluntarily place their reserves, provide a counter-example? Why, or why not?

   (c)   What historical systems, if any, support Bagehot's argument?

5   "The . . . Suffolk Bank . . . arranged for New England country banks to keep with it permanent deposits of $5,000 plus a further sum sufficient to redeem notes reaching Boston. The Suffolk undertook to receive at par the notes of banks that made such deposits, and the notes of country banks who refused to come into the scheme would be sent back for redemption. The Suffolk Bank, moreover, refused admit-

tance to its clearing agency to banks whose integrity was not above suspicion." (Smith 1990)

(a)   Why would the Suffolk have wanted the country banks to keep deposits with it for redeeming notes, rather than simply redeeming all notes by sending them back to the countryside?

(b)   Why would the Suffolk have refused its service to suspect banks?

5

Should Government Play a
Role in Money?

We have seen that there are political and historical reasons why central governments around the world today run the bankers' bank, monopolize the production of currency and reserve money, and regulate the provision of bank-issued money. The *status quo* did not materialize by accident. But are there any good reasons why governments *should* do these things? Is there a utilitarian or consumer-welfare-enhancing role for government to play in the monetary system? (A separate question, on which chapter 4 provides some evidence, is whether any such rationale actually accounts for why a particular government historically chose to become involved. That is, even if a good reason for intervention were found, it cannot be taken for granted that a realworld government has been motivated or driven by it. Actual government involvement in monetary systems may be better explained by the pursuit of goals other than the general public interest.) This chapter examines a number of theoretical arguments that propose a welfare-enhancing role for government in the provision of base money.[1] Chapter 6 then examines arguments that offer rationales for government regulation of banking.

---

[1] We do not consider, in this chapter, the important set of arguments proposing that government should (actively) control the quantity of base money so that it can pursue macroeconomic stabilization policy. A successful stabilization policy could, no doubt, be viewed as a public good. The main question about stabilization policy, however, is how likely in fact it is to succeed. See chapter 11 for discussion of stabilization policy in the context of the "rules versus discretion" debate.

Is Some Aspect of Money a Public Good?

The theory of public goods

The modern neoclassical economist's standard rationale for government provision of certain goods and services is the argument that they are "public goods." Some authors (van Dun 1984; Schmidtz 1991) have raised important questions about the internal coherence of the theory of public goods, and about its adequacy as a justification for the use of compulsory taxes and other governmental methods, but here we simply ask whether money, or any aspect of money, can be considered a public good. Does money exhibit the characteristics of a public good? The following discussion of the nature of a public good will be a bit informal, but sufficient for our purposes.

The key characteristic of a public good, following the standard analysis, is *non-rivalness in consumption*. Non-rivalness means that my use of the good's services does not diminish the amount of its services available to other consumers. My reception of an over-the-air television broadcast of *The Simpsons*, for example, does not make any less of the broadcast signal available to you. My choosing *not* to receive the signal does not make any more of the signal available. By contrast, a *private* good like a chocolate doughnut clearly exhibits rivalness in consumption: my eating a chocolate doughnut makes one less doughnut available to other potential consumers.[2]

A second characteristic ascribed to public goods is *non-excludability in supply*. Non-excludability means that it is not possible (or not profitable) to exclude non-payers from receiving the services of the good once it is provided to anyone. The benefits of preserving stratospheric ozone, for example, cannot be provided to me without also providing them to you. Non-rival goods, such as broadcast television signals or abatement of ozone depletion, tend to be non-excludable because "consumption" that does nothing to reduce the benefits available to others can be difficult, or impossible, to detect, let alone to meter. The provider of a non-meterable good cannot charge a price to beneficiaries alone, and exclude non-payers from consuming, because he cannot tell a beneficiary from a non-beneficiary. Non-rival consumption is likely to be non-meterable consumption, which in turn is likely to be non-excludable consumption.[3]

---

[2] Mmmmm . . . doughnuts.

[3] Consumption of a non-rival good can sometimes be metered and excluded, however. The British Broadcasting Corporation has been funded by a tax on television use enforced by television detector vans that actually roamed the streets electronically detecting television use (which coincided with the receipt of broadcast signals in the days before cable and

continued on next page

If a good is provided without exclusion, an individual's failure to pay for (or to contribute toward) its provision will not prevent him or her from enjoying whatever amount is provided. The selfishly best strategy in such a case is to "free ride," i.e. not to contribute, letting others make the sacrifices necessary to provide the good. If all individuals adopt the free-rider strategy, however, *no one* will voluntarily cover the cost of producing the good. A "market failure" occurs when the good goes unproduced even though in the aggregate individuals *would* (faced hypothetically with exclusion of non-payers) be willing to pay an amount exceeding the cost of production.

A public good is the limiting case of a good providing *non-appropriated* or *external* benefits, that is, a good whose consumption by one person throws off a set of incidental benefits to other people who are not compelled to pay for them. In a non-limiting case, the good provides primary benefits that are exclusive to one consumer. For example, a sharp-looking red 1963 Ford Falcon Futura convertible provides private transportation exclusive to its driver, and also incidental benefits to those who enjoy seeing it drive by. The private benefits may be sufficient for the primary consumers to provide some quantity of such goods, but the usual prognosis is that a failure to compensate them for the external benefits they provide results in "market failure" to provide enough of the goods. At the level produced by the market, the external beneficiaries are hypothetically willing to pay more than the marginal cost for an additional unit. (If admiring pedestrians were to toss coins, even only half as great in value as the pleasure they received, into the back seats of sharp-looking classic convertibles driving by, more drivers would be willing and able to bear the cost of keeping such cars on the road.) The usual prescription is a system of taxes and subsidies that compensate providers appropriately.

Money as a medium of exchange

A specific piece of currency or a checkable bank balance, as a privately owned good, clearly provides some benefits exclusively to its holder. The services of ready-to-spend balances of a generally accepted medium of exchange, as such, do not exhibit non-rivalness. As Roland Vaubel (1984) emphasizes, my enjoyment of the services from a pocketful of money *does* diminish that

---

satellite television) inside houses and apartments. Detected users were fined heavily if they had not paid the television use tax. For a photograph of such a detector van, see Heilemann (1994).

Bryan Caplan points out (in private correspondence) that admission to an uncrowded movie theater (where an additional patron does not interfere with the consumption of other patrons) can be considered a non-rival but excludable good. From that perspective, markets provide many non-rival goods. It is only non-excludability that makes market provision infeasible.

money's availability to others. You do not receive the same facilitation-of-exchange benefit regardless of whether you or I, or someone else, holds an additional dollar. (The less stringent idea that you nonetheless receive *some* benefit from my holding of an additional dollar is discussed below.)

Similarly, money balances are an eminently excludable good. I can cheaply exclude you from using dollars in my pocket or my bank account. Owners of money balances have no special difficulty commanding something in exchange for them. Market failure due to public-goods problems does *not* occur in the provision of media of exchange. Private mints and banks have for centuries been able to make a business of producing and selling money.

Money is therefore clearly not a *pure* public good. Authors nevertheless who argue that "money is a public good" really mean to argue that there is some public-good *aspect* to money. This is usually equivalent to saying that there are non-appropriable external benefits conferred by using a money. It will often be more convenient, in what follows, to frame the discussion in terms of external benefits, rather than public goods. Our discussion will draw extensively on Vaubel (1984), who has patiently categorized, and criticized, various ascriptions of "public good" characteristics to money.

Monetary stability

Some authors have suggested that monetary stability is a public good. Assume that "monetary stability" here means the stability of the purchasing power of a money. The argument for regarding monetary stability as a public good is that I cannot enjoy the benefits of holding stable money without you also enjoying those benefits. But surely I can, if you hold no money, or a different money. The benefits of monetary stability are provided only to those who (rivalrously) hold the money, and in proportion to their holdings. Stability of purchasing power is a *quality characteristic* of a money good, rather than itself a good (private or public). Monetary stability is unlike a broadcast television signal, which is not a quality characteristic of the television set needed to receive it. To use the chocolate doughnut analogy again: the tastiness of my chocolate doughnut may correspond to the tastiness of your doughnut, provided both have come from the same batch, but that does not make doughnuts (or "tastiness") a public good.

There is one sense, however, in which "monetary stability" can be said to be a public good. Where government monopolizes money production, monetary stability *does* become a public good in the sense that *any improvement in a government policy that benefits the entire public* is a public good. *Given* an effective government monopoly, we are both compelled to hold the same money (if we both hold money at all). I cannot then have money with one inflation rate while you have money with another. Efforts to bring about good behavior by the monetary authority (to increase monetary stability) are subject to free riding, each user of money preferring to let others bear the cost of those efforts. Such an interdependence among money users is due to the statutory monopoly in production, not to the nature of the good. If government monopolized, and standardized, all production of chocolate doughnuts, that would make improvements in "doughnut policy" a public good. It would not make chocolate doughnuts, as such, a public good.

Are There Relevant External Benefits in the Choice of Which Money to Use?

The choice of a common medium of exchange

Several economists have argued that there are important external benefits conferred by using a *common* medium of exchange. As Vaubel (1984, p. 33) summarizes the case, they argue that "if A decides to accept and use the same money . . . which B accepts and uses, he confers an external benefit on B." This external benefit is taken to be *non-appropriable*, meaning that A has no way to charge B for it, and *Pareto-relevant*, meaning that B would be willing to pay an amount sufficient to induce A to use the same money.[4]

The same idea is expressed – for example by Hellwig (1985), and others cited by Vaubel (1984, p. 30) – in the argument that the social consensus to use good x as money generates useful nonproprietary knowledge, and is thus a public good. The knowledge that every trader in an economy accepts x as money is useful to me for facilitating planning and trade. If I know that everyone I will meet in a market uses money x, I do not have to incur costs to find out what exchange media others will accept. My possessing that knowledge is nonrival to your possessing it.

This argument does not yet establish, however, that there is a welfare-enhancing role for government in fostering consensus on a medium of exchange. As Vaubel points out, at least some methods of producing knowledge of what other traders will do are not worth the cost, for example the method of central planning that restricts what other traders are allowed to do. It may be that consensus on a generally accepted medium of exchange is best reached through the market, following the Mengerian convergence process discussed in chapter 1. It seems likely, in fact, that those in government would have no superior knowledge of what good to establish as the conventional money. In a pre-monetary economy, neither those in government nor anyone else has even conceived of such a convention.

---

[4] Buchanan and Stubblebine (1962) elaborate the distinctions between marginal and inframarginal externalities, potentially relevant and irrelevant externalities, and Pareto-relevant and Pareto-irrelevant externalities.

Markets can accomplish consensus on a particular money, in the Mengerian fashion, because self-interest in economizing on the costs of finding a trading partner leads each agent *privately* to seek the most popular medium of exchange. There are private as well as social benefits to using the medium of exchange that the most other traders use: the medium readily accepted by the largest number of my potential trading partners is precisely the medium that most facilitates trade for me. Indeed, there is no apparent divergence between what is socially most beneficial (using the medium of exchange most commonly favored by one's potential trading partners) and what is privately most beneficial.[5]

Spontaneous convergence is possible, à la Menger, because the benefit conferred on others by using the medium of exchange they prefer is not showered on them willy-nilly, like broadcast television signals or pollution abatement. It is a transaction cost saving conferred *only* on one's trading partners. Thus it *can* be appropriated. An individual on the margin of a group using a common money can be "bribed" to use that money by those who benefit from her use of it. A trader already using the money, acting in accordance with her self-interest, will offer the marginal trader better prices in terms of the preferred money, implicitly sharing her cost savings from transacting with him in that money.

The decision to use a particular money (rather than barter or another money) is like the decision to join a telephone network, i.e. to rent a phone line and connect a telephone or fax machine to it (Vaubel 1984, p. 34). The benefit to any individual of owning a telephone or fax machine increases with the number of other machine-owners who are thereby accessible; thus a new agent's decision to join confers benefits on others. The potential welfare problem with such a "network good" is that too few may decide to join the network if joining involves significant *fixed* costs to the joiner (i.e. costs independent of the volume of interactions – phone calls or trades – made within the network). There may be a public-good aspect to the sinking of the fixed costs of joining, as each potential network partner will prefer to free ride rather than contribute toward them.[6] Under-joining would clearly

---

[5] In the language of game theory, forming a consensus on a particular money is a co-ordination game. Defection from an established consensus is clearly not a dominant strategy. I thank David Schmidtz for this observation.

[6] An under-joining problem occurs in the case of telephones if, for example, all the children in a family would together be willing to pay enough to cover the fixed monthly connection fee for their parents (who themselves find the fee too expensive), so that they could phone the parents, but each child waits for the others to bear the cost. It is hard to believe that failures to negotiate around such problems (e.g. the children agreeing on a method for sharing the subsidy) are of much practical significance within families, but there could be a problem in a more anonymous network.

not occur in a money network if the costs of using a particular money are entirely variable, i.e. there are *zero* fixed costs of "plugging in" to the network, because then the costs can be recouped by appropriating some share of the transaction cost savings when trading with others in their preferred medium of exchange. Even if fixed costs are not zero, they will still be irrelevant at the margin if the private benefits (the joiner's share of the transactions-cost savings) from joining the network are sufficient to induce *every* trader to join the common money network (exceed the fixed cost for every potential joiner).[7] There is obviously no market failure to produce a common medium of exchange when everyone in an economy spontaneously uses the same money.

Stephen Morrell (1983) has argued that, even so, a dynamic externality may remain. The market convergence process may operate too slowly, providing a rationale for government speeding it up. In this argument, the *information* on which particular good is most highly saleable is a public good (like pure scientific information). Underproduction of this information, due to free-rider problems, results in too-slow convergence.[8] The collective action the argument rationalizes is not government's producing or regulating money, but only publicizing the salability of the most salable goods. (Information or publicity about money, not the money itself, is the public good.) Prescribing such a publicity role to government is somewhat paradoxical: to improve the market outcome, those in government have to know better than those in trade what is the most salable good among traders. Further, to speed the emergence from barter, those in government would have to know that the market process is heading toward convergence on a commodity money, even though they live in an economy in which money has never yet existed. The idea of money would have to be grasped before money has emerged. In any event, the rationalized government role ceases once a common money has emerged.

---

[7] Vaubel (1984) assumes that externalities from the use of a common money are *not* entirely appropriable (though he points out that such externalities cannot be relevant at the margin when everyone spontaneously uses the same money). His formal model makes *A*'s payoff increase with the number of other people who use the same currency, regardless of whether *A* ever transacts with them. His own discussion of the benefits from a common money, however, recognizes them as savings of transaction costs.

[8] Similar concerns exist today about convergence on information-technology standards, like a standard for high-definition television. Should we let competing incompatible standards slug it out in the marketplace, as in the videocassette battle between Beta and VHS, and in the operating standards battle between Macintosh and Microsoft Windows? Can we be confident that the fittest will survive? Or should a panel of experts agree on an industry-wide standard before hardware and software are rolled out? If the latter, should the panel be a private group of industry experts (as in the case of the Motion Pictures Expert Group responsible for the MPEG standards in video compression) whose decisions have no force of law, or should government and compulsory standardization be involved?

Uniformity of money

A similar (perhaps identical) argument holds that there are uncompensated positive external effects from any individual's using a medium of exchange that is uniform with the medium used by others. In other words, *uniformity* of exchange media is a public good. Government, the argument continues, may supply this public good by monopolizing the provision of exchange media or otherwise suppressing the variety of media that prevails under free competition.[9] Carl Menger (1936) himself made this argument with regard to metallic standards and coinage. Immediately after noting that "the sanctioning of money through the authority of the State is alien to the general conception of money," Menger nonetheless endorsed "the perfection of money through the State," i.e. government suppression of excessive variety in metallic monies:

> The automatic development of money usually leads to an extremely detrimental multiplicity of money with regard to the types of metals, the alloys, the weight units and their parts. Once coinage of the monetary metal becomes established, an equally detrimental multiplicity of coins tends to develop. The State fulfills one of its most important tasks by regulating the uniformity of the money system in a way that corresponds to the needs of the population instead of confining itself to the certification of weights.
>
> By satisfying the need of trade for a uniform system of weights and measures in all areas but especially in the area of coined money through the determination of the country's currency, the State creates the basis and precondition for a simplified and secure system of calculation and payments which is a great improvement over the multiplicity of monies that would develop automatically.

Karl Brunner and Allan H. Meltzer (1971, pp. 801–2) have made much the same argument with regard to banknotes, stating that the suppression of rival brands of banknotes in England by the Bank Charter Act of 1844 "raised economic welfare by reducing the costs of acquiring information." Though they make this statement only in passing, it warrants our attention as a rare attempt by leading monetary economists to defend, in welfare-theoretic terms, a piece of legislation that sponsored a central bank.

Uniformity is held to be a good by these authors because it reduces the information costs that transactors bear: if transactors in my economy are compelled to use only money *z*, then I am better off because I don't have to bother finding out about any other monies. This argument, however, seems

---

[9] For a recent example of this argument, see Gandal and Sussman (1997, p. 440), who refer to "standard universally accepted coins" as "a public good".

to prove too much. If it is valid with regard to coins and banknotes, there should also be welfare gains to suppressing rival brands of checking accounts. In fact, there should be gains to suppressing rival brands of any product. It seems to be saying that too much choice makes life difficult for consumers. But it is far from clear how we are supposed to know *a priori* that the optimal number of product varieties is equal to one, or if it is equal to one, why we should believe that the market will inefficiently support more than one. The previous section argued to the contrary that there is no divergence between private and public interest in the choice between using a popular or an unpopular money, because there is not an *uncompensated* external effect.[10]

Still less is it clear that consumers will be better off choosing through a political process, or having government choose for them, which one brand or variety is to survive. Even if the market process will eventually converge on a single type of money, the uniformity foregone while converging is not necessarily a wasteful aspect of competition that may efficiently be supplanted by edict. It is unlikely that anyone, in or out of government, would know ahead of time exactly what type of money the market process will select (White 1989, p. 58). If the eventual winner were obvious, other media of exchange would already have been abandoned (nobody wants to be stuck with a loser), and convergence would already have occurred. It is unclear how a non-market, or political method, for selecting the most suitable type of money would discover what that type is.

Menger's theory of convergence to a generally accepted medium of exchange suggests by extension (though Menger himself appeared to deny this) that an unimpeded market will converge to a single uniform metallic monetary standard. Even with a plurality of competing private mints, all coins *can* conform to a uniform standard provided only that the requisite technical knowledge is not a trade secret. The mintmasters *will* choose to make their coins interchangeable if their customers desire it, that is, if each trader wants to hold money exactly conforming to the standard most readily accepted by his trading partners.[11] Thus mintmasters can be expected to produce coins denominated in multiples of the one standard unit. A variety of competing brands does not imply non-uniformity.

From this perspective, the historical experience of early modern Europe with an inconvenient multiplicity of metals, alloys, and weight units among

---

[10] If the potential positive effect from my choosing to use a popular money is appropriable (I share in the benefit), then the benefit is internalized.

[11] For the same reason – users desire interchangeability – a plurality of competing brickmakers make their products conform to the dimensions of a standard building brick. Even a plurality of competing toymakers produces interlocking plastic toy bricks that conform to a common standard (the Duplo/Lego standard).

its coins (presumably this experience was the source of Menger's concern) should be attributed to the great number of local states involved in granting or operating local mint monopolies that debased their coins at various rates, rather than attributed to the "automatic development" of money in the absence of government involvement. The private bankers of Europe in fact worked to overcome the difficulties created by the variety and non-uniformity of coins, through their development of transferable bank deposits denominated in standardized units (de Roover 1948, p. 250; Glasner 1989, p. 10). The fact that merchants demanded such deposits, as a means of avoiding the non-uniformity of coin, illustrates how private incentives tend to promote a uniform monetary standard.

Competing banks issuing banknotes and deposits in an unrestricted market, as analyzed in chapters 1 and 3, will normally all denominate their liabilities in the same monetary standard. Notes and deposits will tend to trade at par against one another. Information costs associated with additional brands are therefore low. All I really need to know, in deciding whether to accept a note issued by a new bank is whether my bank will accept it at par from me, and whether the issuer is likely to fail before I spend or deposit it. Again, a variety of competing brands does not imply non-uniformity. Brunner and Meltzer might argue that until all brands but one are suppressed, there is a positive information cost to traders of determining whether an additional bank is failure-prone. However, while this is true, the same cost is equally present when deciding whether to accept the liabilities of the one bank (rather than dealing only in coin). Also, there are potential consumer benefits of risk-diversification from additional banks entering the competition.

The welfare question is whether the costs of additional brands of banknotes exceed the benefits at the margin. It is difficult to see why this is a public-good question calling for a collective decision, and difficult to see how it can be answered *a priori* without a market trial. Why are the information costs involved with competing brands of banknotes any different in kind from the information costs involved with competing brands of any other product? (Would Brunner and Meltzer argue that only one brand of checking account should be allowed, to avoid the costs of comparing brands? If not, what is the relevant difference between checking deposits and banknotes?) Individual traders who estimate that the costs of dealing with any additional brand of banknotes do exceed the benefits can refuse to incur the costs, and simply refuse every new brand after the first. If this attitude were widely shared, then the market would support only a single brand even without legal restrictions. Those who choose to undertake the information costs, on the other hand, must believe that the benefits outweigh those costs. Suppression of additional brands prevents the market from supporting multiple brands even when, in the eyes of some consumers, the benefits do exceed the costs (White 1989, pp. 154–5). It is a type of paternalism, harmful to those consumers who value having a choice, and incompatible with competition.

Social consensus on a unit or medium of account

A number of economists, among them Leland Yeager (1983) and Charles Kindleberger (1986), have argued in various ways that the unit-of-account or medium-of-account role of money has public-good characteristics. This subsection considers the case for considering consensus on *any* medium of account to be a public good.[12] In important respects, this case is akin to the above-considered cases for considering commonness or uniformity of the medium of exchange to be a public good. The next subsection considers the public-good characteristics of switching to a *superior* medium of account.

The argument for regarding consensus on a medium of account as a public good runs as follows. The benefits of having a common medium of account are non-rival and non-excludable. Even by a transactor who does not hold any money denominated in the medium can use it for pricing and bookkeeping. More generally, transactors cannot feasibly be charged a fee to use the medium of account. Because those who promote a common medium of account (for example by producing a currency denominated in it, listing prices in it, or calculating and publishing a price index for it) cannot enforce proprietary rights in it, and thus cannot charge fees that fully capture the benefits to others, the market will insufficiently provide common media of account. Put another way, the market will not produce enough consensus concerning media of account.

This argument, were it accepted, would not rationalize government action to suppress alternative media of account, or to supply media of exchange. It would instead rationalize government's promoting one or more common media of account, using them in its own transactions, and perhaps publishing price indices or subsidizing those who do so. Such activity would, the argument goes, provide information of a public-good sort that would otherwise be underprovided (Vaubel 1984, pp. 29–30).

It is doubtful that the problem of *underprovision* applies to media of account as such. If one common medium of account is enough – if the social

---

[12] The unit of account is the unit used for pricing, bargaining, and bookkeeping. The distinction between the *unit* of account and the *medium* of account is that the former consists of a specified quantity of the latter. The term *numeraire* is sometimes used to denote the medium of account. In addition to the benefits from having a common *medium* of account (silver), we might consider separately the benefits from having a common standard *unit* (the dollar, defined as so many grams of silver of specified fineness) in which that medium is measure or counted. In most of what follows, the same arguments apply to both types of consensus.

benefit of having a *second* common medium is close to zero or is at least exceeded by its cost – then no market failure occurs so long as the market establishes *one* common medium of account (Macaulay 1983). If the value of commonality in the medium of account is large, and it is costly for the typical transactor to deal in multiple units, that by itself suggests that the social benefit of a second medium of account is close to zero. But will the market establish even one sufficiently common medium of account?

The Mengerian theory of the spontaneous origin of a standard medium of exchange, supplemented by chapter 1's arguments that this medium will naturally be used as the medium of account, and that one unit of same will be chosen as the unit of account, indicates that the market will, in fact, establish one common medium and one common unit of account, even without proprietary rights in the unit.[13] There is no market failure to deliver a common medium or unit of account because

1   there is no failure to deliver a commonly accepted medium of exchange,
2   each individual will naturally prefer to use the generally accepted medium of exchange as his medium of account, and
3   there will be convergence on a standard unit of that medium as the unit of account.

Thus, there is no apparent divergence between the public interest (in a common unit of account) and the private interests (in using the unit that is most popular with other traders) that govern individuals in their choices of accounting units. Private interests drive a process by which a commonly accepted medium of exchange *and* unit of account emerge.

Some authors, such as Menger (1936) in the passage quoted above, draw an analogy between the role of government in establishing a common unit of account and its role in establishing a common system of weights and measures. The analogy cuts both ways. Government bureaus today do maintain official definitions of weights and measures. But standard units in these areas, as in money, are typically the products of long usage and evolution rather than of *de novo* definition or invention. After standard units have emerged, they may be codified, but codification can take place in the private sector (O'Driscoll 1986, p. 25).[14] A trade association of private mints

---

[13] Where there are economies of standardization, a non-proprietary standard carries the advantage of eliminating the potential for monopoly pricing by the proprietor.

[14] O'Driscoll (1986, pp. 25–6) notes that the creation of standard time zones by joint action of railroad companies is an example of private standardization. He also notes that the metric system is an unusual case of an invented system of weights and measures. But even the metric system could conceivably be *adopted* without governmental action.

would presumably find it in its interest to codify the precise definition of the standard unit of a metallic money, just as trade groups in other industries specify technical standards. Private arbitration or judicial resolution of contractual disputes could resolve the precise meaning of money units named in contracts if any uncertainty remained.

Switching to a better medium or unit of account

The objective of reformers who wish to establish a new medium of account is usually not to secure *additional* media of account, of course, but rather a *better* medium of account. Thus, they argue for government actively promoting a *switch* in the medium of account, on the grounds that *coordinating a switch to a medium of account better than the currently established medium* is a public good. Leland B. Yeager (1983) explicitly makes this argument to explain why market forces, alone, cannot be counted on to assure adoption of his own proposal for a novel index-basket medium of account. (His proposal and associated ideas are discussed at length in chapter 12.) But the argument is independent of any particular medium-of-account proposal. Advocates of switching back to a gold standard – on the grounds that gold represents a better medium of account than the fiat money – implicitly accept the argument when they call upon the government to make the switch, rather than simply calling for the elimination of any legal barriers against private citizens and firms putting themselves on the gold standard.

To actively promote a switch, the government would define a new medium (and unit) of account, publicize it, and make it official by requiring tax payments and other government transactions to be denominated in it. The government would thus do more than simply eliminate legal restrictions against the use of alternative media of account. On the other hand, the switching process does not necessarily require that money denominated in the new medium is made an *exclusive* legal tender (i.e. that contracts in alternative media are prohibited).

The argument that coordinating the switch to a better medium of account is a public good does not deny that a common medium spontaneously emerges in the market. The question is, instead, whether the spontaneously emerged standard is the best among the feasible alternatives. What makes one medium of account "better" than another? Not its superiority a denominator for spot prices: any good with a non-zero relative price can play that role as well as any other. The concern of reformers is rather that media of account differ in their suitability for use in long-term contracts, accounting, and forward-looking economic calculation, due to differences in the stability or predictability over time of their purchasing powers. A better unit of account is one with a more stable purchasing power. Profits are more difficult to estimate accurately, both retrospectively and prospectively, when the value of the monetary unit is more variable. Long-term contracts become more costly to make, and to keep.[15]

The same Mengerian theory that predicts convergence to *some* common medium of exchange, and to a medium of account linked to it, can be used to argue that the invisible hand may fail to select the *best* medium of account.[16] Recall that the theory derives convergence from each individual's strong private incentive to use the medium of exchange that is most popular. A particular good with an accidental "head start" as a popular medium of exchange in the earliest stages of indirect exchange (perhaps it is widely consumed and has at least some of the physical properties that make it suitable for swapping hand to hand) might therefore emerge as money even though a different good would have made a better medium of account. The evolutionary process selected the most popular commodity, not necessarily the best to serve as medium of exchange and account. Even if the best medium of *exchange* tends to be selected, it can be argued that technological advances including the development of banking have now made other properties (namely stability of purchasing power) more important in a medium of *account* than the property (namely linkage to a medium of exchange suitable for hand-to-hand trading) that historically drove the medium-of-account selection process. In any event, each individual's private incentive to use the medium that others use makes it exceedingly difficult to bring about a spontaneous switch to a new medium of account. Once the Mengerian process has converged to a common medium, even unanimous agreement to the proposition that "alternative medium *y* would be superior" will not suffice to bring about a switch to the alternative. The problem is that too few individuals have an incentive to *go first* in switching.

The concept of a "network good" is useful for restating the problem. Users of a common unit of account form a network. The decision to participate in a network provides benefits to one's trading partners in the form of reduced costs of communicating prices, contracting, and accounting with them. If the fixed costs of network switching are negligible, these benefits to others are fully appropriable. If fixed costs are significant, the decision to join a network has a public-good aspect. This holds *a fortiori* when the fixed costs are so high that an individual can economically belong only to

---

[15] For a thoughtful account of the burdens of an unstable medium of account see Leijonhufvud (1981, chs. 9–10).

[16] I am indebted to Israel Kirzner for bringing this argument to my attention. He may not subscribe to the specific version of the argument that follows. Similar arguments are common in the economics literature on the adoption of standards, cited in the following footnote.

To say that the invisible hand *may in principle* fail to select the best medium of account is not to say that it did, in fact, fail. It may be that, fortunately, silver and gold standards are as good as any feasible alternative.

one network. The early switchers to a new network then bear significant extra costs from being in à smaller network. Each trader would rationally choose *not* to be an earlier switcher, but, instead, would wait for others to go first before she incurred the costs of adopting a proposed new unit, especially if there is uncertainty about whether it really will supplant the old. In effect, those who wait are rationally free-riding on the cost-bearing actions of others. Thus Yeager (1983, p. 314) writes that would-be early users "have inadequate incentives to provide what would be in part a public good" of switching to, and thereby raising the benefits to others of switching to, a superior unit of account. A superior potential standard languishes, because people are "locked in" to the network surrounding an inferior standard established by historical chance.[17]

Could not a private entrepreneur bear the start-up costs of launching a new unit of account, just as entrepreneurs have borne such costs to launch telephone, fax, computer, video-game, and other networks? Here the questions of excludability and free-riding arise. Yeager (1983, p. 321) argues that the market would under-reward the private provision of a superior unit of account (assumed to be embodied in a private money) because of non-excludability and free-rider problems: "Because of the free availability of his money as a unit of accounting and calculation even to parties who held little or none of it, a well-behaved issuer could not collect compensation for all the advantages he was conferring on the public in general."

There would seem to be methods for excluding would-be free riders on a unit of account, however, and thereby for enabling the unit's provider to collect compensation from users. Somewhat analogously to a unit of account, a musical melody is a non-rival and non-excludable aspect of a musical recording, and therefore could be considered a public good.[18] The melody can be remembered and hummed, even by those who do not buy the recording. This does not make a recorded disc a public good, but, perhaps, the melody itself is. Do we therefore need government to subsidize the provision of melodies? In practice, of course, our economy relies upon a more market-oriented means for sufficient production of melodies, namely copyright and royalty protection. Those who use a melody (commercially, at

---

[17] A much-cited example of technology "lock-in" of this sort is Paul David's (1985) account of the persistence of the QWERTY layout as the standard typing keyboard despite the later arrival of an alternative – the Dvorak keyboard – that is supposedly known to be significantly faster-typing . For further elaborations and applications of the argument see Katz and Shapiro (1994) and Besen and Farrell (1994). Leibowitz and Margolis (1990; 1994) show that David's QWERTY tale is doubtful, and argue that, in general, the scope of network externalities is empirically more limited than these authors suggest. The lock-in literature has not considered the case of monetary standards.

[18] Or, although a chocolate doughnut is a private good, one could regard a superior *recipe* for chocolate doughnuts as pure information, and therefore a public good.

least) are legally required to obtain permission, or pay a royalty fee (or both). The system provides excludability in a manner that has proven enforceable enough, in practice, to encourage plenty of melodies to be produced.[19]

Similar protection can be, and actually has been, extended to published price indices. Reportedly the Dow-Jones Company has successfully prevented a futures contract in the Dow-Jones Industrial Average from being created, with the legal system recognizing that the company has a proprietary right in its index. Establishing, or enforcing, a similar proprietary right in a unit of account might be a more challenging task. But, in principle, a copyright and royalty protection system could be applied to units of account. The private agencies ASCAP and BMI monitor the airwaves, collect royalties from radio stations, and distribute them to the owners of copyrighted melodies who have engaged the agencies for that purpose. In principle, a similar private agency could monitor advertisements and price tags, collect royalties, and distribute them to the owners of the copyrighted units of account used in the ads and price tags. At least some proprietary rights in a unit of account can apparently be secured already. In the 1980s, a firm (now defunct) called the Gold Standard Corporation (advertising slogan: "Put yourself on the gold standard") issued coins and banknotes bearing marks to indicate that both the symbol and the name of its "Gold Standard Unit" carried trademark protection.

The primary reason we do not see an active market for privately provided media or units of account, today, is therefore not free-rider problems specific to the unit of account *per se*. These problems could be overcome by a copyright and royalty protection system. The reason is, rather, the natural link between a medium of account and a medium of exchange, combined with Mengerian convergence or network effects – and possibly legal restrictions – working against the achievement of critical mass by alternatively denominated media of exchange.

As we saw in chapter 1, markets are not incapable of supplanting one medium of account with a better medium that spreads from the "foreign trade" sector. Cowry and copper standards have given way to silver and gold, and high-inflation countries (such as Israel and Argentina in recent decades) have become "dollarized": the local fiat money has given way to a more stable foreign fiat money. (The US was Argentina's largest trading partner. Under the high inflation of the late 1980s, prices

---

[19] This "intellectual property" system is at least akin to the system of private property rights and contract within which goods composed of atoms (rather than information bits) are normally produced and sold. One might wonder, though, why a composer who *broadcasts* his melody to people with whom he has no contractual agreement is not, like an author who tucks his pamphlet under your windshield wiper, considered to have given it away.

began to be listed in US dollars rather than in rapidly depreciating australs, simply to avoid the costs of changing the nominal price listing every day. Common use of the dollar as a medium of account, which implied that many people were already incurring the cost of tracking the current austral–dollar exchange rate, paved the way for dollar-denominated Federal Reserve notes to become a commonly accepted medium of exchange.) Spontaneous switches of this sort seem to occur, however, only when the original medium of account becomes *much* worse than an alternative (in recent dollarization experience, when the difference in inflation rates exceeds something like 20 percent per year). Apparently, only then are private incentives sufficient for enough individuals to choose to be early switchers.

There is, thus, a case in principle for collective action to switch to a better medium of account.[20] To make a compelling case, in practice, for switching to a specific new medium of account, its proponents must show that it would, in fact, be a better medium, and enough better to justify bearing the cost of the switchover.[21] This is the practical question that, in recent years, has faced Europe in considering the switch from various national currencies to the euro, Argentina in considering the switch from the austral to a US dollar-based peso, and former Soviet republics in considering the switch from the ruble to a dollar- or Deutsche-mark-based currency. As we did in chapter 2 in contrasting gold and fiat standards, one can estimate the size of consumer surplus from lower inflation – if the inflation rate of the new standard can be predicted. In the case of a switch to the gold standard or the US-dollar standard, there is at least a track record to consult. In the case of Europe's switch to the euro, there is not. The citizens of low-inflation European countries (Germany in particular) have been understandably skeptical of promises that euro inflation will be no higher.

There may be other benefits from a new unit of account besides lower inflation: two major selling points for the euro have been the elimination of currency-changing costs in cross-border shopping, and the elimination of exchange-rate risk in cross-border investment. Evaluating the relative benefits of fixed versus floating exchange rates is a book-length topic (see De Grauwe 1997) that is beyond our scope here.

---

[20] The phrase "collective action" leaves it open whether government, or (say) a private group of payments industry experts, is the best body for reaching a consensus decision on a new monetary standard. Obviously, a government the size of the typical modern nation-state (through which passes one-fourth to one-half of national income) is going to have to get on board for any switch-over.

[21] Europe's cost of switching from national fiat currencies to the euro has been estimated at US$200 billion.

Policy implications

To summarize what we have covered to this point: Public goods theory does not provide a rationale for the provision of media of exchange by government. Money balances are not a public good. It can be argued that *pure information about money,* like pure information about anything else, is a public good. However, there are private incentives to acquire the relevant information (about the media of exchange and media of account used by others), and to act on it in a way that produces social consensus and uniformity in money (without anyone necessarily intending this outcome). Government promotion of information to speed up convergence might have been justified on public goods grounds in a pre-monetary economy, but such policy advice has lost its relevance once a standard money *has* emerged of which everyone is aware.

When the benefits to others from an individual's choosing to use a popular medium of exchange and medium of account (reduced transactions and accounting costs for her trading partners) are appropriable (are shared with those trading partners), they are not a source of market failure to converge to a common medium of exchange or medium of account. A problem might arise if there were large fixed costs of adopting monetary exchange, but the problem does not exist where everyone already uses money. Even in developing economies, which are less than fully monetized, if there *were* significant *non*-appropriable external benefits at the margin from inducing more transactors to use money, these benefits would at most argue for subsidization of adoption costs, not government production of money (Vaubel 1984, p. 41). Private incentives could be allowed wider scope to work toward full monetization in incompletely monetized economies, as they were historically allowed to work in the Western economies, through the private issue of banknotes (White 1989, p. 119).

Network effects that "lock in" an established monetary unit do provide a case, in principle, for collective action in switching to a better medium of account. The practical problem is to identify what would, in fact, be a better medium of account.

Are There Relevant External Benefits to the Choice of How Much Money to Hold?

The previous section considered arguments about external effects from an individual's choice of which medium of exchange or unit of account to use. This section discusses arguments that posit external effects not in the choice of which, but in the choice of *how much* money to hold.

Transactions cost reductions

David Laidler, as quoted by Vaubel (1984, p. 29), has argued that holding more money throws off external benefits because "any one agent, holding cash balances of a given average size, is less likely to incur the costs of temporarily running out of cash, the larger are the average balances of those with whom he trades." Trader Joe, this argument suggests, can replenish his cash balance by selling goods to his trading partners. The larger *their* balances, the less likely *they* are to run out of cash, and, hence, the more likely they are to be able and willing to buy Joe's goods when he wishes to sell. Their holding of inventories on which Joe may draw provides him with benefits.

Benefits, yes; but are these benefits really external? A grocery store does not provide me with an *external* benefit by holding a stock of milk that I can buy whenever I need milk. The value of the milk's availability is, presumably, fully incorporated into the price the store charges for the milk. Stores that make milk available in the middle of night charge higher prices to cover their costs of providing additional availability. Likewise, pawn shops, which make cash readily available in exchange for goods, charge higher goods prices for money (pay lower money prices for the pawned goods) than the goods' owners might find (less readily) elsewhere. As an alternative to pawning goods, individuals can avoid running out of cash by borrowing. Banks that guarantee, in advance, an individual's ability to borrow at any time – provide a line of credit, in other words – can, and often do, charge a fee for that service. Otherwise, the value of the service of having cash available to borrow is, presumably, fully incorporated into the interest rate and loan fees the bank charges when money is actually borrowed.

Increases in purchasing power, considered statically

A long-standing and much-debated argument in the literature of monetary theory claims that the uncompensated external effect of private money-holding decisions on the purchasing power of money implies the "nonoptimality of money holding under laissezfaire" (Samuelson 1969). This non-optimality (in the absence of a program to remedy the problem) can be stated in several alternative ways. We will number the alternative statements to facilitate discussion. The first version is:

Statement 1: Real money balances are too small.

An equivalent version is:

Statement 2: The price level is too high (for a given nominal stock of money).

Equivalence between statements 1 and 2 follows from the definitional identity that the stock of real balances equals the stock of nominal balances divided by the price level.

The purchasing-power externality argument, leading to statement 2, runs as follows.[22] Each individual, confronting an opportunity cost of holding money (identified with the higher interest yield available on alternative assets), economizes on real balances so as to equate the marginal benefit of holding them (sometimes labeled their "liquidity service" yield) to the marginal cost. A collective decision to *lower the price level* and, thereby, increase real money balances would provide every money holder with greater liquidity and, thus, make every money holder better off. Unfortunately, each individual acting selfishly would endeavor to restore his private equi-marginal condition by spending his additional real balances (to him, the foregone interest cost exceeds the benefit). The aggregate result of all individuals responding to private incentives in this way is to drive the price level back up, reducing real balances, and nullifying the potential social bonanza from a lower price level. Thus, the price level remains too high.

As stated, the argument is clearly invalid. Consider how it would read as applied to wheat, rather than to money. Would an arbitrary social decision to raise the relative price of a bushel of wheat make every wheat holder better off? No, because some would be unable to sell their wheat at a price above the market-clearing price. Money is no different in this respect from other goods. The price level (which is the inverse of the relative price of a unit of the money good) has an equilibrium value that equates the actual and desired real stocks of money. To lower the price level below that value is to create an unsustainable *disequilibrium*, an excess supply of money that implies an excess demand for non-money goods. The appearance of a bonanza for money-holders is simply an illusion, based on ignoring the other side of the market for cash balances. Because the market is not clearing, money-holders cannot all take advantage of the higher purchasing power seemingly available. The short side of the market rations trading: at the low prices, fewer goods are offered for money than money-holders want to buy. The argument is invalid in suggesting that a lowering of the price level is beneficial even if the price level's *equilibrium* value is not lowered.

This suggests an amended statement of the supposed non-optimality:

Statement 3: The equilibrium price level is too high (for a given nominal stock of money).

---

[22] This version is based on what William P. Gramm (1974, pp. 125–26) calls the "Samuelson Paradox," after what he takes to be Paul Samuelson's (1968, pp. 9–10) statement of it. The following exposition may not be precisely faithful either to Samuelson or to Gramm.

Monetary equilibrium requires that the actual quantity of real money balances equal the quantity demanded. Thus an equivalent statement is:

Statement 4: Real money demand is too small.

A weightier version of the purchasing-power externality argument runs as follows. Assuming a fixed nominal stock of money, any individual in demanding larger real balances of a money increases the purchasing power of that money incrementally, thereby conferring the external benefit of "capital gains to all other holders of [that] money" (Friedman 1969, p. 15). Demanding smaller balances correspondingly "creates a public *bad*" by reducing its purchasing power and inflicting capital losses on others (Yeager 1983, p. 322). Because the individual is not compensated, nor penalized, for these benefits or harms to others, money-holding is under-rewarded and real balances are too small. The market outcome is less than the "optimum quantity of money."

As Vaubel (1984, p. 33) points out, however, the failure to internalize windfall capital gains or losses is *not* a source of allocative inefficiency. Such gains and losses do not signal a failure of the market to put resources to their highest-valued uses. They, rather, constitute an inevitable side effect of the price changes by which resources *are* put to their highest-valued uses. In the terminology of welfare economics, they are not "technological" externalities (that is, they cannot be represented as external effects on others' utility or production functions), and accordingly are not even potentially Pareto-relevant. Capital gains and losses are merely "pecuniary externalities" due to changes in the terms of trade facing individuals. They are a matter of "market interdependence" rather than of "direct interdependence," to use Tibor Scitovsky's (1954) terminology. As Scitovsky remarks, static equilibrium theory *"relies* on market interdependence to bring about an optimum situation."

In this respect, too, money is no different from other goods. Capital gains or losses are felt by money-holders just as they are felt by the holders of any asset whose price rises or falls as the market efficiently registers a change in relative demands. Owners of used refrigerators enjoy a capital gain when the demand for, and price of, used refrigerators rises, but no inefficiency results from the failure of refrigerator demanders to be compensated for bestowing that gain.

Increases in purchasing power, considered nonstatically

Friedman's formulation of the purchasing-power externality argument, and Vaubel's rebuttal to it, place the argument in a timeless or static equilibrium context. In such a setting, we have just argued, the externality is merely pecuniary, and is Pareto-irrelevant. But such a setting abstracts from the very *raison d'être* of money-holding. People hold money in order to be able to resell it at a later date. In a sequential-markets setting, a rise in the purchasing power of money does not just present money-holders with a capital gain, but also *increases the serviceability* of each existing unit of money balances. Martin Hellwig (1985, pp. 572–4) points to this effect as a Pareto-relevant external effect.

Hellwig expresses his argument in welfare-theoretic terms by saying, in accordance with the usual characterization of money as a durable good that yields liquidity services, that a "technological (!) external effect" [exclamation point in the original] or "non-pecuniary externality arises because the liquidity services of money depend on its purchasing power."[23] As a technological externality, this dependence can be represented as an effect on utility or production functions which contain money balances. In Hellwig's view, money is different, in this respect, from other goods. The cooling capacity of an existing refrigerator does not increase with a rise in its price. But money is like "a refrigerator whose refrigerating power depends on its market price." The services of a nominal unit of money *do* increase with an upward shift in its relative price.

It might be objected to this argument that the services of a *real* unit of money balances do not rise with an increase in the purchasing power of a *nominal* unit of money, and it is *real* balances that enter utility or production functions. However, measuring in real units does not make the effect in question go away: although the usefulness of one unit of real balances does not change, an increase in money demand calls *more* real balances into existence in the aggregate. The creation of these additional balances constitutes a net social (technological) benefit, so long as their value exceeds the cost of producing them.

The question of non-optimality of money-holding under laissez-faire thus boils down to the question: does the marginal value of real money balances exceed their marginal cost of production? Following our discussion of com-

---

[23] Hellwig also says that in "a nonstatic [rational expectations equilibrium] setting, there is no presumption that pecuniary externalities are Pareto-irrelevant." What he apparently means is that the shift to a higher purchasing power of money, while providing pecuniary external benefits to contemporary money-holders (which, as we have just argued, are Pareto-irrelevant), *also* throws off nonpecuniary external benefits to those who *anticipate* the shift. He refers to a sequential model in which it raises "the indirect expected utility associated with money holdings at the end of [the previous] period."

Hellwig cites Scitovsky (1954) as establishing "the Pareto-relevance of pecuniary externalities outside the narrow framework of static equilibrium theory." Scitovsky, however, argues the Pareto-relevance of pecuniary externalities to interdependent investment decisions made outside of (but sequentially converging to) an equilibrium. This does not establish that pecuniary externalities remain relevant once an equilibrium is reached.

modity money in chapter 2, it should be evident that such an inequality does *not* hold in a commodity money system in equilibrium. Profit-maximization by mine-owners ensures that the value of additional gold tends to equal its marginal cost of production. Our discussion of profit-maximizing banks of issue in chapter 3 similarly indicates that the inequality does not hold for bank-issued money in equilibrium. Profit-maximization by bankers ensures that the value of additional bank-issued money tends to equal *its* marginal cost of production. The argument that an increased demand for money creates a net external benefit, therefore, cannot apply *generally*, to all types of money. An increase in demand for commodity money, or bank-issued money, will call more real units into existence, not as an external benefit, but by providing incentives for more resources to flow into money production, in the same way that an increase in demand for any ordinary good calls forth an addition to the quantity supplied.

Only in the case of a special sort of money, real balances of which can be created at a near-zero marginal cost, could increasing the stock of real balances represent a pure benefit. Fiat base money (or "outside" money) is often thought to constitute, at least in the abstract, just such a "socially costless" sort of money. Thus Hellwig (1985, p. 573) founds his argument on a model embodying the assumption that the cost of producing real money balances is zero, and is careful to argue specifically that "the demand for *outside paper money* involves a Pareto-relevant externality [italics added]."

Additional real balances of government fiat money are supposed to be available at zero cost by fixing the nominal quantity of money, and letting an increased demand for money (costlessly engineered in a way discussed below) work its effects solely by lowering the price level. Such fixing of the nominal quantity is not possible with a competitively supplied commodity money, or with bank-issued money. Only money with a supply curve that is vertical, its quantity not subject to augmentation by competitive producers, can have its purchasing power increase in response to a demand shift without calling additional resources into money production.[24]

Because government fiat money is not an outcome of laissez faire in monetary arrangements, the "non-optimality of money holding" arguments of Samuelson, Friedman, and Hellwig are *not* actually about the "non-optimality of money holding *under laissez-faire*," despite Samuelson's use of that label (Gramm 1974). Laissez faire is more naturally associated with a commodity standard. There is no suboptimality in economizing on the holding of monetary gold stocks under a gold standard, because it is costly

---

[24] The hypothetical possibility of fiat-type money produced by competing firms is mentioned briefly below in this section, and discussed in detail in chapter 13. The current discussion relates to *government* fiat money.

to mine gold, and to divert gold from industrial uses.

Although it is does not identify any suboptimality that needs to be remedied within a laissez faire monetary system, Hellwig's version of the "nonoptimality of money holding" argument does have two potential uses.

1   Because it *is* about the non-optimality of money-holding *under government fiat money*, it is relevant to determining the best monetary policy within a government fiat money system. We will see below that the argument leads to a case for a *deflationary* policy in place of any other fiat money policy.

2   Once the argument is used to establish the best policy under government fiat money, it becomes relevant to the choice among monetary standards. The "best-case scenario" of a government fiat money system – one that minimizes the suboptimality – can be used to argue that a fiat money system (administered the right way) can provide greater real balances at the same or lower cost than a commodity money system. In discussing the choice between commodity and fiat standards, back in chapter 2, we already noted the argument that a fiat money standard can in principle be administered to mimic the purchasing power behavior of a commodity standard. The "best-case" scenario can be used to argue that a fiat standard can (in principle) do even better than that.

We have indicated above that increasing the real quantity of fiat money requires increasing the real demand to hold money (see statement 4). *Costlessly* increasing the real quantity of money requires *costlessly* increasing real demand. But how is real money demand to be costlessly augmented? The most stripped-down version of the standard approach views real money demand as a function of two variables: a positive function of the real volume of transactions (or a proxy such as real income or real wealth), and a negative function of the opportunity cost of holding money. Only the latter variable is within the reach of monetary policy.[25]

---

[25] Real income depends ultimately on the availability of costly real inputs (labor and capital) and technology for transforming inputs into outputs. If real income *could* be costlessly increased, that would be worth doing for its own sake, regardless of its indirect effect on money demand. Furthermore, if the non-optimality of money-holding is that people are enjoying too little in liquidity services, increasing real income does not alleviate *that* problem; it increases real money demand by increasing the *need* for liquidity services, not by lowering their cost.

In the standard inventory-theoretic (Baumol–Tobin) approach to money demand, a third variable enters: the per-transaction cost of transferring wealth between money and non-money forms. That variable is also beyond the reach of monetary policy. Furthermore, to raise real money demand by that route implies *increasing* the cost of transfers, which is hardly conducive to an improvement in welfare. It lowers the cost of holding money perversely, by reducing the net benefit from temporarily holding wealth in alternative ways.

This way of reformulating the problem leads to a fifth way of stating the suboptimality that is believed to arise when purchasing-power effects of money demand are not internalized:

Statement 5: The opportunity cost of holding money is too high.

This statement implicitly underlies statement 4, that the real demand for money is too low. Real money demand is inversely related to the holding cost, and this cost is held to be needlessly high.

The standard measure of the opportunity cost of holding money is the interest yield foregone on bonds that are the most closely matched in risk and liquidity. The benchmark for government-issued fiat currency is the yield on government bonds denominated in the same currency unit, which are ordinarily assumed to have equivalent (zero) nominal default risk, at the shortest maturity (thus with the least interest-rate risk) and the greatest liquidity.[26] The opportunity cost can be written as $i_b - i_m$, where i_b is the yield rate obtainable on the specified government bonds, and i_m is the explicit nominal interest rate on money. Assuming that the explicit nominal interest rate on money is fixed at zero, we have an alternative version of statement 5:

Statement 5a: The nominal rate of interest on bonds (i_b), if higher than the difference between the government's costs of producing money and bonds, is too high.

If, instead, it is assumed that nominal interest can be paid on money as cheaply as it can paid on other assets, we have yet another version:

Statement 5b: The interest rate on money (i_m), if less than on other assets of equivalent risk by more than the additional cost of issuing money, is too low.

The implication for monetary policy within a fiat regime was enunciated in the classic treatment of Friedman (1969). Each individual equates the marginal benefit of holding real fiat money balances to the opportunity cost of holding them. The availability of net social benefits (in the form of the liquidity services from greater real balances) justifies the *payment of a real*

---

[26] If fiat currency pays interest – just how it might do so is a question we defer to chapter 14 – it begins to resemble a bond, which raises the question of its maturity or duration. In the usual conception, fiat money is always spendable at its face value. Thus, it resembles the limiting case of bond about to mature. The benchmark bond yield should thus be the yield on the bonds closest to maturity. When the yield curve has its normal upward slope, the opportunity cost of holding currency is then the yield rate on the lowest-yielding bonds available.

return on fiat money, so as to reduce the opportunity cost of holding fiat money relative to bonds, increase the demand for real balances, and thereby increase the quantity of real balances to its Pareto-optimal level. The "optimum quantity of money" (OQM for short) is reached when each individual's marginal benefit of holding real fiat money is reduced to the social cost of "producing" them (by paying a higher real return, and, thereby, increasing real demand). If the cost of producing, and maintaining, real balances of fiat money is zero, then efficiency calls for reducing the opportunity cost of holding fiat money to zero, either by paying explicit interest so that i_m rises to meet i_b at a positive number, or – what is sometimes assumed to more feasible because of the difficulty of paying nominal interest on currency – by engineering a deflation at the real rate of interest so that nominal i_b falls to meet i_m at zero. A deflation (falling price level) can be engineered by selling assets from the central bank's portfolio (assuming that it acquired salable assets when it issued the existing money, and still holds them) to buy back and retire fiat money, shrinking the outstanding stock. Under deflation, money balances pay a real return by appreciating in purchasing power.

Deflation reduces nominal interest rates in accordance with the simple Fisher relationship

$$i = r + gP^e$$

which says that in equilibrium the nominal rate of interest equals the real rate of interest (the real exchange rate between present and future, which is determined by non-monetary forces) plus the anticipated rate of growth of the price level.[27] Correct foresight implies $gP = gP^e$. Setting i to zero implies $gP^e = -r$. The dynamic version of the equation of exchange tells us that the sum of the money growth rate and the velocity growth rate equals the sum of price level growth rate (the inflation rate) and the real income growth rate:

$$gM + gV = gP + gy$$

Setting the inflation rate gP to $-r$ by choosing gM appropriately thus implies

$$gM = -r + gy - gV$$

---

[27] The strict equality holds for continuously compounded rates (for annualized rates it becomes an approximate equality) and assumes away effects on real yields from the taxation of interest income.

Under empirically reasonable estimates for the real interest rate r (5%), the rate of growth of real income gy (3%), and the secular rate of growth in velocity gV (0%), the indicated money growth rate gM is slightly negative (−2%).

As Vaubel (1984, p. 33 n. 17) points out, in the final analysis, the prescription to achieve optimality by paying a market rate of return on fiat money balances *does not rest on an externality argument*. It amounts to a prescription for government to pay a competitive, rather than a monopolistic, interest rate on the fiat money it produces. Equivalently, it prescribes that government should avoid taxing, and thereby distorting, money-holding by pursuing a rate of monetary expansion that reduces money's yield below the competitive rate. If the marginal cost of producing and maintaining real balances of fiat money is zero, it follows from the standard case for the efficiency of marginal-cost pricing that the price (cost of holding) fiat money balances should be reduced to zero. It no longer matters whether the zero cost of production is ascribed to an externality, or simply taken as a given.

Calling it a "competitive" practice for government to pay a return on its fiat money equal to the market rate of return on other assets (of equivalent risk and maturity) suggests that *private* producers of money would naturally have to pay such a rate under competitive conditions (assuming zero administrative costs both of furnishing the money, and of paying a return on it). Friedman (1969) and Neil Wallace (1983) point toward this result in their discussions of bank-issued money. Benjamin Klein (1974) and Bart Taub (1985) have developed explicit models of the hypothetical competitive provision of fiat-type monies, or "outside paper monies" to use Hellwig's phrase, from which the result formally emerges. When private fiat-type money is feasible, perfect competition compels its issuers to pay the market rate of return on their monies. (These models and their conditions are discussed in chapter 12.)

The competitive provision of outside paper monies, under the right conditions, thus delivers the optimum quantity of money. There is no divergence between the benefit of additional real balances and the cost (entirely interest costs, under the hypothesized conditions) of maintaining those balances. The purchasing-power effects of demand for outside paper money are fully internalized. With private issuers already paying a competitive return on money, there is no need for government to intervene in order to ensure a competitive return.

The prescription for a deflation at the real rate of interest, so that the nominal interest rate on the shortest-term government bonds meets the nominal rate paid on money balances at zero, rests on the assumption that the cost of thus "producing" additional real balances of fiat money is zero. Is this assumption reasonable? Is it actually costless to engineer a deflation?

Two issues need to be considered: the fiscal ramifications of pursuing a deflationary monetary policy, and the impact of deflation on the economy.

By paying a real return on outstanding balances of fiat money, equal to the rate it pays on short-term bonds, the government pays money-holders funds it might instead have used for government spending. By shrinking the monetary base, it sacrifices the revenue it might have gained from expanding the base. Viewed either way, the government gives up its tax on fiat money balances. (This tax, seigniorage, is the subject of chapter 7.) If we assume that the payout to money-holders is matched by spending cuts, an optimizing citizen would want to count, as a marginal cost of the policy, the value of the services that had been provided by the marginal government spending.[28] Alternatively, assuming that the government replaces the funds with revenue from a different tax, the payout is socially costless only if the new tax carries no deadweight burden.[29] (We will return to the "optimal tax rate" question with respect to seigniorage in chapter 7.)

There is no obvious reason to believe that a mildly falling price level, if anticipated, is harmful to the economy. Business owners and workers who recognize that the monetary unit is rising in purchasing power should not confuse real with nominal profits, or real with nominal wage offers. One concern is sometimes expressed about the prospect of a zero nominal interest rate: why would anyone then bother to invest? The incentive to invest in private capital formation, rather than hold only Treasury bills, would be the same as it is today. The optimum quantity of money (OQM) prescription for a zero nominal interest rate applies only to *short-term, nominally riskless* government securities. It changes the spread between government currency and T-bills, but not between T-bills and other securities. Corporate securities and equities would pay the same risk premia over T-bills that they pay today.

There is a different concern about a zero nominal interest rate that is harder to dismiss. At zero, the nominal interest rate is at its lower bound. (No one would accept a *negative* nominal rate if she can costlessly store currency.) The nominal interest rate would therefore seem to have lost a

---

[28] This does not necessarily imply that less, or no return, should be paid to money-holders. A real dollar returned to money-holders is always worth a real dollar. If the services provided by a marginal real dollar of spending never rise in value to a real dollar – if the government was overspending from a utilitarian viewpoint – it is still optimal to pay a full return to money-holders, even if the services have some small positive value.

[29] If the best new tax involves some deadweight burden, the "optimal tax rate" rule is to find the mix of tax rates that minimizes deadweight burden by equating across taxes the marginal burdens per dollar of revenue raised. A number of theorists have argued (for a variety of reasons) that, even following an "optimal tax rate" rule, the optimal tax rate on money is, or may be, zero. For discussion, see Mulligan and Sala-i-Martin (1997).

degree of freedom in responding to shocks. If, for example, the rate of money growth randomly slips so far negative that anticipated inflation temporarily drops below $-r$, the nominal interest rate can not fall to keep the *ex ante* real market rate from rising above its equilibrium value.

The OQM case for paying a market rate of return on government-issued fiat money has technical limitations that should be mentioned: Friedman's (1969) argument for the optimality of a deflationary scheme is based on a particular model of money demand in which real money enters the utility function of a representative agent who has an infinite planning horizon. Deflation at the real rate of interest induces the agent to hold the optimum quantity of money – to "satiate" herself with costlessly produced real balances – but it does not affect resource allocation in any other respect. These results are not robust across all models of money demand. In other sorts of models, in particular those depicting overlapping generations of finitely lived agents whose interests differ across generations, or sequential markets, the welfare superiority of monetary contraction may no longer obtain. The level of real balances is no longer so cleanly separable from real resource allocation. Switching to a higher level of real balances, by paying a real return, can involve a transfer of wealth from old to young, a policy disadvantageous to the old. A constant rather than shrinking money supply may then be a Pareto-optimal policy for a fiat regime.[30]

Is the Supply of Base Money a Natural Monopoly?

A "natural monopoly" is said to exist when economies of scale in production are so extensive (average costs are still declining at such a large output volume) that a single firm can produce the entire output of an industry at lower cost than a plurality of firms can. Profit maximization may lead a natural monopolist to restrict output, and to raise product price relative to the output and price combination at which the marginal cost of output equals the marginal value to consumers (as measured by willingness to pay for an additional unit of output). The potential inefficiency of monopoly pricing is sometimes held to rationalize government's breaking up the monopoly through antitrust action, or regulating the output and pricing of the monopolist, or government itself assuming the role of monopolist. Just as in the case of public-goods and externality arguments, one might question the adequacy of natural monopoly arguments for justifying government in-

---

[30] For these results, see Lin (1989), Freeman (1989), and Williamson (1996). For an overview, again, see Mulligan and Sala-i-Martin (1997).

tervention (Armentano 1982, pp. 13–48). Again, we will forgo that line of inquiry here, in order to examine, instead, whether the characteristics of natural monopoly plausibly apply to base money. We examine their applicability to bank-issued money in chapter 6.

It is difficult to find arguments asserting unlimited scale economies in the production of base money. For a gold or silver standard, although there are clearly some economies of scale in subsurface mining, there is no reason to believe that mining or coinage is subject to *continually* declining average costs. Gold and silver deposits are geographically dispersed by nature, and history does not show a tendency for the ownership of mines to be most efficiently concentrated in a single firm. As chapter 1 noted, the business of coining gold and silver has, historically, been competitive where private mints were allowed.

The question of scale economies in the production of *non-commodity* base money is difficult, or impossible, to answer empirically, because free entry and private production of fiat-type money have not been observed.

Several economists have argued that there are "social economies of scale in the use" of a money (Vaubel 1984, p. 45). This phrase means that the usefulness of a money increases with the number of users, or the stock of real balances, or the volume of transactions in it. Such arguments are basically the same as the arguments we have already considered concerning the benefits of commonness or uniformity in money, or the network-good properties of a monetary standard. The notion of "social economies of scale in the use" of a money refers to *economies of standardization*, which should not be mistaken for economies of scale in production. Failure to avoid that mistake is common in the literature (White 1989, p. 39). It is only economies of scale in production that imply natural monopoly. "Social economies of scale in the use" of a money promote convergence in the adoption of a particular monetary standard, as explained in chapter 1. However, convergence to a common monetary standard does not imply a single producer of money.

This point should be obvious with respect to a commodity money like silver, and with respect to bank-issued money. A uniform silver standard is compatible with dozens of competing silver mines, dozens of competing private mints, and dozens of banks issuing silver-redeemable liabilities. The concept of "social economies of scale in the use" of a money applies to the monetary *standard*, not to the *brands* of money (bullion or coins or bank liabilities) denominated in a particular standard. So long as the coin you offer me is reliably of full weight, there is no obvious extra benefit to me from its being the product of a mint with a large market share.[31] So long as

---

[31] Historically, there were many private mints during the western US gold and silver rushes, as noted in chapter 1. The trial period during which private mints were neither banned nor confronted with subsidized government mints was brief, however, so that we cannot confidently infer how many mints a private minting industry would support in the long run.

the check or banknote you offer me is denominated in standard money, and is drawn on a reputable bank whose liabilities my bank will accept at par, there is no apparent extra benefit to me from its being drawn on *my* bank. Experience does not show that all banking customers tend to congregate in a single bank out of a desire to bank at the most popular bank. Thus "social economies of scale in use" do not promote natural monopoly in the markets for bank-issued money or full-bodied coins. Neither product market tends to be dominated by a single producer.

In a competition among fiat-type monies, governmental or possibly private, the distinction between economies of standardization and economies of scale is not so clear when each producer's brand constitutes its own monetary standard. Mengerian convergence to a single standard *would* then imply convergence to a single producer's brand. Fiat-type money would then be a natural monopoly, as has been claimed, for example, by Friedman (1960). If a significant part of the costs of producing real balances of a brand of money are the "selling costs" of persuading people to use that brand, and if average selling costs are a declining function of the number of users (for Mengerian reasons), then there may be natural monopoly in the production of real balances of an outside paper money.[32]

It is possible, however, that competition among fiat-type monies will lead to a convergence of standards among brands that nonetheless remain distinct. Hayek (1978) envisions that private producers of outside paper monies would stabilize the values of their respective brands with reference to independently published price indices (see chapter 12 for a more detailed discussion). If there were convergence on a single index, then there would emerge a common monetary standard. This amounts to saying that under private competition each brand of outside paper money would *not* constitute its own monetary standard. Instead, each producer would fix the value of his or her money with reference to an external standard, much as a banknote issuer under a commodity standard does (except that fiat-type issuers would do so without redeemability). Convergence to a common stand-

---

[32] Benjamin Klein (1974) has offered a model of the competitive private production of fiat-type money (which chapter 12 discusses in detail.) Based on Klein's model, Michael Melvin (1988) has argued that an issuer's costs of creating the brand-name reputation necessary to persuade people to "buy" that brand of money are largely fixed costs. Thus there *is* natural monopoly in the production of fiat-type money because average costs continually decline with the volume produced. In the Klein–Melvin framework, however, these costs are in fact *not* fixed, but rise in proportion to the quantity of real balances produced. Because the issuer's potential profit from cheating the public (through hyperinflation) is proportional to the real balances it has in circulation, to convince the public that it will *not* choose to cheat them the issuer must acquire a brand-name reputation proportional in value to its circulation. Reputation-bolstering expenditures are therefore not a fixed cost, and no natural monopoly exists on this account.

ard would not then imply dominance of a single producer's brand of money.

It is also possible that, even without a convergence of standards, the market might support multiple brands of outside paper money. Vaubel (1984, p. 46) offers two reasons. First, individuals may desire to diversify their holdings of outside money in order to spread their risks of capital losses and gains from depreciation and appreciation. Second, individuals with different expenditure patterns may want to hold different brands of money if each brand stabilizes its purchasing power in terms of a different commodity bundle. In an open market, heavy energy consumers could hold a currency tied to crude oil, while heavy eaters could hold a food-indexed currency. Whether such diversification and purchasing-power-specialization motives would overcome the Mengerian motives for convergence is an empirical question. To settle the question, free entry into base money production must be allowed. Natural monopoly arguments do not justify legal barriers to competition in any event.

Questions

1   "Improving the stability of the purchasing power of the dollar is a public good, because one person can not receive the benefit of such an improvement without everyone else who uses dollars also receiving it." Correct? Explain.

2   Gary Becker (1993) has written: "With thousands of banks issuing notes, many resources will have to be allocated . . . to informing the public as to the quality of different notes. Since the conserving of resources used to facilitate transactions is one motivation for a paper currency, it seems desirable to outlaw private bank notes." Identify the strong and weak points (both theoretical and empirical) of Becker's argument. How does it provide, or fail to provide, a persuasive rationale for government note monopoly?

3   "Suppose . . . that . . . [m]any different producers are induced to issue paper money as a claim against commodity money. The social benefit resulting from the use of lower-cost money is partly offset by the higher cost individuals pay to acquire information. The legislation of 1844 in England and of the 1860s in the United States that reduced the number and type of notes in circulation by restricting the right to issue notes are examples of institutional changes that raised economic welfare by reducing costs of acquiring information." (Meltzer 1998)

(a)   Assume that Meltzer is talking about the cost consumers bear to evaluate whether to accept each brand of bank-issued money at par, at a discount, or not at all. How high are these costs likely to be, based on historical experience?

(b)   Does restricting the right to issue redeemable notes to a single government institution lower, or eliminate, this information cost? Does it carry any offsetting disadvantages? On net, is the restriction likely to raise, or lower, economic welfare?

4   Imagine that Sears, the department store chain, decides to launch a new proprietary unit of account (the "Roebuck") which (let's assume) everyone believes will have greater purchasing power stability than the fiat dollar. Sears hopes that many people will want to buy the Roebuck-denominated notes and deposits that only Sears and its licensees provide. Suppose that there are no legal obstacles, and there is no problem of unauthorized Roebuck issuers. What marketplace obstacles might Sears face in persuading potential customers to hold its money?

5   Axel and Bo are regular trading partners, and both use ducats as their medium of exchange. If Axel decides to hold *more* ducats, is it plausible that Axel thereby provides external benefits to Bo? If so, how? If not, why not?

6   According to the "optimum quantity of money" argument, the demand for fiat base money is too small (in the absence of the right policy). Is the argument an externality argument? If so, what is the nature of the externality? If not, what kind of suboptimality is at issue?

7   Individuals normally face a foregone-interest cost of holding fiat money balances. Can monetary policy reduce or eliminate that cost? If so, how? If not, why not?

6

Should Government Play a Role in Banking?

The leading argument against laissez-faire banking is that banks, in an unregulated environment (particularly in the absence of government deposit guarantees), are vulnerable to runs and panics. A bank run occurs when many noteholders, or depositors, of a bank simultaneously seek to redeem their claims out of concern that the bank will default if they wait. Depositors who run, it is argued, impose negative external effects on other customers, and owners, of the bank. A panic occurs when runs simultaneously afflict many banks. If runs are "contagious," then a run at one bank imposes negative external effects on the customers, and owners, of other banks.

Because of its importance, we consider the problem of bank runs in some detail. Later in this chapter, we turn to the question of natural monopoly in banking.

The Problem of Bank Runs

If bank runs were always confined to banks that were already (pre-run) insolvent, then runs would not be a problem, but, instead, largely salutary. In other industries, an insolvent firm's creditors whose debts are overdue, and who wish to cut their losses, can legally force the firm into liquidation through an involuntary bankruptcy proceeding. A run on an insolvent bank serves the same function as an involuntary bankruptcy proceeding: it is an action by the bank's creditors, namely its depositors (or note-holders, but for simplicity we will speak only of depositors), that forces the bank into liquidation. Unlike the rule in a bankruptcy, the assets do not go *pro rata* to all creditors of equal standing, but instead go preferentially to those who are first in line to redeem their claims (a possibly problematic feature of deposit contracts that will concern us later). The run is salutary in that it closes the insolvent bank immediately, before the bank squanders even more depositor wealth, and goes even further into the red. The run cuts the depositors' potential losses in the aggregate. The *threat* of a run, like the threat of bankruptcy in other industries, provides useful discipline. It forces banks to invest smartly, and to work vigorously to avoid insolvency or even the appearance of insolvency.[1]

A problem arises, however, if depositors with imperfect information sometimes run on banks that are not (pre-run) insolvent. In an influential article, Douglas Diamond and Philip Dybvig (1983) emphasized that *a run itself can cause a bank to default that would otherwise have defaulted*. A bank forced to liquidate assets hastily may have to accept less for them than they would otherwise be worth, an event known as suffering "fire-sale" losses.[2] A bank run can thereby be a *self-reinforcing* equilibrium: if enough other depositors are running, the bank will incur large fire-sale losses, default becomes likely, and it becomes each depositor's own best strategy to run.[3] There is a "me-first" scramble as each depositor tries to redeem his claim ahead of others, before the bank's funds are exhausted. In Diamond and Dybvig's model, discussed in more detail below, the bank attempting to meet redemption demands by more than a certain proportion of its depositors will incur fire-sale losses so large that its default is *a certainty*. Any event that makes people anticipate a run, therefore, makes them anticipate insolvency, and so does, in fact, trigger a run. As in a rational speculative "bubble," the induced outcome validates the anticipation, even if the anticipation is triggered by an intrinsically irrelevant event like the appearance of sunspots. The Diamond–Dybvig model is accordingly sometimes described as a "bubble" or "sunspot" theory of bank runs.

An insolvency-causing run is regrettable not only to depositors, some of whom lose wealth, but also to bank shareholders, who lose wealth in the "fire sale" of assets, and even to bank borrowers, if they must incur a significant cost re-establishing credit elsewhere. Merely the *risk* of such a

---

[1] Calomiris and Khan (1991) argue importantly that runable (demandable) deposit contracts have advantageous incentive and informational effects. Alonso (1996) offers a model in which runs occur when depositors respond to indications that a bank may be pre-run insolvent, and it is therefore optimal to have occasional runs.

[2] The label is somewhat odd, because in retail trade a "fire sale" typically takes place after a fire, to get rid of fire-damaged merchandise. In a bank run, the "fire sale" takes place *during* the "fire," in a hasty attempt to acquire the ("liquid") reserves needed to put out the "fire."

[3] In game-theoretic terms, the bank run is a Nash equilibrium.

run is regrettable, because it compels depositors to make costly efforts to avoid being victimized (e.g. to hold less bank-issued money, or to monitor the banks more closely), compels the banks to make costly efforts to forestall runs (e.g. to keep reserves higher), and, in both ways, makes intermediation more costly. In the Diamond–Dybvig model, a run is regrettable because it forces the bank to terminate investments that would be more productive if carried to fruition, and thereby ruins the investment-pooling arrangement among bank customers. A depositor's decision to run, therefore, has negative external effects on other depositors, on shareholders, and possibly on borrowers. The model rationalizes some kind of deposit insurance as a way to hold the bank at the welfare-superior no-run equilibrium.

If "contagion effects" are present, the external effects are doubly severe. The run-induced failure of any one bank, by setting off a panic, has negative spillover effects on the customers of other banks. A panic is regrettable not only because it multiplies the negative effects of runs, but because it can lead to a macroeconomic contraction. A sudden general scramble to redeem bank-issued money shrinks the money stock unexpectedly, subjecting the macroeconomy to a negative monetary shock. The view that undesirable panics of this sort are inherent to an unregulated banking system provides the standard rationale for maintaining a government monetary authority that can act as a lender of last resort (Bordo 1990).

Is laissez-faire banking really as vulnerable to runs, and panics, as these views suggest? There are both theoretical and historical reasons to doubt that it is.

Inherent Fragility in Theory: The Diamond–Dybvig Model

The Diamond–Dybvig (or "DD") model sets up a simple world in order to explicitly derive a useful role for a bank. There is only one bank, and it has basically only one function: to allow depositors to pool a risk (explained below). The bank does not make loans, and does not issue checking accounts or banknotes. Thus the DD model envisions a rather special sort of a "bank."

The DD bank is unstable (run-prone) because it does not know how many deposits will be withdrawn in a particular period, and it holds assets that are less liquid than its deposits. It cannot possibly meet the largest mass redemption demand that depositors may rationally choose to stage. The instability is harmful in the model because it disrupts the production process that the bank oversees, and thereby ruins the beneficial risk-sharing arrangement that the bank provides.

The DD bank operates in a three-period world. The periods are denoted $t = 0, 1, 2$. Table 6.1 shows the life history of the bank.

One feasible contract for the bank, clearly, is to set $r_1 = 1$, which implies $r_2 = R$. But under the assumption that individuals have access to the same investment opportunities as the bank (the bank enjoys neither economies of scale nor an informational advantage), they would find it pointless to use a bank that offered such a contract. They could just as well plant corn in their own backyards, and dig it up in period 1 if need be.

DD show that risk-averse agents prefer an alternative feasible contract. The bank sets r_1 such that $R > r_1 > 1$, and $R > E(r_2) > r_1$, where $E(r_2)$ is the expected value of r_2. Note that $r_1 > 1$ implies $r_2 < R$. Some investments are liquidated at $t = 1$, at which time the physical return is only 1 per unit invested, but the depositors have been promised more than 1 per unit deposited. To pay the extra return additional corn must be dug up, so that the number of units remaining invested becomes less than the number of deposit claims remaining. The final value of the bank at $t = 2$ must therefore end up below R per unit of deposit claims.

With $r_1 > 1$ and $r_2 < R$, the deposit claim provides *insurance* against the unlucky event of being a type-1 agent and needing funds before the investments mature. The type-1 depositor gets more than the autarky payoff $r_1 = 1$, and this is made possible by the type-2 depositor getting less than the autarky payoff of $r_2 = R$. In the same way, someone who never files an insurance claim ends up with less, ex post, than if he or she had never bought the insurance. In the DD model, insurance against the event of being a type-1 agent is the only motive for making a deposit in the first place. DD show that the optimal size of r_1 will depend on the expected proportion of type-1 agents, and on the degree of risk aversion.

The preferred contract, however, is unstable. If too many depositors withdraw in period 1, total claims can exceed the bank's physical payoff from interrupted investments. When total claims exceed the maximum possible payout, DD assume that the bank faces a "sequential service constraint", or, in plainer language, follows a "first come, first served" rule: the bank pays each depositor r_1, in the order in which they have queued, until the funds run out. The depositors who withdraw in period 1 do not all have to be type-1 agents: type-2s have the option to withdraw, and DD assume that the bank can not tell the types apart. Because the last in line receive nothing, running to withdraw – joining the line rather than waiting until $t = 2$ to withdraw – is the smart thing for a type-2 agent to do if it is the strategy that enough other type-2s are playing. Consequently, there are two possible outcomes for the DD bank: the good equilibrium in which only type-1s withdraw at $t = 1$, and the bad equilibrium – a run – in which everyone tries to withdraw.

Table 6.1   The life history of the DD bank

t	
At $t = 0$	• The bank sells claims (of only one type; there is no distinction between depositors and shareholders; we may call all claimants "depositors"). It takes in depositors' funds in the form of a good that is also the only consumption good in the economy. To be concrete, we may think of the bank as taking in corn, and selling claims to future corn.
	• The bank invests the funds it has received into production projects (not to mature until $t = 2$), i.e. the bank plants the corn entrusted to it. There is no uncertainty in production.
At $t = 1$	• Each depositor discovers what "type" he or she is. Type 1 only enjoys consumption in period 1 (is going to die before period 2), so must withdraw in period 1. The risk of being a Type 1 is the risk that depositors are pooling. Type 2 only enjoys consumption in period 2.
	• Type 2 depositors face a choice: leave the deposit in the bank until period 2, or withdraw now and store the commodity at home until period 2. Because the investment project does not mature until period 2, the bank must interrupt production (dig up the corn) to pay depositors who withdraw in period 1.
	• Investments liquidated after only one period physically yield a gross rate of return of exactly 1 (the corn can be dug up intact, but has not grown).
	• Those who withdraw (no matter whether type 1 or 2; the bank cannot distinguish) receive the pre-specified payment of r_1 per unit deposited.
At $t = 2$	• The uninterrupted investments mature, with a gross return of $R > 1$ per unit invested. (There are constant returns to scale in production.)
	• The bank is liquidated, and remaining depositors receive r_2 per unit deposited, which represents a *pro rata* share of the bank's liquidation value.

The Fragility of the Diamond–Dybvig Bank: A Numerical Example

Recall the notation being used:

1 = return per unit to one-period (interrupted) investments
R = return per unit to two-period (uninterrupted) investments, $R > 1$
r_1 = fixed return per unit to those who withdraw at $t = 1$
r_2 = residual return per unit to those who wait to withdraw at $t = 2$

Suppose $R = 1.2$ and $r_1 = 1.08$, and that 100 depositors invest a total of 100 units of corn (one unit per depositor).

If only 50 depositors withdraw at $t = 1$, the bank pays out $(50 \times 1.08 =)$ 54 units. That leaves 46 units invested. Their total final yield is $(46 \times 1.2 =)$ 55.2. Dividing the total final yield among the 50 remaining depositors,

$$r_2 = \frac{55.2}{50} = 1.104$$

Because $r_2 > r_1$, it pays a depositor to wait if he can. This is the good outcome.

If, instead, 75 depositors withdraw at $t = 1$, the bank pays out $(75 \times 1.08 =)$ 81 units. That leaves only 19 units invested. Their total final yield is $(19 \times 1.2 =)$ 22.8. Dividing the total final yield among the 25 remaining depositors,

$$r_2 = \frac{22.8}{25} = .912$$

In this case, because $r_2 < r_1$, it does *not* pay a depositor to wait, even if he can. The return is lower to those who wait, because too many others withdrew early. Any type-2 depositor who suspects that as many as 75 others will withdraw will choose to withdraw early too. A run – all those who could wait choosing instead to withdraw early – is then a self-reinforcing event.

If all 100 depositors seek to withdraw at $t = 1$, the bank clearly must default. It would need 108 units to fulfill its obligation to pay every depositor 1.08 per unit withdrawn, but it can only get 100 units by interrupting all the investments. With 100 units, it can pay only 92 depositors the 1.08 per unit return they were promised. Under a first-come, first-served rule the 93rd depositor receives a partial payoff, and the last seven depositors receive nothing (and thus presumably starve). This is the bad outcome. More investments are interrupted than the number necessary just to meet the withdrawals of type-1 agents, reducing aggregate output accordingly. The danger of being one of the last seven in line and thereby doing worse than under autarky means that participating in the bank does not even insure depositors against risk of being a type-1 the way it is supposed to, but actually increases the risk he or she faces.[4]

Deposit Insurance in the Diamond–Dybvig Model

DD argue that their model provides a rationale for government deposit insurance. They describe a particular form of deposit insurance that preserves the model's good equilibrium by removing the incentive to run. Added to the model, the deposit insurance scheme works in the following way. The bank keeps a list of who withdraws. If so many withdraw at $t = 1$ that the bank must default or pay less than r_1 on the last claim serviced (thus giving type-2 agents an incentive to run), the government intervenes. It taxes away the difference between r_1 and 1 from those who got r_1, and redistributes it so that everyone gets exactly 1. The mere *prospect* of such a redistribution eliminates the incentive of type-2 agents to run. A wait-and-see strategy now dominates. If other type-2s run, every type-2 receives 1 unit back whether he runs or not. If other type-2s do not run, he receives r_1 if he does run, but the higher payoff of r_2 by waiting. Thus he always does at least as well by waiting.

Criticism of the Diamond–Dybvig Model

Later, we consider empirical problems with using the DD theory to explain when runs occur in the real world. First, we consider internal critiques: arguments identifying ways in which the DD bank is so unlike a real-world bank that the key implications of the model (banks are inherently run-prone; government deposit insurance is a useful remedy) may not apply to real-world banks.[5]

1   Claims against the DD bank are a peculiar debt-equity hybrid. Real-world banks have a distinct class of equity-owners (residual claim-

---

[4] A potential depositor who places a sufficiently high value on avoiding the risk of starving, and who estimates a non-zero probability of default, would therefore refuse to participate in a DD bank in the first place. See Huo and Yu (1994).

[5] The discussion that follows draws on Dowd (1992a; 1996, ch. 9), Selgin and White (1994a), and works cited in those surveys.

ants) to insulate depositors from random asset losses. An equity cushion large enough to absorb all but the most improbable losses would ordinarily eliminate the incentive to run. The DD bank, by contrast, has no class of equity-owners distinct from depositors. The bank has *no* equity – all claims are debt – in period $t = 1$, and thus *no* cushion. Its total debts *always* exceed the liquidation value of its assets at $t = 1$. Type-2s who wait are *never* insulated from changes in r_2 as the number of withdrawals varies at $t = 1$.

2   DD find suspension of payments (an alternative to deposit insurance) undesirable because it interferes with the consumption of those who cannot withdraw (they cannot eat if they do not receive any corn back). Holders of claims on a real-world bank (notes, checkable deposits) can usually continue to use their claims to buy things even when claim-redemption is temporarily suspended. They do not starve. In the DD world, suspended deposits would be useless for reclaiming corn, and they have no other function. A bank suspension (no redemption) would be equivalent to a bank holiday (no banking services at all).

3   DD find government deposit insurance welfare-improving over any remedy the bank could devise, because they impose the sequential service constraint on the bank but not on the government. Because of the constraint, the bank cannot reduce r_1 when the number of redemption requests is large. However, the government deposit insurance scheme does this, in effect, by taxing the first in line and topping up the last in line (evidently it springs into action before anyone can consume the corn they have withdrawn). Removing the government's ad-hoc technological advantage removes either the feasibility, or the need, for government deposit insurance. When bank and government both face the sequential service constraint, the deposit insurance topping-up scheme is infeasible. When neither faces the constraint, the bank can institute the scheme by itself, contractually, making deposit payoffs contingent on the number who opt to withdraw in period $t = 1$.

Are Deposit Contracts Inherently Fragile?

The general question raised by these criticisms is whether the DD contract really represents a plausible contract in an unregulated banking system without deposit insurance. In models of the DD sort, a bank and its customers structure the contracts defining claims on the bank in a particular way that exposes the bank to runs. Yet, if non-run-prone contracts are available at low cost, run-prone contracts should not be expected to prevail under laissez-faire. A bank that modifies a relatively fragile contract to make it less fragile has a strong survival advantage. It would be remarkable indeed if a truly fragile banking contract had survived the centuries of Darwinian banking competition before the first government deposit insurance scheme was devised.

It is rational for a depositor to run a bank if the deposit contract is structured so that there is a greater expected payoff to arriving sooner, rather than later, to redeem. This condition will obtain if deposits are:

1 debt claims (claims to fixed amounts of dollars, regardless of how the bank's assets are performing);
2 redeemable on demand, with a first-come, first-served rule for servicing redemption requests; and
3 subject to likely default (less than 100 percent payoff) on the last redemption claim serviced.

Default on the last claim is likely if it is likely either that the bank is insolvent before the run begins, or that a run itself will render the bank insolvent.

Changing *any one* of these conditions can effectively "run-proof" the bank. There are several types of alternative claims, suitable for use as media of exchange, which do change these conditions, as the following examples show.

1 Money-market mutual funds are run-proof, because the checking accounts they issue are equity-share claims, rather than debt-deposit claims. A share in the fund becomes a claim to fewer dollars immediately, and proportionally, whenever the fund suffers a capital loss on its asset portfolio. The realized value of a cashed-in share does not remain unchanged for those first in line to redeem, and fall only for those last in line to redeem, as it does in the case of an insolvent bank. There is, consequently, no reward for rushing to be first to redeem.[6]
2 Claims that a bank is not obligated to redeem on demand are not runable. Their holders cannot rush *en masse* to redeem, but must wait until the claims mature. The leading example of such a claim, suitable for use as a medium of exchange, is a note or deposit which the bank ordinarily redeems on demand, but which gives the bank a contractual option to delay redemption for a stipulated period on stipulated terms. Scottish banks issued "option-clause" banknotes before the clause was outlawed in 1765, and the notes appear normally to have circulated at par. American savings banks in the twen-

---

[6] Goodhart (1988, pp. 89–95), Glasner (1989, pp. 195–201), Cowen and Kroszner (1990), and others have emphasized that a payments system consisting of checkable MMMFs is run-proof, and provides an attractive alternative to a system of government-insured deposits.

tieth century have commonly included in "passbook" account contracts a clause that requires the customer to give prior notice for withdrawals, and have customarily waived the requirement except in banking panics.

An option clause allows the bank to avoid the fire-sale losses from hasty liquidation of assets in the event of an incipient run. The bank can delay redemption for long enough to liquidate assets (or to arrange to borrow reserves) in an orderly manner. With the right sort of compensation built in for invoking the option clause (e.g. the contract obligates the bank to pay the depositor a high interest bonus for the delay), the bank will not invoke the clause, except when it faces a run, or some other extraordinary redemption demand. Depositors should welcome a well-designed option clause because it will not be invoked, except in circumstances where its presence reduces the risk of the bank's becoming insolvent, and thus the risk of any depositor suffering the loss from being last in line for redemption. Should an extraordinary redemption demand, or panic, confront the banking system, despite the option clause's deterrent effect against runs, invoking the clause allows the system to avoid a sudden contraction of the money stock. In the event of a panic, as Friedman and Schwartz (1963, pp. 163, 329) have noted, the restriction of redemptions can be a "therapeutic measure." The option clause allows a restriction to take place without breach of contract, on terms that are mutually agreeable to banks and their customers *ex ante*.[7]

A promissory note or a time deposit with a definite maturity date, e.g. a certificate of deposit, is not runable. However, such a claim is not normally suitable as a medium of exchange, and so does not solve the problem of providing a run-proof payments instrument. (In the DD context, a deposit not redeemable at $t = 1$ would not be suitable for providing insurance.)

3   A number of strategies are available for assuring depositors that a bank is solvent, or that the likelihood of bank default, due to insolvency, is negligibly small. Default due to insolvency occurs when the value of assets falls below the value of liabilities. The obvious strategy for assuring solvency is, therefore, to hold ample assets for each dollar of liabilities, i.e., to maintain *adequate capital* in the form of a high equity ratio. A second strategy is to hold *safe*

---

[7] For detailed treatments of option clauses see Dowd (1988; 1996, pp. 152–5) and Shah (1997). For discussion of their historical use in Scotland, see Gherity (1995) and Selgin and White (1997).

assets, i.e. a diversified portfolio of assets, little exposed to the risks of default or capital loss. A money-market mutual fund pursues both strategies to the extreme: it cannot become insolvent because it has 100 percent equity (zero debt liabilities), and it holds a diversified portfolio containing only assets of high grade (low default risk) and short maturity (low risk of capital loss due to interest rate swings).

Historical precedents can be found for two contractual arrangements, beyond simple capital adequacy and portfolio diversification, for assuring solvency in a debt-issuing institution. First, bank shareholders can retain extended (double, triple, or even unlimited) liability for the firm's debts, providing a pool of "off-balance-sheet" equity. Second, demand-debt customers can be given first claim on a group of safe and easily monitored assets that are segregated on the bank's balance sheet. This sub-portfolio, managed like a money-market-mutual fund to minimize risk of capital loss, serves as "collateral" for, and should therefore always exceed in value, the bank's demand liabilities. Whether either of these arrangements is enough to suppress bank runs is an empirical question. Empirical evidence is considered below.

Contagion effects – where one bank's failure inspires customers of other banks to run – are rational if the first bank's default provides information relevant to assessing the probability that a second bank is about to default, but not otherwise. The first bank's default could provide such information if

1 in DD fashion, news of the first bank's failure acts as a "sunspot," triggering a run because each depositor thinks it will inspire *other* depositors to run, or
2 the two banks are believed to have very similar asset portfolios (which are not themselves directly observed), so that the first bank's failure acts as a (noisy) signal that the second bank may be pre-run insolvent.

We have already suggested that the survival of DD-type run-prone contracts, given the availability of hardier alternatives, is very doubtful under laissez-faire. As for similar asset portfolios, they are seen where banks are subject to common geographic or portfolio restrictions, but, in the absence of such restrictions (and without a safety net), banks would have strong incentives to avoid herding behavior, and to maintain distinct reputations. Thus, it is not obvious that one bank's failure would normally concern other banks' customers, or that contagion effects would occur under laissez-faire. In the next section, we consider what history indicates about runs, panics, and contagion effects.

Historical Evidence on Inherent Fragility

In the Diamond–Dybvig view, as we have noted, *anything* that makes people anticipate a run, in fact causes a run, because a run will cause the bank to fail and, thereby, validate the anticipation. Runs can therefore be triggered by intrinsically irrelevant events (like the appearance of sunspots), which can occur with apparent randomness. If the DD model makes any prediction about *when* runs occur, it thus suggests that runs are random events, or possibly linked to other events that could happen at any time. A different explanation of when runs occur would be needed if historical runs and panics have, in fact, followed a definite non-random pattern .

Likewise, the DD model suggests that runs could happen in *any* fractional-reserve banking system. A different explanation would be needed if, in fact, runs were a persistent problem in some historical banking systems but not a problem in others.

Banking panics were clearly a problem in the USA during the National Banking era (1863–1913), and during the Great Depression. The panics of these periods figured prominently in the arguments for the establishment of the Federal Reserve System and federal deposit insurance. However, few other countries have had similar experiences. The absence of panics in numerous countries which had neither a government central bank nor government deposit insurance indicates clearly that "panics are not inherent to banking" (Gorton 1989, p. 5).

Gary Gorton (1985b) has emphasized the "sunspot" nature of the Diamond–Dybvig account of bank runs. Gorton (1988) finds that the panics during the US National Banking era do not, in fact, fit such a random or inexplicable pattern. Each of the panics (he counts seven) occurred when information arrived that reasonably foreshadowed a business downturn and that, correspondingly, would have raised bank customers' estimates of the likelihood of bank failures due to pre-run insolvency.

In considering whether panics are "costly market failures justifying government intervention" Gorton (1989, pp. 6–10) points out that private arrangements effectively limited the damage done by the National Banking era panics. As noted in chapter 4, commercial bank clearinghouses developed techniques for supervising member banks, for assuring depositors of their banks' solvency, and even for acting as lenders of last resort . Based on a counterfactual simulation, Gorton argues that the US banking system would have suffered far less damage (fewer failures, smaller depositor losses) during the 1930s under the evolved private clearinghouse system than it suffered under the Federal Reserve System. It is unnecessary, and on this evidence inadvisable, to turn to nationalize depositor protection and lender-of-last-resort services.

Bank runs and panics have *not* been a common problem outside the USA, even before the advent of lenders of last resort and deposit insurance. Scotland, Canada, Sweden, and Switzerland, to cite four leading examples of less regulated banking systems, provide a striking contrast to US experience. Before central banks were established, all four had stable, and competitive, financial systems. There were occasional bank failures and rare runs on individual banks suspected of pre-run insolvency, but neither led contagiously to widespread runs nor to system-wide panic. Bordo (1990, pp. 25–6) suggests that the success of Scotland, Canada, and Switzerland can be explained by "access to a governmental authority which could provide high-powered money in the event of . . . a crisis." In fact, Scottish banks did not in fact have any such access to the Bank of England (White 1995, pp. 58–9), and it is far from clear that Swiss banks had any to the Bank of France. The Canadian government intervened twice in the twentieth century, but did not intervene in the nineteenth. Sweden, remarkably, had no private bank failures during the era of competitive note issue, so the question of access to a lender of last resort never even arose.[8]

The most plausible reason why the US banking system was unusually fragile was the unique set of destabilizing legal restrictions placed on banks by federal and state authorities. Limitations on branch banking especially weakened US banks by reducing their abilities to diversify assets, to diversify deposit sources, and to allocate reserves. As noted in chapter 3, the National Banking regime placed a special collateral requirement on banknotes, preventing banks from freely converting deposit liabilities into currency liabilities. The result was that seasonal demands to switch from deposits into currency – demands that could have been easily satisfied absent the collateral requirement – became scrambles for high-powered money that occasionally escalated into panics.

Is There a Natural Monopoly in Bank-issued Money?

The longest-standing case for expecting to find scale economies in the production of bank-issued money goes back at least to Edgeworth (1888). It argues that the variance of reserve losses, against which costly reserves must be held, increases less than proportionately with the number of depositors or noteholders because of the law of large numbers. A bigger bank can manage with a lower reserve ratio, and thus has lower average reserve-holding costs. A second argument cites similar stochastic eco-

---

[8] On these experiences, see Dowd (1992b).

nomies from the diversification of bank assets. A bank twice as large can achieve greater diversification with less than double the transaction costs, and thus has lower average asset-default-risk costs (Baltensperger 1972; Vaubel 1984, p. 46).

These economies of scale no doubt exist, but they are probably trivial beyond some minimum viable bank size. Economies of scale from these two sources may easily be swamped by diseconomies of scale, such as those associated with internal hierarchy, or with diminishing returns in cultivating a clientele, once a bank exceeds a certain size. Presumably, this explains why historical experience does not show survival of only one or a few banks under open competition, and thus contradicts the hypothesis of natural monopoly in banking.

Can Government Produce Currency More Efficiently?

Eugene Fama (1983) has argued for the efficiency of letting government collect the (float) profit from issuing currency. There is no loss to consumers from a government currency monopoly, he suggests, because consumers will face the same price of holding currency (receive the same zero interest rate) as under competitive issue. The monopoly is therefore a source of government revenue without the relative-price distortions, or deadweight losses, associated with other taxes.

Scott Sumner (1993) builds Fama's point into a natural monopoly argument: government can produce currency more efficiently as a monopolist because it need not engage in non-price competition. It can produce a $1 coin or note for a few cents. Under free entry into currency production, by contrast, banks battling for market share (and not paying interest on their notes) are compelled to expend resources on differentiating their products and making them more appealing to potential noteholding clients. A competitor's costs rise until, in equilibrium, marginal cost equals price, i.e. until the present value of the cost of producing, and keeping in circulation, a $1 coin or note equals $1. Production costs are therefore higher, and the revenue from currency issue is dissipated in wasteful "combative competition". Just as US banks' non-price competition for deposits was inefficient when deposit interest rates were capped by Regulation Q, Sumner argues, non-price competition in currency is wasteful.

Fama's and Sumner's arguments, however, rest on a *non sequitur* (White and Boudreaux 1998). Creating a monopoly through legal restrictions does maximize industry profit, but it reduces benefits to consumers. Competitive profit dissipation *promotes* economic efficiency, because it delivers greater benefits to consumers. True, in the case of currency, the benefits are delivered to consumers exclusively via non-price competition, rather than via price competition. True, non-price competition can be associated with waste where the manner of competition is legally restricted (as by Regulation Q). It does not follow that non-price competition is wasteful in absence of legal restrictions.

Non-price competition (quality enhancement, image advertising, distinctive packaging, and other forms of product differentiation) survives even in markets where price competition is not restricted. Consider shampoo. Assuming that consumers are rational, we must infer that those who pass up generic shampoo actually value the special features of higher-priced shampoo (fragrance, stylish bottle, clever ad campaign, whatever) more than the added price. Shampoo makers have every incentive to seek out and provide only the features that customers really are willing to pay for. Successful forms of non-price competition will be those that deliver valued product features to consumers, not that waste resources on pointless "combat." Like shampoo makers, currency issuers will seek the forms of non-price competition that best attract clients, hence the forms consumers value most.

If banks use non-price competition simply because price competition (paying interest on currency) is more costly (at attracting clients, hence at delivering benefits to currency-holders), it means that price competition is inefficient and non-price competition is efficient in that market. It is an error to argue that efficiency can be promoted by legal restrictions against non-price competition. Absent legal restrictions, firms that survive will be those that only use non-price competition where it is efficient. Competitive currency issuers will add costly features to their currency only up to the point where marginal revenue (reflecting marginal consumer benefit) equals marginal cost. A government monopoly for the express purpose of eliminating expenditures on non-price competition in currency would therefore inefficiently eliminate the delivery of benefits to consumers that consumers deem worth having.

Questions

1   "If a bank is insolvent, it ought to be closed promptly. A bank run forces an insolvent bank to close promptly. A bank run is therefore generally something to celebrate, not something to regret." Correct or incorrect? Explain.

2   "It is the side-effects (or externalities, in economists' jargon) associated with bank failures that make them such a special case. When say, a steel producer collapses, its disappearance is unlikely to cause trouble for other steelmakers; indeed they should benefit by picking

up some of the failed firm's clients. But when a bank suddenly goes bust, its rivals may experience problems too." (Giles 1996)

(a)   Why and how might one bank's failure cause problems for its rivals?

(b)   What regulations have been rationalized as methods for preventing such side effects?

(c)   Other than relying on such regulations, what methods have banks, historically, used to minimize side effects from the failure of rival banks?

3   (a)   What, in the Diamond–Dybvig model, makes the bank run-prone?

   (b)   What remedy do DD suggest for bank runs?

   (c)   Why haven't banks already instituted this remedy themselves, in DD's view?

4   What, in the Diamond–Dybvig model, makes a bank run a *self-reinforcing* or *self-justifying* event?

5   Tyler Cowen and Randall Kroszner (1994) write that when checking accounts are linked to mutual fund shares rather than to traditional bank deposits, account-holders "do not facet the me-first problem that creates bank runs."

(a)   What is the "me-first problem" that creates bank runs with traditional accounts?

(b)   Does linking checking accounts to mutual fund shares really solve the problem? Why or why not?

(c)   What are the most important alternative ways banks might try to lessen or eliminate the "me-first problem"?

6   "It is important to stress that the [Diamond–Dybvig] bank is a mutual fund in which there is no distinction between depositors and shareholders. . . . Runs arose in the Diamond–Dybvig model precisely because the zero value of capital meant that . . . the bank has insufficient [assets] to redeem all its deposits." (Dowd 1989)

(a)   Why does it matter that there is no distinction between depositors and shareholders in the Diamond–Dybvig bank? That is, how does the absence of the distinction matter in deriving the conclusion that the bank is inherently run-prone?

(b)   A mutual fund cannot become insolvent: it always has assets sufficient to repay all its claims, because the claims are defined as shares that must add up to 100 percent of the assets. Is there then a contradiction between Dowd's two sentences? How can a Diamond–Dybvig bank *both* be a mutual fund *and* have insufficient assets to redeem all its deposits?

7   What does historical evidence from around the world indicate about whether banking panics are inherent to an uninsured fractional-reserve banking system?

8 "The $1 bill looms large in the stock of US currency: more than one-third of the bills outstanding are $1 bills ... The need to maintain such a large stock of $1 bills in circulation makes the provision of currency unnecessarily costly to the monetary authority and thus ultimately to taxpayers. ... [Because coins are much more durable] the government (and thus the taxpayer) could realize significant savings from replacing the $1 bill with a $1 coin." (Wynne 1997)

Does it follow from the fact that coins would be cheaper that it would be efficient to replace the $1 bill with a $1 coin?

9 "[I]n the short term, it may be difficult for us to determine whether profitable and popular new [electronic money] products are actually efficient alternatives to official paper currency or simply a diversion of seigniorage from the government to the private sector. Yet we must also recognize that a diversion of seigniorage may be an inevitable byproduct of creating a more efficient retail payment system in the long run." (Greenspan 1997)

(a) Under what conditions would competition from, and among, issuers of electronic money generate economic inefficiency?

(b) Under what conditions would the competition instead improve efficiency?

(c) Which case is more plausible, and why?

7

Seigniorage

In Chapters 5 and 6, we considered the normative question of what (if anything) a government *should* do with respect to the provision of money. In this chapter, we begin to explore the positive question of what government *does* do when it exercises discretionary power to produce fiat money. How can we explain the behavior of modern government central banks? In particular, what determines the rate at which a central bank expands the stock of base money? The natural approach for an economist, trying to answer these questions, is to treat the central bank, like the other agents of economic theory (e.g. the consumer and the firm), as a self-interested agent who pursues some set of objectives subject to constraints.

But what objectives does a central bank pursue? Where, in its view, do its interests lie? Economists have proposed at least four positive theories of central bank behavior, each focusing on a different goal as the overriding objective of the central bank:

1 *Seigniorage*: the central bank pursues the fiscal interest of the government, generating revenue by printing money.
2 *Bureaucratic*: the central bank seeks to maximize its own power or comfort subject to political constraints.
3 *Political business cycles*: the central bank pursues the reelection of the incumbent, or seeks to satisfy the preferences of the party in power, through its influence on macro-economic conditions.
4 *Time-inconsistency*: the central bank seeks to manipulate the economy into the best combination of inflation and unemployment through discretionary policy, but when it faces a public that understands the game, its options are so limited that discretion turns out to be a trap.

This chapter considers the first of these theories: seigniorage. Chapters 8–10 consider the remaining three approaches in turn.

The Sources of Seigniorage

The basic concept of seigniorage is fairly straightforward: a government reaps profit when it produces new money at an expense less than the value of the money produced. The government can finance additional expenditures by spending the new units of money into circulation. If new money is interchangeable with old, the expansion of the money stock implicitly taxes money holders by diluting the value of existing money balances. Defined as the net revenue or profit from producing money, seigniorage is equal to the difference between the exchange value of the money produced and the cost of producing and maintaining it in circulation.

Under a specie standard

Historically, under gold and silver coin standards, seigniorage was the difference between the face value of coins minted (in bullion units of account) and their actual bullion content, minus the cost of minting. Algebraically, mint operations were subject to the accounting identity

$$M = PQ + C + S$$

where

> M = the nominal value (e.g. one hundred "pounds") assigned to a batch of coins ("shillings")
> P = the nominal price paid by the mint per ounce of precious metal
> Q = the number of ounces of precious metal embodied in the batch of coins
> C = the remaining average cost of operating the mint (called "brassage")
> S = the nominal seigniorage

If out of every M's worth of shillings minted, PQ is paid for the silver, and C covers other mint expenses, then S is retained as seigniorage profit, available for spending by the duke or king. Total seigniorage revenue per year depends on how many batches of coins are produced per year.[1]

---

[1] For further discussion of medieval and modern seigniorage, see Selgin and White (1999).

In a perfectly competitive minting industry, competition would enforce the condition of price equal to marginal cost, $M = PQ + C$, implying $S = 0$. If government took no steps to force their acceptance, then underweight coins (Q below the standard) would be rejected or accepted only at a discount. If bullion owners were free to choose where to take their bullion to be coined, rivalry would bid up P until every mint, even the government's if it operated one, would earn zero seigniorage at the margin. If new mints could produce as cheaply as incumbent mints, then profits on inframarginal production would be eliminated by the entry of new competitors. A royal mint can earn seigniorage permanently, only if it has a legally protected monopoly, which allows it to maintain P or Q below the competitive level without losing its business.

A monopoly mint can increase its seigniorage per batch of coins by *debasement*, a reduction in the bullion content or "fineness" of newly minted coins, because debasement allows the mint to produce the same number of shillings more cheaply.[2] By mixing in cheaper "base" metal (copper, zinc, tin) to replace some silver, the mint can continue to use the same dies to produce coins (nearly) identical in appearance. Debasement means that Q is reduced for a given M. If the public notices the difference, and accepts debased coin only at a proportionally reduced value (in terms of old coin or an ideal bullion-weight unit of account), this effectively amounts to insisting on a proportionately lower M (or higher P, if new coin is the unit of account), which eliminates the boost to seigniorage. Governments have historically countered by using "legal tender" laws to compel public acceptance of new (lighter) coin at par with old coin.[3] In a debasement, P can remain constant.[4] C rises slightly with the purchase of more base metal, but only by a fraction of the reduction in PQ (because base metal is cheaper than silver), implying an increase in seigniorage S.

Greater seigniorage per batch can be earned *without* debasement if the mint can arbitrarily reduce P, while keeping Q and C constant. However, reducing P will mean that less silver is brought to the mint, allowing

---

[2] If we think of seigniorage being captured per ounce of silver coined, rather than per nominal batch of coins produced, debasement increases seigniorage by allowing the mint to produce more coins from each ounce of silver purchased.

[3] Boyer-Xambeau et al. (1994, pp. 49–59) note: "Until the sixteenth century princes in most countries prohibited the weighing of coins and made people accept them all, even when used up, simply in view of their imprints and inscriptions." McCulloch (1982, p. 63) notes that the term "seigniorage" itself derives from the French *seigneur* or lord, reflecting the feudal lord's prerogative of extracting revenue from his subjects by compelling them to accept debased coins at face value.

[4] Government mints often increased P for old coins slightly above its legal-tender value, giving owners an incentive to bring old coins to the mint rather than to melt them down or export them for their bullion content.

fewer coins to be produced, so total seigniorage revenue per year may fall if P is pushed too low.[5] Once the profit-maximizing P is found, debasement still remains an option for further increasing total seigniorage per year.

Under a fiat money standard

Today, under fiat money standards, the bullion content of base money is zero, and production costs are almost zero.[6] Setting $Q = 0$ and (for simplicity) $C = 0$, it follows that $M = S$. Nominal seigniorage equals one dollar for each dollar produced. A government's nominal seigniorage per year is then simply equal to the change in the stock of base money per year. We can write the relationship

$$S = \Delta H$$

where Δ (the Greek letter delta) in ΔH indicates the change in H, the stock of "high-powered" or base money in existence. Real seigniorage is

$$s = \frac{\Delta H}{P}$$

where lower-case letters represent real (deflated) variables, and P is the price index used as a deflator.

The budget constraint for a government that issues fiat money is

$$G = T + \Delta D + \Delta H$$

where

G is government spending (including debt service)
T is tax revenue

---

[5] The result depends on the elasticity of silver supply to the mint with respect to the mint price of silver. A profit-maximizing mint would lower P until supply became elastic enough to make it unprofitable to lower P further. To reduce the elasticity along the entire supply schedule, medieval governments gave their mints monopoly privileges: silver miners and importers could not legally sell to any other mint, and sometimes not to any other enterprise at all.

[6] Printing costs are in fact about 3 cents per note for the smaller denominations of US paper currency. Other nations produce higher quality notes, and the US its new $20 and $100 bills, with their greater anti-counterfeiting devices, at a cost of about 6 cents each (at 1996 prices). Worn $1 bills have to be replaced almost annually; higher denominations less frequently. I thank Peter Garber for this information.

ΔD is the change in interest-bearing debt held by the non-government public

ΔH or nominal seigniorage is the change in non-interest-bearing debt (fiat base money) held by the public.

The way in which seigniorage helps to finance government spending is most obvious where the central bank simply prints up new notes to pay the government's bills.[7] Where the monetary base expands through open market operations, the connection remains, but is a bit indirect. By purchasing ΔH worth of Treasury bills in the open market, the central bank effectively retires that much debt (interest on it now goes to the central bank, which largely or entirely rebates it back to the Treasury), and makes it possible for the Treasury to finance a stream of new spending whose present value is equal to ΔH. To do all the new spending in the current period, the Treasury can sell new debt to the public, replacing the debt the central bank just bought (and restoring the Treasury's annual interest payment on the debt, net of central bank rebates, to its former level). The central bank's open market purchase increases H and reduces D. The Treasury's issue of new debt brings D back up, and allows G to rise. The net impact (just as if the central bank had simply printed up new currency and given it to the Treasury to spend) is an increase in G financed by ΔH.[8]

Two somewhat technical controversies regarding the measurement of seigniorage should be noted. First, for some purposes, it is convenient to treat the government's revenue from issuing fiat money as an annual flow from the outstanding stock of base money, rather than as the change in the stock. The revenue flow is $i_b H$, where i_b is the nominal interest rate on government bonds, because this is the government's "float" profit from having non-interest-bearing base money rather than interest-bearing bonds in circulation. Under this approach, seigniorage is positive, even during a year in which the monetary base does not change. The approach counts the holding of central bank liabilities as an interest-free loan to the government, which is the proper way to count profits from the issue of central bank money where that money is *redeemable*, say in gold or silver coin or a foreign currency. Under redeemability, the money issued really is a liability, and the public and the commercial banks can "call in" the "loan" to the government by redeeming the central bank money. In a fiat regime, however, central

---

[7] A recent real-world example, from West African nation of Guinea, is described by Kerfalla Yansane, governor of the Central Bank of Guinea: "The issuance of currency in the previous regime was not under the authority of the central bank but was under the discretionary authority of the president, who would send the necessary papers to the central bank as an order to pay." (White 1993, p. 75)

[8] For a more detailed discussion and a numerical example, see Greenfield (1994, pp. 40–4).

bank liabilities are not redeemable. The issue of additional fiat money increases the government's net worth once and for all, rather than giving it a merely temporary flow of revenue. Accordingly ΔH is properly counted as a once-and-for-all profit.[9] The central bank's net revenue flow, though a useful concept, is not the same as what we are calling seigniorage.

Second, some economists have suggested that commercial banks share in seigniorage, due to their "privilege" of issuing money in the form of banknotes and demand deposits, whenever the reserve requirement is less than 100 percent. This is not generally correct. Only under extreme and implausibly effective legal restrictions could commercial banks share in seigniorage. To imagine such an extreme case, suppose that legal restrictions compel a zero interest rate on deposits, and banks are (implausibly) effectively prevented from engaging in any non-price competition to attract the interest-free deposits. If banks then find it costless to issue non-interest-bearing deposits apart from holding reserves of H_b, issuing deposits gives the banks an interest-free loan, just as issuing fiat money gives the government an interest-free loan. If we treat the loan as permanent (as though deposits in the aggregate were as irredeemable as fiat money), total seigniorage would be

$$\Delta H + \Delta(D - H_b)$$

of which government would get only the share corresponding to ΔH. The banks would get the rest. If banks are not so effectively restrained, competition will compel them to pay explicit interest on demand deposits, at a rate that eliminates any pure profit on bank-issued money. If there are legal ceilings on deposit interest rates, but entry is free, potential profits will be dissipated through "nonprice" competition. Banks will give customers free, or underpriced, ancillary banking services, and amenities, to attract a clientele. The same competitive forces toward profit dissipation apply to banknotes, which may be non-interest-bearing even in the absence of legal restrictions (as discussed in chapter 6). As a result, commercial banks do not ordinarily earn seigniorage. Ordinarily, the only seigniorage-earning money is base money produced monopolistically.

Maximizing the Take from Seigniorage

A classic article by Martin J. Bailey (1956) analyzed the "welfare cost of inflationary finance" in a fiat money regime. Our interest, here, is not in the

---

[9] I am indebted to Fernando Alvarez for discussion on this point.

welfare implications for money holders of various rates of seigniorage, but rather the revenue implications for government. We can, nonetheless, use the essential elements of Bailey's analysis as an illustrative model for examining how a seigniorage-maximizing government will behave. We focus, initially, on steady-state equilibria. For simplicity we assume that money holders correctly anticipate the inflation rate. This assumption is not supposed to be perfectly realistic, but is useful for deriving at least a first approximation to the seigniorage impact of variations in base money growth. We will later discuss the consequences of relaxing the assumption that the inflation rate is always correctly anticipated.

Under these assumptions, and with a reasonable money demand function, the *revenue-maximizing rate of expansion* of the nominal monetary base is finite. Its height depends on a particular aspect of money demand, namely the elasticity of real base money demand with respect to the inflation rate. This elasticity is closely related to the elasticity of real money demand with respect to the nominal interest rate, a measure more familiar to macro-economists.

The revenue-maximizing rate of monetary expansion is not infinite (given our assumption that the inflation rate is always correctly anticipated) basically for the same reason that the revenue-maximizing tax rate on cigarettes, or income, is less than 100 percent. A higher tax rate creates an incentive for greater tax-avoiding actions, which shrink the "tax base," the volume of activity subjected to the tax. Beyond some tax rate, the tax base begins to shrink so rapidly that the product of rate times base, total tax revenue, declines. This effect has become well known from being depicted by the "Laffer curve." It applies to the taxation of real money balances through seigniorage. (In fact, long before Laffer ever drew the curve on a cocktail napkin, a "Laffer curve" appeared in Bailey's 1956 article.)

The problem of solving for the revenue-maximizing rate of monetary expansion is formally equivalent to finding the revenue-maximizing rate for any tax. More revealingly, perhaps, it is also equivalent to the problem of profit maximization for a monopolist, who has to consider how much sales will shrink as he raises price. Here, government is the monopoly producer of base money. The inflation rate is the "price" of holding money. As the price is increased, the real quantity of base money demanded shrinks. The profit-maximizing price is consequently not infinite. We will discuss this monopoly-pricing view of the problem again shortly.

We adopt our algebraic notation in part from Bailey, and in part from McCulloch (1982, ch. 5). The flow of real seigniorage to government is again

$$s = \frac{\Delta H}{P}$$

where

s = real seigniorage
ΔH = change in the nominal stock of base money
P = the price level

We can transform this expression to isolate the "tax rate" and "tax base" aspects of seigniorage:

$$s = \left(\frac{\Delta H}{H}\right)\left(\frac{H}{P}\right)$$

where $(\Delta H/H)$, the growth rate of H, represents the "tax rate," and (H/P), the real base money stock, represents the "tax base."

We can simplify the notation, by rewriting this last equation as

$$s = Eh$$

where

E = rate of monetary base expansion = $\Delta H/H$
h = real money stock = H/P

We assume for simplicity that the rate of inflation (expected and actual) varies one-for-one with the rate of monetary base expansion. The growth-rate version of the equation of exchange, where H is the relevant measure of the stock of money, and where V is correspondingly the income velocity of base money, tells us:

$$\frac{\Delta H}{H} + \frac{\Delta V}{V} \approx \frac{\Delta P}{P} + \frac{\Delta y}{y}$$

In light of this approximate identity, assuming that

$$\frac{\Delta P}{P} = \frac{\Delta H}{H} + k$$

where k is a constant, is equivalent to assuming that

$$\frac{\Delta V}{V} - \frac{\Delta y}{y} = k$$

i.e. that there is no change in the difference between the rate of velocity growth and the rate of real income growth. This would be true, for example, if both real income growth and velocity growth were independent of the inflation rate. These assumptions imply that if the monetary authority increases the monetary base expansion rate by 5 percentage points, the resulting inflation rate will also rise by exactly 5 percentage points. Accordingly, we can speak almost interchangeably of an increase in the monetary expansion rate, and an increase in the inflation rate.

The real base money stock (h) accommodates itself to the real quantity of base money demanded (h^d), through adjustment of P. This proposition – that, in a fiat money system, the equilibrium h is determined entirely on the demand side – has been called "the fundamental proposition of monetary theory." Recall that, under our assumptions, changes in E are matched exactly by changes in the expected rate of inflation. The higher the expected inflation rate, the greater the "price" paid, in the form of lost purchasing power, for each unit of real balances held. Thus, the real quantity of base money demanded falls as the rate of monetary expansion E rises.

A seigniorage-maximizing government wants to maximize s with respect to E, taking into account the negative effect of higher E on real base money demand. A higher rate of monetary expansion E has the direct effect (taken by itself, that is) of generating more seigniorage, but it also reduces h (by increasing expected inflation and reducing h^d), which has an offsetting effect. This offsetting effect, under at least one reasonable specification of the money demand function (spelled out below), grows larger and eventually exceeds the direct effect as E is pushed ever higher. A seigniorage-maximizing rate, denoted E^*, is reached where the offsetting effect just begins to outweigh the direct effect. That is, the h-shrinking effect of increasing E another notch would more than cancel out the direct effect, though that was not true of increasing it the last notch.

Another way to express this idea, familiar to those who remember monopoly pricing theory, is to reason in terms of elasticity, which brings out the parallel to monopoly pricing more clearly. As the monopoly producer of base money, the government wants to set a profit-maximizing "price," paid by holders in the form of depreciation, of E^*. Where marginal production costs are zero, the profit-maximizing price is simply the revenue-maximizing price. (Production can be profitably expanded until marginal revenue goes to zero.) The revenue-maximizing price is found where the elasticity of demand with respect to price is -1. In the case of fiat money produced at zero marginal cost, the revenue-maximizing E is therefore found where the elasticity of real base money demand with respect to E is -1.

"Elasticity of demand" is measured by the percentage change in the quantity demanded of a good when its price is raised by 1 percent. An elasticity of -1 means that quantity demanded falls by 1 percent with a 1 percent increase in price (thus the seller's revenue does not increase; it has reached a maximum). In the case at hand, the elasticity of h^d with respect to E is the percentage change in h for each 1-percent change in E:

$$\eta = \left(\frac{\Delta h}{h}\right)\left(\frac{\Delta E}{E}\right)$$

$$= \left(\frac{\Delta h}{\Delta E}\right)\left(\frac{E}{h}\right)$$

where η denotes elasticity of h^d with respect to E. It is a feature of at least one reasonable money demand function that η becomes increasingly large (in absolute value) as E rises. Revenue is then maximized by the finite price at which η crosses -1.

Graphical Illustration

To illustrate this problem graphically, we can plot a demand curve (see figure 7.1) showing h, the real quantity of base money (demanded and actual), as a function of E, the base money growth rate (and implicitly the expected inflation rate plus a constant). To maximize seigniorage, $s = Eh$, is

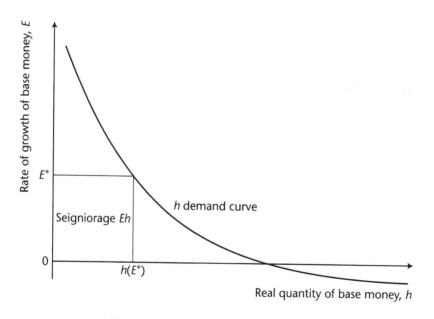

Figure 7.1 Maximum seigniorage is represented by the largest rectangle that fits under the h demand curve

to find the value of E (call it E^*) that makes for the largest rectangle of area Eh, whose opposite corners lie at the origin (0, 0) and on the demand curve $(h(E), E)$. Increasing E makes the rectangle taller, but also narrows it by reducing h. Above E^* the area of the rectangle begins to shrink.

Algebraic illustration

To illustrate the problem algebraically, we can write out a specific base money demand function, including E as one of the arguments, and use calculus to find the s-maximizing value E^*. For at least some reasonable specifications of the base money demand function, there is a unique E^*. Bailey used a function of the following form, used earlier by Philip Cagan:

$$h^d = e^{\beta - aE}$$

where e is the natural logarithmic base (e = 2.71828 . . .), and a and β are constants. A demand curve of this form is plotted in figure 7.1.[10] A convenient feature of this form is that In $e^x = x$, so we can equivalently write the Cagan function in the loglinear form

$$\ln h^d = \beta - aE$$

Given our simplifying assumption that changes in the monetary expansion rate E are matched exactly by changes in actual and expected inflation, we can view a as an inflation-rate sensitivity parameter. The larger is a, the more h^d shrinks for a given increase in the rates of monetary expansion and inflation. (To be precise, $-a$ is the "semi-elasticity" of h^d with respect to E).[11] The other parameter β is a scale parameter: the higher is β, the greater is real base money demand for any given inflation rate. At the inflation rate corresponding to zero growth in the monetary base, $\ln h^d = \beta$.

For the Cagan money demand function, the seigniorage-maximizing value

---

[10] The demand curve and other figures in this chapter were plotted by using a spreadsheet program to plug a range of values for E into a Cagan-type money demand function with arbitrarily chosen values of a and β.

[11] The elasticity of h^d with respect to E is $(dh^d/dE)(E/h^d)$. The semi-elasticity is defined as $(dh^d/dE)(1/h^d)$, which is equivalent to d(ln h^d)/dE. Given the Cagan demand function ln $h^d = \beta - aE$, the semi-elasticity d(ln h^d)/dE $= -a$.

It is more common for money demand functions to include a nominal interest rate rather than the inflation rate or the money expansion rate, but all three rates move together, ceteris paribus. In equilibrium, under simplifying assumptions, the "Fisher effect" insures that the nominal interest rate i changes at the margin one-for-one with the inflation rate and the money expansion rate, so $dE/di = 1$. We can consequently think of $-a$ as equivalent to a nominal-interest-rate semi-elasticity parameter.

E^* is conveniently simple. Reasoning in terms of elasticity, it can be shown that

$$\eta = - aE$$

Where η is the elasticity of h^d with respect to E. Thus, for revenue maximization, we have E^* where

$$- 1 = - aE$$

and thus

$$E^* = \frac{1}{a}$$

(See the appendix to this chapter, parts 1 and 2, for derivations both directly and in terms of elasticity.) The seigniorage-maximizing rate of monetary expansion E^* depends only on a single parameter, a. The more sensitive the real quantity of base money demanded is to anticipated inflation, the lower the equilibrium revenue-maximizing rate of monetary expansion.

We denote s^* the maximum quantity of seigniorage revenue the government can receive. The value of s^* is given by

$$\begin{aligned} s^* &= E^*h \\ &= \left(\frac{1}{a}\right)h \end{aligned}$$

Thus the maximum seigniorage revenue is inversely related to the sensitivity of real base money demand to inflation, and positively related to the scale of real base money demand.

The Bailey curve

Given the Cagan money demand function, figure 7.2 maps steady-state real seigniorage as a function of the correctly anticipated inflation rate E.

We have already noted the analogy to the "Laffer curve," which shows how tax revenue may peak with respect to a tax rate. Here, E is the tax rate, and s is revenue, peaking at expansion rate E^*. We may call this graph the "Bailey curve" in recognition of Bailey's authorship.[12]

---

[12] McCulloch (1982) calls it the "monetary Laffer curve." We follow here the spirit of his suggestion (p. 78) that the usual "Laffer curve" might be more appropriately called the "fiscal Bailey curve" in light of Bailey's priority.

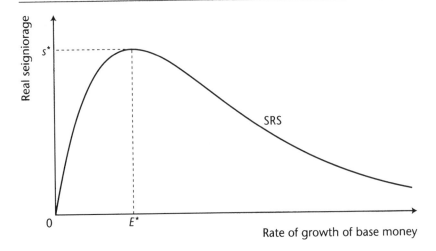

Figure 7.2   The Bailey curve: Steady-state real seigniorage (SRS) rises, peaks, and then declines as the rate of monetary expansion increases

The shape of the Bailey curve relates to the Cagan money demand function in the following ways. The greater the Cagan parameter β, the steeper the "take off" or slope of the Bailey curve at the origin, and therefore the higher is s^* (for a given value of a). Thus s^* is not independent of β, even though E^* is.[13] The greater the parameter a, the more rapidly the curve droops toward the horizontal axis, and thus the smaller are s^* (for a given β) and E^*. The right-hand tail of the curve approaches the horizontal axis only asymptotically because h^d goes to zero only as E goes to infinity.

Having mapped out the Bailey curve, we can examine the impact of various policies on seigniorage by considering how they cause the Bailey curve to shift.

Reserve Requirements

One way for a government to enhance its seigniorage is to impose a reserve requirement on banks, which enhances the real demand for base money h^d by compelling banks to hold more base money than they otherwise would.

---

[13] The slope of the Bailey curve is ds/dE. Given $s = Ee^{\beta - aE}$, $ds/dE = e^{\beta - aE} - aEe^{\beta - aE}$. At the origin $E = 0$, so at "take off" the slope expression reduces to e^{β}. For more algebraic detail on s^*, see the appendix to this chapter, part 3.

In terms of the money demand function, a reserve requirement increases h^d by increasing the β parameter. Less obviously, a reserve requirement also increases the a parameter, the inflation-sensitivity of real base money demand h^d. At higher rates of inflation, the demand-reducing effect of a higher a increasingly counteracts the demand-enhancing effect of a larger β.

Why does a reserve requirement increase a? As inflation rises, banks receive higher nominal interest rates on their assets. Under perfectly competitive conditions, the increased nominal interest earnings will be entirely passed on to depositors. In the limiting case of a bank that holds zero reserves, an increase in the monetary expansion rate E, and thus in the inflation rate and the nominal interest rate on bank assets (i_L), will be fully matched by an increase in the nominal deposit interest rate (i_D). With a positive prudential reserve ratio, the bank receives increased nominal earnings on only a subset of its assets, so the increase in the deposit interest rate i_D will less than fully match the increase in the inflation rate. A *reserve requirement* means that a bank must hold an *additional* quantity of non-interest-bearing base money, on top of its prudential reserves, proportional to its deposits. From the point of view of depositors, the reserve requirement acts as a percentage tax on deposit interest: it increases the wedge between the interest rate the bank earns on its assets, and the rate it can pay on deposits.

For example, consider a bank that voluntarily holds $10 in reserves and $90 in interest-earning assets against each $100 in deposits. The initial nominal interest rate i_L is 10 percent. The bank earns $9 in interest, all of which (assuming zero operating costs for simplicity) it passes through to its depositors, making i_D equal to 9 percent. With a 10 percent reserve requirement (of a sort that makes the required reserves unavailable for meeting the bank's liquidity needs) imposed in addition, the bank holds $20 in reserves and only $80 in interest-earning assets, earns only $8 in interest, and can pay only i_D of 8 percent to its depositors. The $i_L - i_D$ wedge is 2 percentage points rather than 1 point.

A reserve requirement makes the wedge increasingly large at higher inflation rates. Continuing the example, consider an increase of 10 percentage points in the rate of monetary expansion E, and correspondingly in the inflation rate, that raises the nominal interest rate i_L to 20 percent. Absent a reserve requirement, the bank earns $18 in interest, and pays 18 percent on deposits. Under the 10 percent reserve requirement, the bank earns $16 in interest, and pays 16 percent on deposits. The increase in inflation, interacting with the reserve requirement, increases the $i_L - i_D$ wedge – which represents the opportunity cost of holding base money to individuals who could be directly holding assets paying i_L – by 2 percentage points, up to 4 from 2 point. With a zero reserve requirement, the wedge only increases by 1 percentage point (up to 2 from 1). This illustrates the general point that the higher the reserve requirement, the faster grows the wedge as E rises. As a result of the faster-growing wedge, base money demand becomes more sensitive to inflation (a increases) as the required reserve ratio rises.

The higher β, from a higher reserve requirement, means that real base money demand, and therefore seigniorage, are higher at low rates of monetary expansion. The higher a means that h^d falls off more and more at higher and higher rates of expansion. Under simplifying assumptions (the public holds only deposits, the banks hold only the required level of reserves, intermediation is perfectly competitive and costless), the second effect precisely catches up with the first, so that maximum real seigniorage s^* is unchanged, although it occurs at a lower expansion rate E^*. This outcome is shown graphically in figure 7.3 by the contrast between curve B (representing steady-state real seigniorage with a higher reserve requirement) and curve A (lower reserve requirement). (For an algebraic derivation, see Part 4 of the appendix to this chapter). The takeoff angle is steeper for curve B because β (the parameter for real base money demand at zero inflation) is higher with a higher reserve requirement. Curve B droops more quickly because a is higher (real base money demand is more sensitive to inflation) for reasons spelled out above. However, the curves reach the same maximum height.

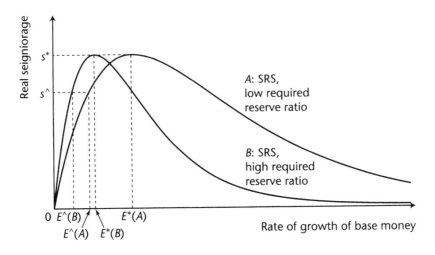

Figure 7.3 Required reserve ratio: raising the required reserve ratio compresses the steady-state real seigniorage (SRS) curve

Increasing the required reserve ratio increases real government seigniorage, at any rate of monetary expansion below the new E^*, by forcing banks to hold more base money and thus increasing the real seigniorage "tax base". Real seigniorage is higher in case B at any expansion rate lower than $E^*(B)$.

Correspondingly, increasing the required reserve ratio reduces the expansion rate, and hence the inflation rate necessary to capture any given amount of real seigniorage. This is shown graphically in figure 7.3 for the rates necessary to achieve a target seigniorage level of $\hat{s}$: the expansion rate $\hat{E}(B)$ lies to the left of $\hat{E}(A)$. In this sense, high reserve requirements are "anti-inflationary." The combination of a higher reserve requirement and lower inflation does not, however, reduce the welfare burden to the public from a given amount of seigniorage. For depositors, the burden is felt from the wedge between alternative interest rates i_L and the rate on deposit balances i_D. That difference is the same in case B. A higher reserve requirement only means that the seigniorage is extracted by a higher tax wedge at any given inflation rate rather than by a higher inflation rate.[14]

As an alternative to increasing the required reserve ratio, but with basically equivalent aggregate effects, the government could increase the share of banks forced to hold required reserves, if not all banks are already forced. This also increases the seigniorage "tax base." The Depository Institutions Deregulation and Monetary Control Act of 1980 in the USA broadened the application of reserve requirements in this way.

Other Legal Restrictions

Other government methods for increasing seigniorage work to increase real base money demand, by placing restrictions on substitutes for base money. Any monopolist's ability to raise price profitably (without losing too many sales) is greater, the smaller the price-elasticity of demand for his product. The price-elasticity of demand is smaller, the less available are close substitutes for the product in question. With few substitutes, the monopolist has a "captive market." In the case of base money, the relevant price is the monetary expansion or inflation rate. If the government can reduce the availability of close substitutes for base money, it can increase real base money demand independent of the expansion rate (increase β), and especially lessen the inflation-sensitivity of real base money demand (reduce a), thereby further increasing its real seigniorage at any rates of monetary expansion.

Graphically, the imposition of heavier restrictions on substitutes shifts the Bailey curve from A to C in figure 7.4. Curve A represents the case in which more good substitutes for government money are available. Curve C

---

[14] Grilli (1988) provides evidence that the government of Italy increased reserve requirements in order to preserve its seigniorage when adherence to the EMS compelled it to reduce its rate of base money expansion.

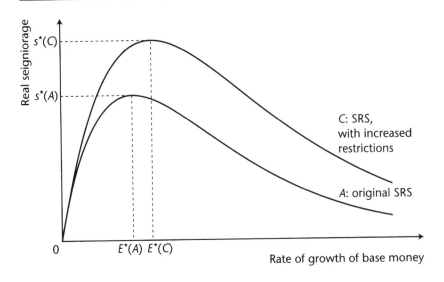

Figure 7.4 Restrictions on *H* substitutes: increasing restrictions on *H* substitutes shifts out the steady-state real seigniorages (SRS) curve

represents the case of fewer good substitutes. Unlike in the impact of an increase in the reserve requirement, s^* rises in case *C*. The effects on a and β are reinforcing rather than offsetting.

Donald Nichols (1974) has pointed out that seigniorage enhancement may explain why many governments impose various restrictions on their financial markets. One close substitute for domestic base money is foreign currency, and many governments restrict their citizens from acquiring, holding, or doing business in foreign currencies. A seigniorage-motivated government would certainly seek to prevent a widespread substitution from domestic to foreign currency, a phenomenon known in Latin America as the "dollarization" of the economy. Dollarization shrinks the real demand for domestic currency and, thereby, reduces potential seigniorage. A second close substitute for government-issued base money is bank-issued money. Government may restrict interest rates legally payable on demand deposits. Both measures reduce the availability or attractiveness of substitutes for the government's currency, shifting the seigniorage curve from *A* to *C*, and increasing the government's seigniorage revenue.

The same effects result from policies that keep government-issued and private bonds a poor substitute for fiat currency. Examples include a policy of refusing to issue small-denomination negotiable bonds (US Treasury Bills come no smaller than $10,000), and a policy of restricting the transferability of small bonds (neither US Savings Bonds nor small bank certificates of deposit are legally negotiable in the USA). Bryant and Wallace (1983) have characterized these policies, enhancing the inelasticity of demand for fiat currency by segmenting the markets for large interest-bearing and small non-interest-bearing government liabilities, as part of a "price discrimination" fiscal scheme.[15]

The Dynamics of Hyperinflation

Following McCulloch (1982), we can also use the Bailey curve to explore, graphically, the possible movement of a monetary system outside the steady state. Instead of assuming that the inflation rate is perfectly anticipated, we consider what might happen if inflation-rate expectations were static, or adapted with a lag to the actual inflation rate. Greater real seigniorage s is available under such "imperfect" expectations than under correct foresight, because when the tax rate E is surprisingly high, the tax base h remains larger than it would otherwise be.[16] If the high E were correctly anticipated, h would be smaller when it arrived.

We continue to assume that actual inflation varies one-for-one with the rate of base monetary expansion, but now *expected* inflation (upon which money demand implicitly depends) need not equal actual inflation. We denote E^e the expansion rate corresponding to the *expected* inflation rate. Base money demand is accordingly given by

$$\ln h = , - \cdot E^e$$

We continue to assume that the price level P always clears the market, so that we can use the variable h to denote both actual and demanded real balances of base money.

Consider, first, the seigniorage implications of inflation-rate expectations that are fixed, regardless of the actual inflation rate. (This assumption is not meant to be realistic, but gives us a benchmark for analysis of other cases.) As E varies, there is no change in E^e, and hence no change in real base money demand h. Because real seigniorage $s = Eh$, s varies proportionately

---

[15] The "legal restrictions theory" of money demand (Wallace 1983) goes to the extreme of saying that demand for government-issued non-interest-bearing currency goes to zero when such restrictions are relaxed, or when private intermediaries are allowed to undo them (by splitting Tbills up into small bearer bonds).

[16] See Barro (1983) for a model in which the public knows that monetary authority would be tempted to choose surprise inflation if the public's inflation-rate expectations were low, and so the public rationally expects high inflation.

with E. Graphically, the relationship between the expansion rate and real seigniorage can be shown as a ray with slope h. Figure 7.5 shows four such rays. The steepest ray represents the case of $E^e = 0$ (the expected inflation rate would be correct at a zero expansion rate). Moving clockwise, the rays become progressively less steep as the expected inflation rate becomes positive and increasingly high.

We denote the h corresponding to ($E^e = 0$) as h_0 (note that $\ln h_0 = \beta$). Along the ray for $E^e = 0$, $s = Eh_0$. Real seigniorage is proportional to the actual base money expansion rate E. Only one point on this ray is consistent with correct expectations $E = E^e$, namely the origin, where $E = 0$, $s = 0$. For $E^e = E_1$, we denote the corresponding h as h_1. Note that $h_1 < h_0$. Again, as E varies, s varies proportionately, $s = Eh_1$. This time, the only point consistent with correct expectations has the coordinates (E_1, E_1h_1). The steady-state "Bailey curve" traces the set of all such correct-expectations seigniorage points.

So long as E^e remains fixed, h remains fixed. The monetary authority may travel out along the relevant ray to generate any level of seigniorage desired, simply by choosing a large enough E (i.e., printing money fast enough). This implication of the model seems absurd in the limit: the government could potentially buy up the economy's entire output by printing up enough money to do so at today's prices. This absurdity raises the ques-

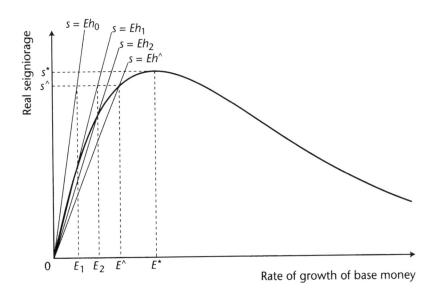

Figure 7.5 Steady state convergence: the economy converges to a steady-state when $s^\wedge$ is less than $s*$

tion: what, in practice, does (or would) limit a government's ability to buy up all existing goods, and services, by printing money? For how long, and to what extent, have seigniorage-seeking governments ever been able to exceed the rate of seigniorage $s*$ available to them under correct expectations?

Suppose that inflation-rate expectations are fixed only for one period, and adapt to experience: members of the public adjust E^e toward E when they discover that the two differ. We can now tell a story of adjustment through time. Assume for simplicity that the public sets E^e for the current period equal to realized E in the previous period. When the government decides to pursue a fixed target rate of seigniorage $s\hat{}$ each period, two types of cases can arise. The first, depicted in figure 7.5, is the case in which $s\hat{}$ is positive but less than the correct-expectations maximum ($0 < s\hat{} < s*$).

To choose an arbitrary starting point for the hypothetical dynamics, assume that, in the first period the public expects zero expansion, $E^e = 0$. The government can move out the ray defined by $s = Eh_0$. To generate the target level of seigniorage $s\hat{}$, given real money demand h_0, the government chooses expansion rate E_1, which exceeds E^e. The public discovers that inflation is greater than had been anticipated. In the second period, the public sets $E^e = E_1$, and the government can move out the ray defined by $s = Eh_1$. Now the government chooses E_2, sufficient to generate $s\hat{}$ given h_1. E_2 exceeds E_1,

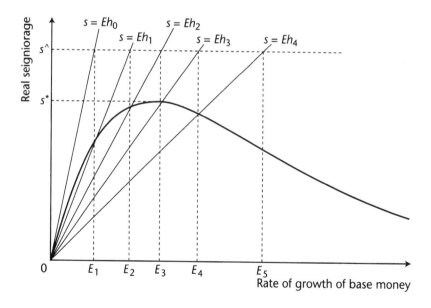

Figure 7.6 Runaway monetary expansion: hyperinflation results when $s\hat{}$ is greater than $s*$

and the sequence repeats. In the limit *the system converges* on a steady-state equilibrium in which expectations are correct. In the steady state, government chooses $E^{\wedge}$ sufficient to generate $s^{\wedge}$ given $h^{\wedge}$, and the public correctly expects the inflation rate: $E^e = E^{\wedge}$.

In the second case, depicted in figure 7.6, government decides to pursue a target rate of seigniorage $s^{\wedge}$ that exceeds the correct-expectations maximum ($s^{\wedge} > s^*$). To achieve $s^{\wedge} > s^*$, each period, E, must always be surprisingly high ($E > E^e$). The period-by-period story is similar to the first case, except that *the system explodes in hyperinflation* rather than converges.

There is no steady-state correct-expectations equilibrium in the second case, because the government is aiming at a level of seigniorage too high ever to be consistent with correct inflation-rate expectations. With E^e rising adaptively each period, E must increase without limit to keep E above E^e. The result is runaway monetary expansion and hyperinflation. The second case, thus, yields a theory of hyperinflation: acceleration to hyperinflation results when the public has adaptive expectations, and the government tries to get a level of seigniorage so high that it requires continually outrunning the public's inflationary expectations.

The Transition between Steady States: Is Honesty a Government's Best Policy?

Suppose that the economy is in a steadystate equilibrium with the expected inflation rate equal to the actual inflation rate, so $E^e = E$. Then a change to a higher E is credibly announced at date t^*, and E^e jumps accordingly. We know that a rise in E^e implies a fall in h, the real stock of base money, because real base money demand falls. But how does the drop in h come about?

There are two polar possibilities, recalling that $h = H / P$. The first is a once-for-all jump in the price level P, with no change in the nominal monetary base H. Such a jump in P means a capital loss to the holders of base money, as the purchasing power of their existing cash balances has been cut. In focusing on the steady-state equilibrium tax on cash balances, we have been neglecting the capital levy on money-holders imposed by this type of transition between equilibria.

The second possibility is a discrete drop in H, avoiding the need for a change in P. Leonardo Auernheimer (1974) calls this an "honest government" policy, because it avoids the capital loss to holders of government-issued base money. It means, instead, a one-shot expense to the honest government, which must "buy back" money balances to reduce the stock of real base money to the lower level desired at the higher inflation rate. Figure 7.7 shows the alternatives graphically.

The government faces corresponding alternatives when it announces a

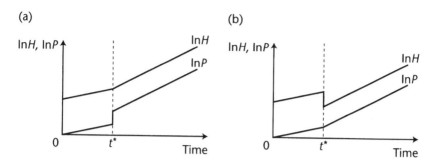

Figure 7.7 Raising the expansion rate: (a) when a "dishonest" government raises the expansion rate, the equilibrium price path jumps; (b) when an "honest" government raises the expansion rate, it "buys back" the unwanted base money

reduction in E. It can sell the additional real balances demanded, reaping one-shot revenue, or it can let P drop.

The "honest government" steps in to change H appropriately whenever it announces a change in E, avoiding jumps in P. It "sells" added H when a lower E is announced and h^d rises, so as to support the existing P through the transition. It "repurchases" excess H when a higher E is announced and h^d falls, so as to hold down P through the transition. Its commitment to bear the cost of repurchase, rather than to "cheat" base-money-holders by making them bear the capital loss from a jump in P, represents "honesty" in Auernheimer's terminology.

An "honesty" constraint lowers the government's seigniorage-maximizing rate of monetary expansion, as compared to the "dishonest" policy of letting the price level change. To show this result, we assume the same Cagan-type base money demand function, and continue to assume that actual h is always equal to h^d (the price level is always at its equilibrium value). We return to focusing on steady states, in which the actual inflation rate, still equal to the rate of base money expansion E, is equal to the anticipated inflation rate.

An "honest" government, in comparing the profitability of any particular rate of monetary expansion E_1 with the profitability of a higher rate E_2, must subtract a discrete once-and-for-all Δh (the difference between h_1 and h_2) from the revenue flow s_2. Or, equivalently, it gets to add Δh to the revenue flow s_1. To add a once-and-for-all stock change to a flow, we calculate the present value of the flow. After making this calculation and addition (see part 5 of the appendix to this chapter), we find that the seigniorage-maximizing rate of monetary expansion under an "honest government" policy, which we denote E^{**}, is given by

$$E^{**} = \frac{1}{a} - r$$

where r = the real discount rate in the economy, and a is the same money-demand parameter (for inflation-rate sensitivity) discussed earlier. E^{**} is lower than our previous solution E^*, the difference being r.

Intuitively, the reason that the "honest government" finds a lower E more profitable is that it can "sell" additional real money balances at a lower E, and must "buy them back" if it announces a higher E. The discount factor r is applied to convert this one time expense or gain into an annualized flow, so that rh is the flow cost or revenue loss from a marginal fall in the real monetary base h. At E^*, the marginal loss in flow revenue from reducing E is zero, but the "honest" government gains rh by reducing E. It will want to notch E back until it is losing flow revenue just equal to rh by doing so, and this occurs at the value of E given by E^{**} above.

The "honest government" analysis has an important implication for a government introducing a new currency (for example, in a newly independent country, or following a hyperinflation). The more credibly it can commit itself to a low-inflation monetary policy, and thus the lower is the public's expected rate of inflation, the greater the real balances of the new currency the government can initially sell.

The analysis also alerts us to the idea that an increase in E, *not* compensated for by a reduction in H, imposes a capital levy on base-money-holders (by contrast with "honesty"). Base-money-holders are "cheated" if P jumps. We miss this if we focus only on steady-state equilibria. An "honesty" constraint on government is a form of binding pre-commitment not to impose such levies. Without such a pre-commitment, a revenue-driven government wishes to inflate to a greater extent in the steady state. Just as importantly, the government is tempted to surprise the public with increases in the rate of monetary expansion and inflation, particularly if the capital levy can be imposed more than once.[17]

If a capital levy is always available, and government wants to maximize its revenue, what can limit E to a finite value? A seigniorage-maximizing government in this setting will, in fact, choose an infinite E (Calvo 1978). An infinite E is ruled out so long as we deal with steady-state solutions where $E = E^e$. If government were driven to choose an infinite E, and the public correctly understood the situation, no one would hold the government's money.

If the government were concerned not only about its own revenue, but

---

[17] Again, see Barro (1983). Chapter 10 in this book discusses temptations of this sort more fully under the label of "time-inconsistent" government policy.

also about the burden that higher inflation imposes on moneyholders, and the public understood that this situation held, there could be an equilibrium with a finite rate of monetary expansion E limited by the marginal welfare cost of higher actual inflation (Barro 1983). However, this E will be higher than where the temptation to impose capital levies is removed by a binding pre-commitment.

We can take the analysis of transitions a bit further, and ask what happens if, under a "dishonest" policy, P does not jump immediately to its new equilibrium path, but instead reaches it gradually. A transition path of that sort is shown in figure 7.8.

If P does not jump immediately when E rises at moment t^*, but P continues to grow at its old rate, the real base money stock h will not only not fall immediately to its new equilibrium value, but will actually rise, because H is growing faster than P (recall $h = H/P$). Graphically, the size of the real base is shown by the vertical difference between the $\ln H$ and $\ln P$ paths in figure 7.8, because

$$\ln H/P = \ln H - \ln P$$

For some length of time after t^*, real seigniorage s therefore increases with E (recall $s = Eh$). The government's short-run revenue from an increase in the monetary base growth rate is greater the more "sluggish" are adjustments in nominal prices (Khan and Knight 1982).

Larry Sjaastad (1976), in an analysis of "Why stable inflations fail," considers the case of a government that pursues the "honest" policy and the

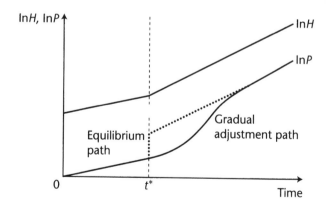

Figure 7.8 When a "dishonest" government raises the expansion rate and the price level gradually adjusts to its equilibrium path, the real monetary base ($\ln H - \ln P$) temporary swells

"dishonest" policy alternately, causing instability of the inflation rate. When E is at E^* (the flow-seigniorage-maximizing level as analyzed by Bailey), it pays to announce a lower E, à la Auernheimer's "honest" government, and pocket the profits from selling the additional real money balances demanded (assuming that the announcement is believed, even in view of the oneshot jump in H). When E is at the lower level, government profits from expanding at a higher rate dishonestly, with h adjusting via a jump in the price level P rather than a through a buy-back of money balances.

Oscillating E, in this manner, increases seigniorage. The Bailey solution E^*, says Sjaastad, represents a strictly "negligent" government. The Bailey government foregoes the capital gains available from a credible disinflation program. It takes account of flows, but ignores stock adjustments. The Auernheimer solution, by contrast, represents a strictly honest government. The expansion rate is lower because government treats the foregone gains from more rapid expansion as an investment needed to preserve its honesty. Sjaastad's "semi-honest" government tries to play both sides of the street, selling h when falling E is announced, and "looking the other way" when E is rising.

Considered seriously as an account of how governments continue to behave over time, Sjaastad's "semihonest" scenario supposes somewhat implausibly that the public can be repeatedly being tricked by the government's announcements. Sjaastad does not say explicitly how often the government can pull its trick. In the limit, government could make continuous announcements, and never actually lower its money expansion rate. It could thereby harvest the economy's entire stock of wealth, with the public continually buying base money to restock its real balances as the price level keeps jumping. An obvious objection to this scenario is that the public will not continue to believe the announcements of a government that has tricked it before. (The public has to believe the announcement of lower E if the government is to sell more h and thereby profit from the announcement.) Unlimited repetition of "semi-honesty" is therefore not feasible, but a single play might be possible. Perhaps the capital levy from "dishonesty" is available only once per administration. If a new administration has more credibility, it should be more likely than an old administration to disinflate. Later in its term, the administration can be expected to "cash in" its credibility by "dishonestly" stepping up the monetary expansion rate. Of course, citizens should come to learn that the commitment to disinflation by a new administration will be short-lived at best, and therefore should not expect it to persist. The public will form some expectation of the later expansion that will reduce, or negate, the attempted capital levy. If a monetary authority's response is to attempt to impose the capital levy by reinflating before it is expected to, the public will come to expect that, too, and even the credibility of the initial disinflation will unravel. (For a survey of game-theoretic models of monetary policy that deal with conundra of this sort, see Cuikerman (1986).

The government of Argentina elected in 1989 seemed to experience this last problem. It would have liked to sell more real balances to the public by announcing a lower E. The public refused to believe any such announcements, having been burned by disinflation announcements before. E^e remained high, so h remained low, and the government could not get much seigniorage, even with a high E. The Argentine government even appeared to have exceeded E^* – gone to the wrong side of the Bailey curve – in April–June 1989 (Kiguel and Neumeyer 1995, p. 680).

How Well Does Seigniorage-maximization Explain Actual Governments' Behavior?

Argentina before 1990 was an unusual case.[18] Click (1998) reports that, for a list of 90 countries, over the period 1971–1990, only ten relied on seigniorage for more than 20 percent of government spending. In increasing order, they were Paraguay, Uganda, Ghana, Israel, Nicaragua, Burma, Peru, Chile, Argentina, and Yugoslavia. The USA, Canada, and most other industrialized nations financed less than 3 percent of government spending with seigniorage. Western Europe's most seigniorage-reliant countries were Switzerland, Italy, Spain, Iceland, and Portugal, at 6.7 percent to 10.1 percent of government spending. In only eight countries did seigniorage exceed 5 percent of GDP: Egypt, Poland, Malta, Nicaragua, Argentina, Chile, Yugoslavia, and Israel. The median country in the sample collected seigniorage equal to 1.7 percent of GDP and 7.8 percent of government spending.

Inflation rates in all but a few countries appear to be far too low to be consistent with seigniorage maximization. Cagan (1956), based on study of several historical hyperinflations, estimated the seigniorage-maximizing inflation rate to be in the neighborhood of 12 percent to 40 percent per month. Barro (1972), based on the German hyperinflation of the 1920s, estimated a higher figure: 140 percent per month.[19] There are few episodes with observed inflation rates that high. The same conclusion emerges from

---

[18] Argentina has since instituted a monetary reform making the Argentine peso 1:1 convertible to the US dollar, which has brought inflation down to the US level.

[19] Compared to Cagan's, Barro's more forward-looking model of expectations yields more rapidly rising estimates of the German public's expected inflation rate as actual inflation accelerated. If, for a given change in real balances, the rise in the expected inflation rate is higher, money demand must be less sensitive to inflation. Thus Barro's estimated α is smaller, and E^* ($= 1/a$) is larger. German inflation did, by the way, go well above 140 percent per month by the end of the hyperinflation.

studies of the elasticity of the real demand for money using recent data from countries with moderate inflation. If a government is actually maximizing steady-state seigniorage, i.e. E is at E^*, then the elasticity of (base) money demand with respect to the inflation rate should be -1. In fact, empirical estimates suggest that a one-percentage-point increase in the inflation rate reduces the real quantity of money demanded by far less, perhaps one-quarter of one percentage point. Thus the USA and other nations, have been underinflating relative to E^* (McClure and Willett 1988).

Why might a government be below the revenue-maximizing rate of monetary expansion? This is akin to asking why *any* tax might be below its revenue-maximizing level. The most obvious answer is that political pressure from the electorate keeps government generally from raising all the revenue it could. Equivalently, the "welfare burden" of the inflation tax could be taken into account by a benevolent government.

Alternatively, the appearance of $E < E^*$ may be deceptive. McClure and Willett note that the estimated revenue-maximizing expansion rate is lower when we take into account (as the above-mentioned estimates do not) the negative impact of inflation on h^d (and on other tax receipts) via the effect inflation has in reducing real national income. As E increases, real income falls due to distortions induced by unindexed tax rates and noisier relative price signals. Therefore, h^d falls faster than the parameter a (the inflation-rate semi-elasticity of money demand) alone would suggest. The fall in real income also brings other taxes down, and that loss must be figured in the marginal impact of E relevant to a government seeking to maximize overall revenue. Still, it is not clear that an E^* estimate adjusted in this way would yet be as low as the rates lately observed in developed countries.

A third possibility is that a rational government does not maximize seigniorage in the observed short run because it wishes to preserve its ability to raise seigniorage in future periods of peak need for revenue (e.g. wartime). The government wants to keep in reserve the ability to levy, in a pinch, a seigniorage tax at a rate higher than the maximum steady-state seigniorage s^*, even at the expense of getting less than s^* in other periods. Such a time-varying seigniorage policy need not involve fooling the public on average: they may be aware that they live in such a regime (but they, like the government, do not know in advance which periods are going to be high-E periods). In such a regime, the observed semi-elasticity a reflects the belief that E will fall after periods of high inflation. Investments in cash-economizing fixed capital are small, because inflationary bouts are viewed as temporary. Observed short-run a is smaller than long-run a. The "tax base" of real balances is kept larger so that it can be hit for larger short-run revenues, as needed. To test the adequacy of this explanation would require a run of data including periods of peak seigniorage demand.

Some countries occasionally seem to be above the seigniorage-maximizing rate of monetary expansion. Recent examples include Bolivia, Argentina, Israel, and Yugoslavia. To explain such behavior, we would look for modifications of the basic model which make $E > E^*$ preferable to a government, at least in the short run, even if it knows that such a run cannot be indefinitely sustained.

A body of work in monetary economics suggests that people generally treat their money balances as a "shock absorber:" unexpected bulges in real money balances are only gradually worked off. Such behavior allows h to rise when E increases unexpectedly, by preventing P from jumping, as discussed above. Seigniorage ($s = Eh$) rises initially when E is increased. Not only does the tax rate E increase, but even the tax base h rises in the short run. As already noted, without some additional theoretical restriction, there is no upper bound on the seigniorage-maximizing rate of monetary expansion.

One possible restriction, suggested by Khan and Knight (1982), is accelerated "learning" by the public, in the specific sense that the time required for h to adjust to its new steady-state equilibrium value shrinks to zero as E approaches infinity. This yields a determinate equilibrium, but with greater seigniorage and a seigniorage-maximizing rate of monetary expansion even higher than the s^* and E^* of the simple Bailey approach.

Hyperinflation results when a government seeks to maximize short-run seigniorage even at the expense of long-run seigniorage. Why might a government so myopically focus on the short run? Because it is at war, or in a domestic crisis that makes it fear for its long-run survival unless it raises more revenue immediately.

Questions

1 Suppose the government of Poland, which (let us suppose) has higher inflation than neighboring countries, begins to allow its citizens to use other European currencies, should they want to. How would this likely affect the Polish central bank's ability to earn seigniorage?

2 Suppose the Brazilian economy begins to "dollarize," i.e. begins to use US dollar bills as a medium of exchange. How would this affect the seigniorage of *the USA* in the short run? How would it affect the seigniorage of the USA in the steady state, once the dollarization is complete?

3 Under what conditions is the seigniorage-maximizing rate of expansion of the monetary base (E^*) infinite? Under what conditions is it finite?

4 When might it be in the interest of a seigniorage-maximizing government to *lower* its rate of monetary expansion?

5   Given a standard money demand function with empirically typical parameters, consider a surprise increase in the rate of monetary expansion to 10 percent per year from 5 percent per year. The new rate begins at t^*, and persists indefinitely thereafter.

   (a)   What are the implications for annual real seigniorage in the long run? Does it double, less than double, or more than double?

   (b)   What are the implications for annual real seigniorage in the short run, during which the price level is "sluggish" to adjust to its new long-run equilibrium path?

6   Suppose that the government of Italy has a seigniorage target $\hat{s}$ that is less than the maximum steady-state seigniorage s^*. Why does an increase in reserve requirements reduce the steady-state inflation rate associated with achieving $\hat{s}$? Does the combination of higher reserve requirements and lower inflation make an Italian bank depositor better off, or worse off?

7   Other than reserve requirements, name one other legal restriction on banks, or the public, a government can use to increase its real seigniorage. How does that restriction work to increase seigniorage?

8   Explain how a government of a country (call it "Lebanon") can generate a hyperinflation by attempting to maintain a constant level of real seigniorage in the face of a diminishing real demand for its base money.

9   "The takeoff in [Bolivian] inflation after 1981 followed closely upon the jump in seigniorage. . . . During 1982–1985 the inflation rate continued to accelerate even though seigniorage did not rise steadily after its one-time jump" (Sachs 1987). Explain these events. That is, take a simple model relating inflation dynamics to seigniorage and use it to show how

   (a)   a sudden takeoff in inflation can be associated with a jump in seigniorage, and

   (b)   subsequent increases in inflation can associated with no steady rise in seigniorage.

Appendix

Part 1: The seigniorage-maximizing rate of monetary expansion E*

Assume the Cagan-type demand function

$$h^{\mathrm{d}} = e^{\beta - \alpha E}$$

where e is the natural logarithmic base, or equivalently

$\ln h^d = \beta - aE$

where a, β are constants, both greater than 0.

The maximization of s is fairly simple. Recall

$s = Eh$

Take natural logarithms of both sides, and substitute for h under the equilibrium assumption that $h = h^d$:

$$\ln s = \ln E + \ln h$$
$$= \ln E + \beta - aE$$

Maximize $\ln s$ (which for positive numbers is equivalent to maximizing s) with respect to E by setting the first derivative equal to zero:

$$\frac{d(\ln s)}{dE} = \frac{1}{E} - a$$

$$0 = \frac{1}{E} - a$$

$$E = \frac{1}{a}$$

Thus $1/a$ is the seigniorage-maximizing value E^*.

Part 2: Derivation of E* in terms of elasticity

The definition of η, the elasticity of h^d with respect to E, is

$$\eta = \left(\frac{dh}{dE}\right)\left(\frac{E}{h}\right)$$

Given the Cagan demand function, and the equilibrium assumption that $h = h^d$,

$$\frac{dh}{dE} = -ae^{\beta - aE}$$

so

$$\eta = - a e^{\beta - aE} \left(\frac{E}{e^{\beta - aE}} \right) = - aE$$

For revenue maximization

$$\eta = -1 = - aE$$
$$E^* = \frac{1}{a}$$

as before.

From the definition of η, and its value given the Cagan demand function, we can see that

$$- aE = \left(\frac{dh}{dE} \right) \left(\frac{E}{h} \right)$$

$$- a \ = \left(\frac{dh}{dE} \right) \left(\frac{1}{h} \right)$$

Thus the parameter a in the money demand function is, as mentioned in the main text, the negative of the semi-elasticity of real base money demand with respect to the inflation rate.

Part 3: The size of maximum seigniorage s*

The value of s^*, the maximum value of s, reached at E^*, is

$$s^* = E^* h$$
$$= E^* e^{\beta - aE^*}$$

Substituting for E^*

$$s^* = \left(\frac{1}{a} \right) e^{\beta - 1}$$

$$= \frac{e^{\beta}}{ae}$$

So we see that the size of s^* depends

1 positively on β, the scale parameter for base money demand that is independent of the inflation rate, and
2 inversely on a, the inflation-rate sensitivity parameter for real base money demand.

Part 4: Derivation of E* with no base money held by the public, no excess reserves, and a required reserve ratio q

Denote the banks' required reserve ratio q. Adopt the same Cagan money demand function, but assume that the public holds money only in the form of deposits. (Currency held by the public is zero, and all base money is held by the banks.) Assume that the base money held by banks is at the legal minimum (if $q = 0$, no base money would be held). Then $H = qM$, and in real terms $h = qm$, implying that the real monetary base is $1/q$ of what it would be in a world where the public held the same quantity of money in the form of outside base money. Assume that banks intermediate with zero operating costs. In this limiting case, perfect competition implies

$$i_D = i_L (1 - q)$$

because the fraction q of deposits must be held by banks as required reserves of non-interest-bearing base money, banks can invest, and competitively pass earnings back to customers from, only the remaining $(1 - q)$ share of their deposits. Assume finally that $i_L = E$. Then

$$i_D = E(1 - q)$$
$$= E - Eq$$

The foregone-interest opportunity cost of holding a dollar of money (deposit balances) is thus Eq. Let Eq (rather than E, as before) enter the money demand function as the opportunity cost variable. That is, assume that the public will act just as if all money were non-interest-bearing and expected inflation corresponded to an expansion rate of Eq. As a result, the seigniorage-maximizing base money expansion rate E^* is $1/q$ times higher than under a purely-outside-money case:

$$s = Eh = Eqm$$

where

m = real stock of money
q = required reserve ratio

So

$$\ln s = \ln E + \ln q + \ln m$$

Now, $\ln m = \beta - aEq$ (modified money demand function), so

$$\ln s = \ln E + \ln q + \beta - aEq$$

Differentiating gives

$$\frac{d(\ln s)}{dE} = \frac{1}{E} - aq$$

Setting this to zero, to maximize s, gives

$$E^* = \left(\frac{1}{q}\right)\left(\frac{1}{a}\right)$$

The right-hand side is $(1/q)$ times that of the result $E^* = 1/a$ for the case without inside money.

But the maximum real seigniorage s^* is independent of q.

$$s^* = E^*h$$
$$= E^*qm$$
$$= \left(\frac{1}{q}\right)\left(\frac{1}{a}\right)qm$$
$$= \left(\frac{1}{a}\right)m$$

as before. Note that this expression does not contain q.

The switch from a purely outside-money economy, to a purely inside-money economy, in which transactions balances are entirely provided by a costless competitive banking sector holding fractional reserves, thus raises E^*, because the opportunity cost of holding money no longer rises one-for-one with E but only by the reserve ratio q times the change in E, where $q < 1$. Once in a pure inside-money economy, a rise in the reserve ratio q lowers E^*, and has no effect on s^*. (For the case where the public holds both inside and outside money, see Dwyer and Saving 1986.)

Part 5: Maximization for the "honest government"

The flow of steady-state seigniorage is, as before,

$$s_t = E_t h_t$$

where t represents a subscript that will be needed to distinguish between two periods. An announcement of the inflation rate E that will prevail for all time thereafter is to be made at date t^*. We denote earlier dates by $t = 0$, later dates by $t = 1$. The problem is to find the E_1 that maximizes the present value of seigniorage at t^*, taking into account the "honest government" constraint that base money must be injected or withdrawn at t^* to avoid a jump in the steadystate path of the price level then. The size of the injection, or withdrawal, is denoted the difference $h_1 - h_0$, where h_1 is the post-announcement real stock of base money, desired and actual, and h_0 is the pre-announcement real stock of base money, desired and actual. (We assume that the price level P is continuously at equilibrium.) This difference is positive (an injection is called for) when $E_0 > E_1$, (a disinflation is announced). It is negative (a withdrawal is called for) when $E_0 < E_1$ (higher inflation is announced).

The present value of seigniorage at t^*, denoted V, combines the present value of the post-announcement perpetual steady-state flow with the size of the necessary injection or withdrawal. The present value of a perpetual flow s is s/r, where r is the continuous discount rate. Here $s_1 = E_1 h_1$. Thus

$$V = \left(\frac{E_1 h_1}{r}\right) + (h_1 - h_0)$$

Under the Bailey approach, we maximized only the first term on the right-hand side. Auernheimer's innovation, the difference "honesty" makes, is to add the second term appearing to the right of the plus sign.

This way of stating the problem may seem to violate the principle that bygones are bygones. Why should the inherited stock of base money h_0 affect the choice of E_1? We will see that, in fact, h_0 drops out when we go to choose the E_1 that maximizes V, because h_0 does not vary with E_1.

Maximizing V with respect to E_1 means finding the E (denoted E^{**}) that satisfies

$$0 = \frac{dV}{dE} = \frac{d}{dE}\left[\frac{(E_1 h_1) + (h_1 - h_0)}{r}\right]$$

Substituting in the Cagan-type money demand function for h_1 and h_0 makes this

$$0 = \frac{d}{dE}\left[\left(\frac{1}{r}\right)(E_1 e^{\beta - aE_1}) + (e^\beta - aE_1) - (e^\beta - aE_0)\right]$$

$$= \left(\frac{1}{r}\right)(e^\beta - aE_1 - aE_1 e^{\beta - aE_1}) - ae^\beta - aE_1$$

$$= (e^\beta - aE_1)\left[\left(\frac{1}{r}\right) - \left(\frac{aE}{r}\right) - a\right]$$

Dividing both sides by $(e^{\beta} - a\,E_1)$, and multiplying by r, we have

$$
\begin{aligned}
0 \;\;&= 1 - aE - ar \\
aE \;\;&= 1 - ar \\
E^{**} &= \left(\frac{1}{a}\right) - r
\end{aligned}
$$

Thus an "honest government" constraint lowers the seigniorage-maximizing rate of monetary expansion by r, the discount factor (both rates, for example, expressed as percent per year).

8

Central Bank as Bureaucracy

A modern central bank is a bureaucracy: it is an agency of the national government, directed by appointed officials, which, unlike a private business firm, does not answer to profit-seeking shareholders.[1] Because a central bank (as discussed in chapter 7) earns revenue, it can be self-financing, and need not receive an annual budget from the legislature as a typical government bureau does. A number of economists have theorized that the bureaucratic nature of the central bank, or its budgeting process, helps to explain its behavior. In considering these theories, we first briefly summarize some bureaucratic explanations for aspects of central bank behavior other than the rate of base money expansion. Then, we turn to the role of bureaucratic features in explaining the rate of base money expansion. The hypotheses we will consider were formulated with an eye to the US Federal Reserve System in particular, but may apply to any similar national central bank.

Bureaucratic Explanation of the Fed's Operating Procedures

Edward Kane (1980) contrasts two viewpoints on the Federal Reserve System's monetary policy operations: "utopian" and "cynical." The utopian viewpoint treats the Fed as seeking single-mindedly to promote the public interest. The choice of a monetary policy then becomes an exercise in ap-

---

[1] The Bank of England, however, began as a private bank and was not officially nationalized until World War II.

plied welfare economics, or optimal control theory. The Fed's objective function is defined over policy goals, e.g. values of inflation, unemployment, and interest rates. Its ongoing task is to quantify, more accurately, the linkages between its goals and its policy instruments (open market operations, the discount rate, reserve requirements). The economics profession is invited to join in the search for better models of how policy works its effects. This conception of the policy process is nurtured in Fed publications, and reflected in money-and-banking texts.

The cynical viewpoint regards the Fed as a politically pressured institution. (In particular, Kane suggests, the Fed is pressured to dampen movements of nominal interest rates.) Business periodicals and "Fed-watching" newsletters (some very expensive) reflect this view. Statements by the Fed chairman, by other Fed governors, by Congressmen, and by Treasury officials are dissected for indications of which way the policy winds are blowing: whether the balance of forces will compel the Fed to "ease" or to "tighten." The perception of the Fed as operating through interest rates, and as open to persuasion on which way rates should move, invites lobbying effort by economic sectors particularly affected by interest rates. Kane suggests that the Fed is pressured to dampen short-run increases in nominal interest rates by spokesmen for the construction industry, financial institutions that have borrowed short to lend long, and securities dealers whose leveraged balance sheets make them averse to any sudden movement in interest rates.

Stepping back to consider the broader institutional context within which the Fed operates, Kane offers the hypothesis that the Fed's ultimate political function is to serve as an economic-policy scapegoat for incumbent politicians. In Kane's view the scapegoating role explains the Fed's

1   incomplete monetary control strategy
2   tendency to obfuscate rather than clearly explain its own actions, and
3   independence.

The Fed has a not-fully-specified (and possibly incoherent) strategy for open-market operations because the incompleteness (or even incoherence) of its strategy gives the Fed room to tailor this month's policy to this month's advice from elected officials. It also gives elected officials room to tailor this month's advice to this month's economic performance. Congress, and the President, evidently value the incompleteness, for they have not forced the Fed to announce, or to adopt, any fully specified strategy procedures. A fully specified strategy would force incumbents to take a position on the strategy as such. Without it, they can easily change from praising to blaming the Fed's policy, based on their constituents' current concerns.

The Fed does not try to educate the public to recognize that easy monetary policy, reducing nominal interest rates today through the liquidity effect, increases inflation and thus raises rates later. Instead, the Fed cites rising rates as evidence of tight-money policies supposedly in effect. They do so because they (and elected officials) value the leeway that confusion confers on them.

The Fed has an "independent" institutional structure because its policy-setting autonomy, together with its lack of a fully specified strategy for using its autonomy, allows Congressmen to blame the Fed for bad policy outcomes. Putting Kane's view bluntly, the Fed is a political institution designed by politicians to serve politicians. Fed officials have been given lofty but impossible policy responsibilities (by the Employment Act of 1946, and the Humphrey-Hawkins Act), and are expected to submit to Congressional blame for failing to meet them. In exchange, Fed officials enjoy long terms in office, and budgetary autonomy.

Milton Friedman (1982) has offered bureaucratic explanations for a number of features of the Fed's operating behavior.

Friedman observes the curious fact that the Fed "churns" its portfolio: for each $1 permanent addition to its assets, the Fed may make $184 worth of open-market purchases and $183 of sales. Friedman proposes that constant churning mostly serves the open-market desk's sense of its own importance. It also creates profits for bond dealers with whom the Fed trades. These dealers provide "informed Wall Street" opinion supporting discretion for the Fed.

The Fed, likewise, postpones release of its open-market directives, Friedman suggests, because the mystery about the Fed's current objectives – and the fact that billions of dollars ride on guesses about what Fed is up to – enhances the perceived importance of the Fed. The mystery also creates well-paid jobs for ex-Fed-officials as "Fed-watchers" who can "read the tea leaves" for signs as to whether the Fed is leaning toward looser, or tighter, monetary policy.

The main puzzle for Friedman is why the Fed produces such highly variable money growth, and has not adopted his long-standing advice (discussed in more detail later in chapter 10) to commit itself to a specific growth path for a single monetary aggregate. He concludes that the Fed resists unambiguous targeting because Fed officials prefers not to face a clear benchmark against which they could be held accountable. The Fed's top officials have no interest in adopting a mechanical monetarist rule that would reduce the open-market desk to one employee (who would no longer churn the portfolio) because to do so would make the Federal Open Market Committee (FOMC) far less important. The perception that the Fed is not precommitted to any particular course of action means that politicians, market players, and academics all have reason to compete for the Fed's attention. Fed staff economists (and outside economists) tend not to push for such a rule because it would reduce the demand for their services in briefing regional Fed presidents for their monthly FOMC meetings (and in consulting with the Fed). This argument complements Kane's idea that the Fed's lack of accountability serves the desire of Congress, and the executive branch, to be able to fault the Fed *ex post* for unwanted policy outcomes.

Friedman notes that the Fed even has a bureaucratic interest in macroeconomic volatility. The Fed chairman is all the more important when the economy lurches from crisis to crisis. This is not to say that Fed officials deliberately aim to produce crisis, but their importance does rise when they pursue an activist (and, in practice, destabilizing) policy. The Fed chairman would not be "the second most important man in Washington" if he were not perceived to be a crisis manager.

Bureaucracy and "Inflationary Bias"

The Federal Reserve System's budget is not specified, reviewed, or approved by the US Congress. The Fed derives income from its holdings of interest-bearing Treasury securities (which it has purchased by creating high-powered money). The Fed spends as much of this income as it chooses on its own operations, and "rebates" the rest to the Treasury. Mark Toma (1982) has analyzed the incentives for monetary expansion that this self-financing mechanism creates, and argues that it gives the Fed an "inflationary bias."

If the Fed's expenses were "given", and independent of the Fed's earnings, 100 percent of the marginal seigniorage dollar from debt monetization would go to the Treasury. Pressure to generate seigniorage through monetary expansion would come only from the administration, or from the Congress. The Fed itself would have no stake in the amount of seigniorage collected. Most discussions of the Fed's fiscal role implicitly make this assumption.

Suppose, instead, that the Fed can capture some percentage of the marginal seigniorage dollar, using the additional income to "pad" its own budget with perquisites and amenities (higher salaries, plusher offices, larger travel budgets, more vanity publications, more employees) that raise its costs of operation above the minimum necessary costs. In that case, the Fed itself would have an inflationary bias. Toma argues that this sort of budget-padding is plausible because the monitoring of Fed expenditures is a public good. Any individual Congressman who worked to reduce Fed expenditures would capture only 1/nth of the benefits (where n is the number of Congressmen) as extra expenditures on his own constituents. It is individually rational for the Congressman, instead, to free ride.

The Treasury has an incentive to monitor Fed expenditures, however, if monitoring (to reveal the true minimum cost of Fed operations) can be used to force the Fed to rebate its profits to the Treasury. If monitoring is costly, the Treasury may prefer to induce the Fed "voluntarily" to make a rebate by simply threatening to monitor. According to Toma, this is a stylized story of how Fed rebating actually began. The Fed must thus share its revenue with the Treasury, but the terms of the sharing are not explicitly established. It is unlikely, under such an arrangement, that the Fed is compelled to rebate 100 percent of the marginal seigniorage dollar.

In similar fashion, Shugart and Tollison (1983) view the amount shared as a choice variable for the Fed. The Fed faces a trade-off between greater amenities (budget padding) and greater rebates to the Treasury. By rebating profits to the Treasury, the Fed buys enhanced autonomy. Monetary expansion expands the Fed's budget, and allows the Fed to choose more of both goods.

So long as the Fed derives benefits at the margin from money-creation, the Fed itself has a seigniorage motive. The Fed will prefer more seigniorage to less, other things being equal. Toma's model of the Fed's discretionary profit-maximization – where the Fed keeps some fraction of marginal seigniorage – has the same implications for the rate of base money growth as an ordinary seigniorage model, where the Fed acts as the agent of the Treasury.[2] The central bank will maximize seigniorage, subject to some kind of political constraint, and will vary the rate of monetary expansion as the parameters of base money demand vary.

Just as the ordinary seigniorage-motive model does, Toma's model implies that the authorities have an incentive to impose legal restrictions on the payment system that increase real seigniorage. They can increase the real demand for base money, and thereby real seigniorage, by reserve requirements or restrictions on the availability of close substitutes for base money.

Toma's approach appears to have two useful, and distinct, implications that the ordinary seigniorage-motive model does not. The first is that the central bank's inflationary bias differs under different arrangements for financing the central bank budget (whether it receives a set allocation from the legislature, or chooses its own self-financed budget). If the central bank were purely an agent of the fiscal authorities, or motivated purely by public interest, the budgeting system would not matter. Toma (1982, pp. 179–85) cites episodes from Fed history to show that "revenue-related alterations in the monetary constitution" have, in fact, affected the Fed's behavior in ways that are consistent with the Fed's seeking discretionary profits, but are inex-

---

[2] Toma draws a "wealth-transfer curve" that is essentially the Bailey curve familiar from Chapter 7.

plicable under the public-interest view. Second, if a costly-to-monitor Fed is "skimming" a percentage of annual seigniorage, but not if it acts purely in the public interest, Fed expenditures should vary with its seigniorage revenue or its wealth position. Toma finds that Fed expenditures have historically varied with its revenue or wealth. The estimated regression coefficients indicate that, in a typical year, Fed revenues have risen by $138million, of which Fed officials have skimmed $1.9million to $2.6million in additional discretionary expenditures (that is, expenditures increased $1.9–2.6million more than they would have had seigniorage revenues not increased). Because it can skim these profits, the Fed has an inflationary bias.

Shugart and Tollison (1983) investigated where the Fed has spent its revenue from base money expansion. They found that Fed employment varies significantly with, and "Granger-causes" changes in the monetary base, and so conclude that the Fed has expanded the base at least partly in order to add extra employees to its payroll. Unnecessary employees are a form of budget-padding.

Like the ordinary seigniorage model, Toma's model faces the problem of explaining why the actual rate of base money growth in the postwar USA appears to be well below the seigniorage-maximizing rate. Toma suggests that the Fed's maximization of discretionary profits is constrained by potential competition from alternative management teams or monetary regimes. Formally, he assumes that the current Fed management team is constrained to provide total net benefits to the public (consumer surplus to money-holders minus Fed expenditures) at least as great as is offered by the next-best alternative. Expressing the same constraint in another way, the Fed cannot impose a burden on the public (lost consumer surplus from the tax on cash balances, plus Fed expenditures) any greater than would be imposed by the next-best arrangement. If the next-best regime, or team, offers total benefits equivalent to the consumer surplus at an expansion rate of E^* (with zero administrative expense), the Fed must expand less rapidly in order to have room to pad its budget.

The kernel of truth in this explanation for E below E^* is that the Fed does not want to be perceived as an engine of inflation and a den of high living. (When the Second Bank of the USA was so perceived during the Jackson administration, its federal charter was terminated.) However, it is difficult to believe that the Fed is *tightly* constrained by the alternative regimes actually available. One such alternative, involving virtually no ongoing administrative expense, would be to freeze the monetary base. If Congress recognized that alternative, Toma's constrained model implies that the Fed would have to shrink the monetary base, in order to provide equivalent benefits (no greater burden) to the public, yet have room for expenses. This implication is not borne out empirically.

Questions

1   Why might a central bank's top officials have little interest in committing themselves to a mechanical, and predictable, rule governing the rate of monetary expansion?

2   What aspects of the Fed's behavior do *not* appear to be consistent with the hypothesis that Fed officials act from bureaucratic motives?

3   A few members of Congress have recently made noises about scrutinizing the Fed's budget more closely. According to Toma's theory, what would be the impact on inflation if the Congress were to limit the Fed to a fixed level of spending?

4   What predictions are made by Toma's model of the "inflationary bias" of a seigniorage-financed central bank that are not also made by the theory that the central bank's aim is to provide the Treasury with seigniorage?

5   Several studies have found that "independent" central banks are less inflation-prone. In "measuring" independence, these studies often give a positive score to an institutional arrangement under which the central bank finances its own budget, rather than relying on an appropriation from the legislature. Is there a conflict between such studies and Toma's theory? If not, why not? If so, how might it be resolved?

9

Political Business Cycle Hypotheses

The idea behind "political business cycle" theories is that monetary policy-makers in a representative democracy deliberately pursue political goals in a way that generates a business cycle. In the early Nordhaus–MacRae model, the monetary authority acts systematically to maximize the re-election chances of the incumbent president, or prime minister, by producing the best short-run combination of inflation and unemployment possible on the eve of an election. In the more recent "partisan" theory of monetary policy, different political parties pursue different monetary policies once in office, with systematic cyclical side-effects on aggregate output.

The Nordhaus–MacRae Model

William D. Nordhaus (1975) and C. Duncan MacRae (1977) formalized the idea of a cycle due to vote-seeking monetary policy in similar models using a pre-rational-expectations (namely, adaptive-expectations) version of the Phillips curve. A synthesis of the essential features of their models produces a model with the following features, depicted in figures 9.1–9.3.

The mechanics

Unexpected inflation reduces the actual unemployment rate below the natural rate through the now-familiar short-run Phillips curve effect: unexpected inflation makes nominal wage offers unexpectedly high, fooling job-searchers into accepting job offers sooner than normal, and thus shrinking the pool of unemployed job-searchers. For any given public expectation of the inflation rate, there exists a short-run Phillips curve (SRPC), a negative relationship between the actual inflation rate and the unemployment rate.

The authorities treat the currently expected rate of inflation, gP^e, as given. Because (as in chapter 7) they can perfectly control the actual inflation rate through their choice of the rate of base money expansion, they face an exploitable short-run trade-off between the unemployment rate (U) and the actual inflation rate gP. We assume that this trade off, the SRPC, is linear.

$$U = U_n - c(gP - gP^e)$$

where

U = the current unemployment rate
U_n = the natural rate
c = a positive constant
gP = the current inflation rate
gP^e = the currently expected inflation rate

The authorities can treat the currently expected rate of inflation as given (pre-determined) because, in the model, the public's expectation of the inflation rate is formed adaptively (in backward-looking fashion) based solely on experience of past actual rates. For simplicity, we assume that this period's expected inflation rate equals last period's actual inflation rate. An actual inflation rate lower than anticipated this year, $gP < gP^e$, therefore lowers the inflation rate that will be expected next year, and so improves the tradeoff next year. A drop in expected inflation makes the (SRPC) shift down. A higher-than-expected inflation rate has the reverse effect. In figure 9.1, $SRPC_2$ represents the trade-off when $gP^e = 0$. $SRPC_1$ represents the tradeoff when $gP^e = A > 0$.

Voters dislike both unemployment and inflation, and vote accordingly. The contours of the aggregate voting function, the electoral popularity isoquants, are shown in figure 9.2. Each curve represents combinations of U and gP, as perceived by voters, that yield the incumbents the same percent of the vote. To motivate a cyclical macroeconomic policy, we assume that the voters' perceptions are myopic. Voters care about the (U, gP) combination that prevails on election day, and not about the rates that prevailed earlier in the incumbents' term. The closer to the origin (0, 0) is the isoquant attained on election eve, the greater is voter support for the incumbents. Greater support is shown by the voting percentages attached to the curves in figure 9.2.

The incumbents, who control monetary policy, choose a sequence of money growth rates that enhances their vote plurality at the next election. The vote-maximizing policy, given this set-up, is to attain a point on an isoquant as close to the origin as possible on election day. Figure 9.3 combines the elements of the earlier figures, and shows point D to be the incumbents' best attainable point on $SRPC_2$. The political business cycle results

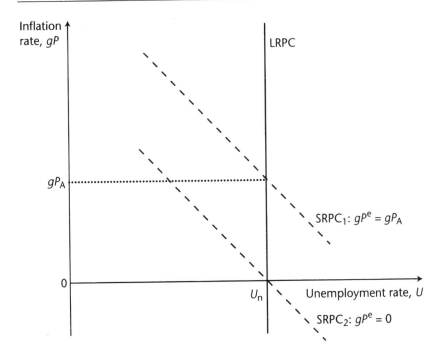

Figure 9.1   Long-run and short-run Phillips curves (LRPC and SRPCs)

from the preparations necessary for the incumbents to reach point D. Assuming a vertical long-run Phillips curve (LRPC), and an economy that begins at point A, the incumbents must lower the SRPC. This implies pushing the economy along the following sort of path shown in figure 9.3: point A to point B to point C to point D.

Suppose that the incumbent government finds itself at point A following its election, with actual and expected inflation both equal to gP_A. To reach point D will require shifting the SRPC down from $SRPC_1$ to $SRPC_2$. This means reducing the expected rate of inflation to zero. (Recall that, by construction, $SRPC_2$ represents the tradeoff when $gP^e = 0$). Under the simple adaptive expectations scheme, the authorities can lower the expected inflation rate to zero only by first lowering the actual inflation rate to zero. In the short run, lowering the inflation rate to zero moves the economy southeast along $SRPC_1$ to point B, raising the unemployment rate U temporarily. Once gP^e drops to zero, the SRPC shifts down, and the economy moves from point B to point C. The new SRPC is $SRPC_2$. The economy has returned to the LRPC, but with a lower rate of inflation.

The stage is now set to maximize the prospects for re-election by increas-

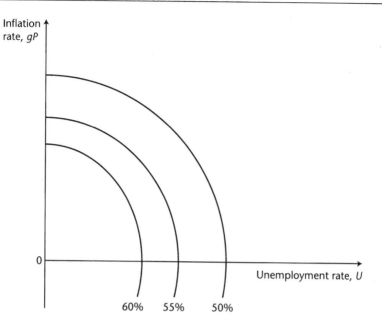

Figure 9.2   Electoral popularity isoquants

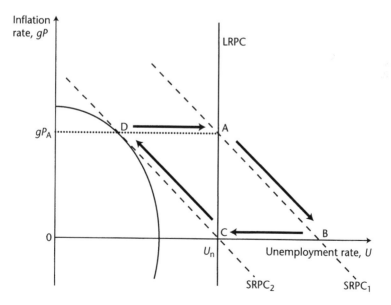

Figure 9.3   The Nordhaus political business cycle

ing the rate of inflation unexpectedly on the eve of the next election, moving the economy northwest along $SRPC_2$ to point D. Of all the points on $SRPC_2$, point D achieves the highest level of electoral popularity, as shown by the tangency of $SRPC_2$ with the electoral popularity isoquant. After the election, in the next term of office, the cycle repeats.

Discussion

One of the necessary conditions for rationalizing a political business cycle of this sort is that the government is chosen periodically in democratic elections. (A president-for-life would have no reason to generate a political business cycle.) However, the term between elections need not be fixed. The policy would seem to suit, at least as well, a variable-term parliamentary system (such as Great Britain's) under which the incumbent government has some discretion regarding the date of the next election.[1]

Nothing in the theory as specified thus far limits the incumbent's aim to the combination of U and gP represented by point D. Given the voter preference map as drawn, the origin $(0, 0)$ is the unconstrained vote-maximizing point. To reach the origin requires a SRPC that intersects the LRPC below zero. It therefore requires lowering gP^e below zero, which given the adaptive expectations scheme requires a period of negative inflation. The whole cycle would be shifted down, so that, in election years, the inflation rate would be zero, and, in midterm years, there would actually be deflation. Needless to say, this pattern has not been observed historically. The Nordhaus model implicitly relies on the presence of some constraint that makes D the best *attainable* point. One constraint that would do the job would be the constraint that gP never fall below zero, but the rationale for such a constraint is not clear.

We have noted that the voters "myopically" disregard macroeconomic experience early in the incumbents' term. They also disregard next year's likely experience. Voters do not forecast (or do not care about) what will happen after the election. If they recognized, and disliked, the fact that the stimulus from moving along the SRPC was only temporary, they would vote differently.

The most fundamental objection to be made to the model is that the public forecasts the current inflation rate naively, oblivious to the game the government is playing. Model-consistent ("rational") expectations would undercut the incumbent government's ability to play the game successfully. If the public rationally expected a spurt in inflation as an election approached,

---

[1] With typical macroeconomic and electoral lags, the theory implies that, in such a system, economic booms should regularly precede (or "Granger-cause") election date announcements. See Keil (1988, pp. 93–4).

the SRPC would shift up. An increase in actual inflation equal to that anticipated would leave the economy on the LRPC. We further elaborate the rational expectations critique below.

Introducing rational expectations raises a host of questions that go beyond the subject of this chapter. Knowing that a cyclical policy would raise the SRPC, would the government abandon it, because points above C on the LRPC can only harm electoral popularity? Or, would it be tempted to increase actual inflation even more than expected, to reach the vote-maximizing point on the now-higher SRPC? But, if the public knew that it was so tempted, then what inflation rate would the public rationally expect? We defer these game-theoretic problems to the next chapter, where we analyze a model in which potential moves and counter-moves are resolved conjecturally (before any moves are actually made) in a rational expectations equilibrium.

A long-run equilibrium

Nordhaus discusses a long-run equilibrium solution to an adaptive-expectations sequence that unfolds through time, move by move. If the *government* is also "myopic," in the sense that it is unwilling ever to incur the temporary loss of popularity from increasing unemployment through the disinflation necessary to lower the SRPC, the best a government beginning at point A can do is to move on the eve of the next election to point E in figure 9.4. The SRPC will subsequently rise to $SRPC_3$. The next government will face a worse SRPC, and if similarly myopic will end up at point F. Note that both U and gP are worse at F than at point E: "stagflation" is being produced by myopic macroeconomic policies.

A series of myopic-government outcomes will move along the "election outcome line" (EOL), formed by tangencies between electoral popularity isoquants and SRPCs, until it reaches the intersection between EOL and the LRPC at point M. Point M represents a myopic government's long-run resting point. The SRPC through M can no longer be exploited to increase electoral popularity, because it is tangent with the electoral popularity isoquant; M is the best point on the SRPC through M. Compared with point G, which is the "golden rule" (non-myopic) optimum, the outcome at M has higher inflation, but the same unemployment rate (given a vertical LRPC). In the long run, the higher inflation brings no offsetting benefit. We will meet a similar equilibrium, reached through rational expectations, rather than through the combination of voter and incumbent myopias, in chapter 7.

Supporting evidence

Nordhaus inquired into where, and when, countries have conformed to his model of the political business cycle. The theory implies (Nordhaus 1975,

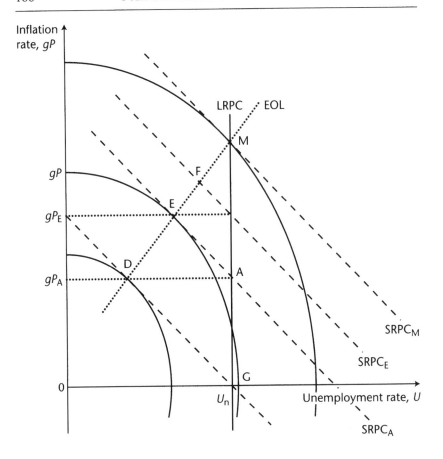

Figure 9.4　Myopic long-run equilibrium at point M

p. 185) that inflation and unemployment rates will display a specific pattern in phase with the electoral cycle: "unemployment and deflation in early years followed by an inflationary boom as elections approach." Nordhaus looked at nine countries, using annual data for 1947–1972, seeking a pattern of unemployment rising in the first half of the electoral period and falling in the second half. The empirical challenge is to distinguish episodes that look like political business cycles from random events. For three countries – Germany, New Zealand, and the USA – he found that the actual pattern matches the predicted pattern in a way that has less than a 10 percent chance of having occurred randomly.

The Rational Expectations Critique

Bennett McCallum (1978) criticized Nordhaus's theory on the grounds that the public is not forming its expectation of the inflation rate rationally, recognizing the regime under which it lives. As applied to a country with a four-year presidential term, the A–B–C–D–A–B–. . . cycle depicted in figure 9.3 suggests that the public fails to anticipate a hike in the inflation rate that occurs like clockwork every fourth year. Job-seeking workers systematically overestimate the real value of nominal wage offers in presidential election years, and are, thus, fooled into taking jobs sooner, shortening the length of job search, and, thus, the measured unemployment rate. Workers could be easily avoid such a mistake by considering the phase of the electoral cycle in forming their gP^e forecasts. Expected inflation gP^e would then rise every fourth year, no systematic forecasting error would occur, and systematic deviations from the LRPC would be avoided. As McCallum notes, this is a simple application of the "policy ineffectiveness" proposition associated with rational expectations macroeconomics. Any systematic, and hence anticipated, monetary policy is ineffective at moving real variables, like unemployment and real income, away from their natural rates.

Nordhaus's model yields the testable hypothesis that the changing phase of the electoral cycle helps to explain the behavior of the unemployment rate over time. McCallum's method of testing the hypothesis is, first, to estimate an auto-regressive model for forecasting U, then to see whether adding in the contemporaneous values of an electoral-phase dummy variable helps to improve the forecast significantly. McCallum constructs six different EVs (electoral variables), each representing a different possible profile to the cycle. All fail to be statistically significant. McCallum concludes that the evidence fails to reject the policy-ineffectiveness proposition, and thus fails to support the political business cycle theory.

McCallum's failure to find corroborating evidence of an electoral cycle in the US unemployment rate inevitably leaves unanswered questions. Is this the right way to look for a cycle? Did McCallum simply not look hard enough for an EV dummy that "works" in explaining the US unemployment rate? Does the unemployment rate in other countries exhibit an electoral cycle? Is the unemployment rate the right dependent variable to examine?

Manfred W. Keil (1988) questions McCallum's method of testing for an electoral cycle. He nonetheless finds an electoral cycle in UK unemployment data using a McCallum-type test.

The absence of a predictable electoral cycle in US unemployment rates might simply mean that not *all* administrations have tried to influence the (U, gP) mix in an election-timed way, not that *none* of them have. Or, it might mean that they have tried but not succeeded, either because of the public's rational expectation of the ploy, or simply because of bad timing. Several investigators have found electoral policy cycles in monetary growth rates, suggesting that some administrations have at least *tried* to generate a favorable cycle. David Meiselman (1986) presents graphical evidence of a rough electoral cycle in US M1 growth from 1960 to 1986. He warns that researchers should not expect to find a perfectly regular cycle in light of the rational-expectations insight that money growth must be unexpected to influence the real variables that matter for voters and incumbents. Kevin Grier (1987) offers econometric evidence that money growth is systematically higher just before US elections that just after. Stuart D. Allen (1986) finds an electoral cycle in US money growth 1954–1980 by estimating equations in which the EV dummy interacts with the size of changes in the federal debt. Daniel J. Richards (1986) finds some evidence that the pattern of unexpected money growth in the USA was consistent with political business cycle theory between 1960 and 1974, but not after 1974. Richards speculates that the apparent disappearance of an electoral cycle in monetary policy may actually reflect the efforts of Nordhaus, McCallum, and other economists. Their studies of the political business cycle, and rational expectations, "put the authorities on notice that the public was aware of the political game, and that continuing to play it would require increasing large fluctuations in the Fed's behavior to produce the necessary monetary shocks."

An Alternative Formulation: Wagner's Political Seigniorage Cycle

Richard Wagner (1977) suggests that an observed political business cycle (or political monetary growth cycle) may be only an unintended consequence of policies aiming at greater seigniorage near election time. The re-election prospects of the incumbent party will be better enhanced by monetary injections that finance targeted government expenditures than by injections that simply finance open-market bond purchases. An open market purchase, unmatched by increased government spending, would (if unanticipated) provide the "benefit" of reduced unemployment all across the economy. This would be inefficient as a strategy for maximizing the re-election chances of the incumbent. An efficient re-election strategy specifically targets constituencies where the vote-value of an additional dollar in government spending is high, and where the marginal value of the vote won is high. For example, the incumbent might generate seigniorage, and use it to provide a new job-training program in an electoral "swing district."

In Wagner's electorally-driven-seigniorage theory of monetary politics, as in the Nordhaus–MacRae model, cyclical monetary expansion is explained by attempts to get re-elected. However, the intermediate goal is to finance government spending, rather than to alter the inflation and unemployment rates. Wagner calls this a strategy of "influencing relative prices rather than the general price level." Politicians try to "buy" votes with spending programs rather than to gain them by hitting (U, gP) targets. This sort of vote-buying is more effective if a voter cares about local conditions, and not just about economy-wide conditions.

On Wagner's theory, any cycles in the economy-wide unemployment rate would be the *unintended*, rather than the intended, outcome of the incumbent's policies. If cycles are synchronized with elections, it is because (with myopic voters) attempts to raise more seigniorage to spend are concentrated near election time. The hypothesis that seigniorage, and government spending, show electoral cycles remains to be empirically tested.

The "Partisan" Political Business Cycle Theory

Alesina and Sachs (1988) note two sources of dissatisfaction with the Nordhaus–MacRae model. First, as McCallum (1978) argued, the Nordhaus–MacRae model is inconsistent with rational expectations. Second, the empirical support for the theory is weak or fading. "Partisan" political business cycle theory (so called because it distinguishes between two political parties) hopes to remedy these problems.

In partisan theory, consistent with rational expectations, only *surprise* inflation drives the economy off the LRPC. Surprise inflation can occur, despite rational expectations, because there are two parties with different inflation-unemployment preferences, and the outcomes of elections are uncertain. (All that matters about the candidates is their respective party affiliations, so we will speak as though it is the political parties that are standing for election.) Compared to the "R" party, the "D" party has a lesser distaste for inflation, and a greater distaste for unemployment below the natural rate[2], and is, therefore, facing a SRPC tradeoff, prone to choose a higher

---

[2] Alesina and Sachs actually describe the two parties' preferences in terms of the rates of monetary expansion and real income growth. We describe them in terms of inflation and unemployment to facilitate comparison with the Nordhaus–MacRae model, and with the model to be discussed in chapter 10 (where such preferences are mapped, and are given an explicit algebraic formulation in the appendix).

inflation rate than the "R" party. The public does not know, for certain, which party will win the next election. Consequently, the public must form its expectation of the post-election inflation rate gP^e as an average of the higher rate the D party would pick (gP_D) if elected and the lower rate the R party would pick (gP_R). Whichever party is elected, there is a post-election inflation "surprise:" if the D party is elected, realized inflation in the following period will be gP_D, higher than expected, and unemployment will be reduced below its natural rate. If the R party is elected realized inflation will be gP_R, which is lower than expected, and unemployment will exceed its natural rate.

The post-election inflation-rate surprise lasts only until wage contracts are adjusted to the election results. If this takes half as long as the electoral term (a reasonable assumption for the USA, say Alesina and Sachs, citing evidence that the average union wage contract in the USA is two years long), then the unemployment rate returns to the natural rate in the second half of the term.

The economy thus exhibits two types of four-year cycles. Following the election of the D party, the economy "booms" for two years, and then returns to its natural rates of output and unemployment for two years, with inflation high for all four years. Following the election of the R party, the economy slumps for two years, then returns to its natural rates of output for two years, with inflation low for all four years.

The partisan political business cycle theory is illustrated in figure 9.5.

The position of the SRPC depends on the height of gP^e, which is determined as an average of gP_D and gP_R, weighted by each party's probability of victory. Specifically, let v be the probability of electing the D party (and $1 - v$ the probability of electing the R party). Then, for the period immediately after the election,

$$gP^e = v(gP_D) + (1 - v)\,(gP_R)$$

The SRPC, as shown, therefore crosses the LRPC between gP_D and gP_R.

Before the election, the economy is at D_2 under a D-party administration, or at R_2 if the R party is in office. If the D-party candidate is then (re-)elected, the economy moves to point D_1 on the SRPC, where inflation is higher than the weighted-average expectation and unemployment is consequently below the natural rate. If the R-party candidate is instead elected, the economy moves to point R_1 on the SRPC, where inflation is lower than expected and unemployment consequently exceeds the natural rate.

Notice that the more surprising the electoral result, the bigger the deviation of realized gP from gP_e, and consequently the bigger the deviation of U from U_n. The more likely the wage-contractors think a D-party victory (the higher the value of v), the higher is the SRPC, the smaller is the post-election inflation surprise ($gP_D - gP^e$) if the D's do in fact win, and the smaller is the boom. Likewise, the more likely a D-party victory, the greater is the recession if the R's pull an upset, because the greater the negative surprise in the post-election inflation rate.

In contrast to the Nordhaus–MacRae model, boom or bust (movement off the LRPC) occurs only in the immediate post-election period, which corres-ponds to the first two years of a US presidential term. Wage contractors (whose expectations determine the position of the SRPC) know the preferences of the ruling party in office, and form their expectations accordingly, so, in the second half of the administration, there can be no surprise in-flation, and no movement off the LRPC.

Alesina and Sachs offer a striking fact as empirical evidence for the partisan model: there is a significant difference in real GNP growth between Democratic and Republican presidential terms, but only (as the theory predicts) in the first halves of the terms. In the first halves of Democratic administrations (1949–1984), real growth averaged 5.0 percent per year, well above the mean growth rate for all administrations (approx. 4.2 percent per

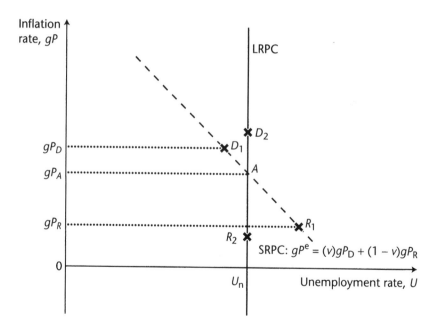

Figure 9.5 Partisan post-election results

year). In the first halves of Republican administrations, real growth averaged only 1.2 percent.[3]

The larger deviation from the mean, when Republicans take office, implies that Republican elections have been a bigger surprise. Alesina and Sachs, in fact, derive a value for v (the probability of a Democratic victory) over the entire sample of 81 percent. This figure seems implausibly high. They do not check the model's prediction that the size of the deviation varies with v, which should be possible to check by constructing v from polling data (rather than deriving it *post hoc*).

Questions

1 Why, in the Nordhaus political business cycle theory, do incumbent politicians not try to get re-elected by *eliminating* business cycles, i.e. by keeping the economy at its natural rate of unemployment?

2 On a single graph, plot annual (unemployment rate, inflation rate) pairs for the USA (or any other democratic country) over the last 30 years. Under which presidents (or prime ministers), if any, do you find the election-cycle pattern predicted by

    (a)   the Nordhaus PBC model, or

    (b)   the Alesina–Sachs partisan theory?

3 "One of the pieces of 'conventional wisdom' among economists has always been that to win elections politicians should depress the economy soon after a general election to squeeze inflation down in time for the next general election and then should boost the economy as this new election approaches." (Minford 1985) Why have many economists nonetheless been dissatisfied with the Nordhaus PBC model that rationalizes this "conventional wisdom?"

---

[3] Alesina and Sachs also offer evidence that there has been a statistically significant difference in rates of money growth between Democratic and Republican administrations. In a simple regression for money growth, with an intercept, trend, and Republican party dummy, the dummy has a significant (at the 5 percent level) and negative coefficient. The Kennedy (tight-money Democrat) and Nixon (loose-money Republican) administrations do not fit this pattern; separately dummying those years, the Republican dummy becomes even more negative and more statistically significant.

10

Discretion and Dynamic Inconsistency

In the Nordhaus political business cycle model, the monetary authority uses inflation surprises to cause deviations away from the natural rate of unemployment, shown as movements along the short-run Phillips curve (SRPC). We noted McCallum's (1978) rational expectations critique of the model: the public, in setting its expected inflation rate (and thus the position of the SRPC), unreasonably acts as though it is oblivious to the game the authority is playing. What happens if we modify the model to give the public rational expectations? That is, suppose the public prefers zero inflation, and an unemployment rate below the natural rate, and the monetary authority (benevolently) seeks to reach such a combination. What then happens if the public chooses its expected inflation rate with full awareness of the monetary authority's objective, and Phillips-curve constraint? A model developed by Finn Kydland and Edward Prescott (1977), and further elaborated by Robert J. Barro and David B. Gordon (1983b), shows that, in such a setting, the monetary authority can be trapped by its own good intentions. The authority generates what both the public, and the authority itself, regard as excessive inflation with no offsetting benefit.[1]

The argument that discretion is a trap has added a powerful strand to the case for monetary policy rules. Kydland and Prescott (1977) emphasize this normative implication of their model, a topic we return to below. Barro and Gordon (1983b) use the model to explain (rather than prescribe) monetary policy. For example, they seek to explain why money growth in the postwar USA has tended to rise following a rise in the unemployment rate – when a

---

[1] Remarkably, neither Kydland and Prescott, nor Barro and Gordon, cited, or appears to have been consciously responding to, the Nordhaus model.

predictable policy response of this sort would seem to be pointless at best. A policymaker who understands that we live in a "natural rate" world, where agents have rational expectations, should understand that such an easily anticipated change in money growth has no effect on real output, or employment.

The choice variables for the monetary authority modeled by Kydland and Prescott, or Barro and Gordon, are the same as those of the Nordhaus monetary authority. As in the political business cycle literature, the authority chooses the inflation rate through its control of the money growth rate. Choosing a higher inflation rate, taking the public's inflation-rate expectation as given, implies a lower unemployment rate. The set of attainable (unemployment, inflation rate) combinations is shown by a SRPC. The authority chooses the best of these combinations, namely the combination that achieves the highest "social preference" score. As before, the SRPC, embodying expectations of a particular inflation rate, is distinct from the long-run Phillips curve (LRPC), which shows the natural unemployment rate for various correctly anticipated inflation rates.

The key difference from the political business cycle literature lies in the way the public forms its inflation-rate expectation. The public no longer has naive, or adaptive, expectations that can be exploited by the monetary authority. Instead, the public has "rational" or model-consistent expectations. That is, the public forms its expectation of today's inflation rate, not by any form of extrapolation, but by correctly solving the model that determines the rate chosen by the monetary authority.

Because expectations are rational rather than adaptive, there can be none of the cycling produced by the Nordhaus political business cycle model. Instead, in the absence of unanticipated money demand, or aggregate supply shocks (which we abstract from here, to simplify the analysis), the public is never confused, and all outcomes lie on the LRPC. The monetary authority's desire to reduce unemployment below the natural rate cannot be fulfilled, but instead drives the authority to the analog of Nordhaus' myopic equilibrium, i.e. drives it to produce pointlessly high inflation. In this case, the outcome does not reflect myopia, but rather reflects the discretionary monetary authority's inability to commit credibly to low inflation. The public expect high inflation, because they know that were they to expect otherwise, the monetary authority would be tempted to reduce unemployment through surprisingly high inflation.

The Kydland–Prescott Model

To flesh out the argument just sketched, we present a graphical version of the model. We will then interpret the results. A simplified algebraic version of the model is presented in the appendix to this chapter. Kydland and Prescott (1977) first presented the graphics; Barro and Gordon (1983b) offered an algebraic version.

The graphical elements of the model are as follows.

1   Linear short-run Phillips curves (SRPCs) – see figure 10.1
2   Social indifference curves – see figure 10.2

Each SRPC shows the set of (unemployment rate, inflation rate) combinations available to the monetary authority by choosing the inflation rate, *given* that the public expects a particular rate of inflation. The expected rate of inflation associated with any shortrun Phillips Curve is the *y*-coordinate of the point at which the curve crosses the vertical LRPC.

Each social indifference curve represents points of equal macroeconomic "misery," where the "misery index" is a function of the unemployment and inflation rates. (The curves thus play the same role as the voter isoquants in the Nordhaus model.) The misery index represents the public's preferences,

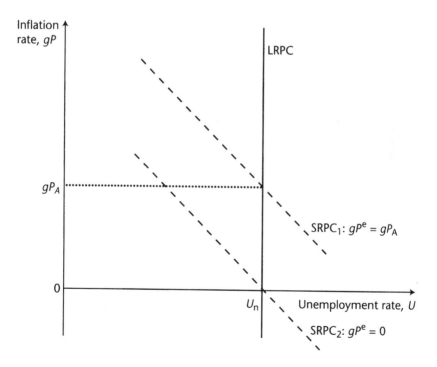

Figure 10.1   Long-run and short-run Phillips curves (LRPC and SRPCs)

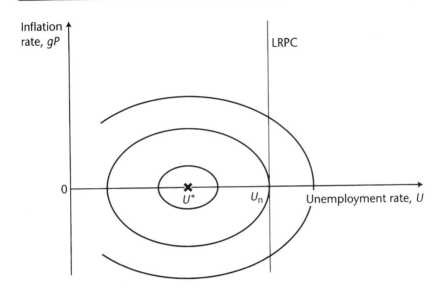

Figure 10.2   Social indifference (isomisery) curves

and the benevolent monetary authority seeks the point of minimum misery on whatever SRPC it faces, shown as the tangency point with the innermost indifference curve. The curves are drawn as ellipsoids in order to produce nice tangencies with the linear SRPCs. Drawing them as ellipsoids means that the misery index is a weighted sum of the squared distances of the inflation rate and unemployment rate from a most-preferred point. The unemployment and inflation rates at this "bull's-eye" point may conveniently be called the "target" unemployment and inflation rates.

As drawn, the target unemployment rate U^* is below the natural rate U_n, implying that the public believes the natural rate to be undesirably high. Such a belief may be rationalized (see below) as a response to an externality created by unemployment compensation, income taxation, or other policies.

The target inflation rate is assumed to be zero. A zero target can be rationalized by the desire to minimize price-changing costs (a common example is the cost of reprinting menus; hence, these costs are sometimes called "menu costs"). The model could easily be modified to incorporate a nonzero inflation-rate target. As we have seen in earlier chapters, the target rate might be negative for optimal-quantity-of-money reasons, or positive for seigniorage reasons.

The *policymaker's instrument* is the growth rate of the money supply.

Under the simplifying assumption that there are no lags in the effect of money growth on inflation, so that the authority has direct, and continuous, control over the inflation rate, we can treat the inflation rate itself as the instrument. By implication, we abstract from any temporary effects of a change in money growth on real income. The economy is always on its long-run money demand curve, and the inflation rate always equals its steady-state equilibrium value.

The *policymaker's objective* is to choose the inflation rate that (together with the associated unemployment rate) minimizes the level of the misery index, denoted Z. Graphically, the authority wants to reach the innermost social indifference curve. Given that the target unemployment rate is below the natural rate, this objective means that the authority would be tempted to choose an inflation rate higher that the public expected if the public expected a low inflation rate. For example, if the public expected zero inflation, and so the authority could move along the SRPC passing through $(U_n, 0)$, Z-minimization implies that the authority would choose a positive inflation rate, moving the economy to the northwest along the short-run Phillips Curve. If the target rate were to equal the natural rate, there would be no reason to try to reduce unemployment below the natural rate through unexpected inflation.

The authority faces a simple one-period choice problem, because, by assumption, each period is independent of past and future. Today's unemployment rate, and the inflation rate expected for today, are independent of yesterday's outcomes, and tomorrow's values for these variables are independent of today's outcomes. Today's unemployment rate, U, depends only on today's natural rate of unemployment U_n, and on the difference between today's inflation rate gP, and the inflation rate expected for today gP^e. The public chooses gP^e by solving the model that determines the rate chosen by the monetary authority. The chosen rate depends only on the monetary authority's preferences between inflation and unemployment (which are assumed to be the same as the public's preferences, as depicted in figure 10.2), and the constraint the authority faces in choosing (the SRPC, as depicted in figure 10.1). Both pieces of information are assumed known to the public.

To solve for the misery-minimizing inflation rate, the monetary authority must calculate the public's expected inflation rate gP^e in order to know along which SRPC its choice is constrained. The authority recognizes that gP^e is not simply "given," but that the public forms gP^e by solving the relevant model for the authority's choice of gP. That is, the public knows that gP will emerge from the policy-maker's minimization of Z, has the same information on U_n and the Phillips tradeoff that is available to the policy-maker, and knows the authority's preferences (which it shares). It is in the formation of the public's inflation-rate expectations that the crucial break is made from the early-type political business cycle models. For Nordhaus, gP^e was formed adaptively by extrapolating from the previous period's gP. The monetary authority could take advantage of the public's "locked-in" inflation-rate expectations, and the public failed to recognize the game the authority was playing. The assumption of rational expectations rules out such naïveté. The public knows exactly what game the authority is playing. The authority knows that the public knows, and so on.

With the monetary authority, and the public, playing an informed game against one another, equilibrium requires that each party to the game choose an action that is best, given what the other party chooses.[2] The authority must choose the inflation rate that minimizes Z given the authority's preference map and the SRPC as determined by the public's choice of an expected inflation rate. The public must choose an expected inflation rate for which it knows that the monetary authority facing such an expectation will choose to fulfill it. For the authority to choose not to deviate from the inflation rate the public expects (a requirement sometimes called "time consistency"), it must be that in equilibrium

$$gP^\sim = gP^e$$

where

> $gP^\sim$ = the inflation rate that minimizes Z given the authority's preference map and the SRPC
> gP^e = the public's expected inflation rate, which determines the height of the SRPC

Only such an outcome is time-consistent. The appendix to this chapter gives an algebraic representation of this problem of solving for $gP^\sim$. Graphically, the solution is seen in figure 10.3.

The "best" (Z-minimizing) point on any SRPC is the point tangent to a preference ellipse. The dashed line LL' represents the locus of such best points on various SRPCs. The authority's choice must lie somewhere on this locus. The time-consistent solution is the positive inflation rate shown by point M, where the LL' locus crosses the LRPC. Only at an inflation rate of M does the authority have no incentive to deviate from the expected rate of inflation (and thus from the natural rate of unemployment). M is the only point that is both on the LRPC (consistent with correct expectations by the public), and on the LL' locus (the best point on its SRPC, consistent with Z-minimization by the monetary authority).

---

[2] This is the "Nash equilibrium" concept familiar to students of game theory.

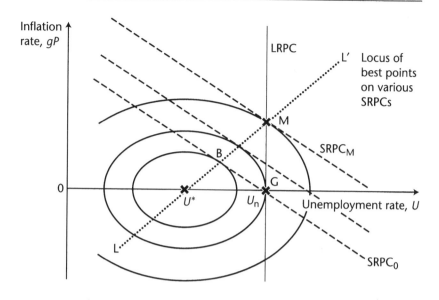

Figure 10.3   Time-consistent equilibrium M versus optimal outcome G

Positive Implications: Using the Model to Explain Changes in Inflation

Barro and Gordon (1983b) emphasize the positive implications of the model, that is, its ability to explain changes in the actual inflation rate. In standard fashion, we can examine the impact that changing each parameter of the model has, *ceteris paribus*, on the chosen inflation rate. In graphical terms, the key parameters, all evident in figure 10.3, are

1   the position of the LRPC relative to U^*,
2   the shape of the social indifference ellipses, and
3   the slope of the SRPCs.

The inflation rate rises with an increase in the difference between the natural rate of unemployment and the target rate

Suppose the natural rate increases, but the target rate does not increase, or does not increase by as many percentage points. With higher unemployment in prospect, a monetary authority that balances the marginal miseries from inflation and unemployment along the SRPC is tempted to "buy" a somewhat greater reduction in the actual unemployment rate U, with somewhat greater surprise inflation. Because the public observes the shift in the natural rate U_n, and has rational expectations (understands how the shift will affect the authority's inflation-rate choice), however, the resulting increase in inflation is not unexpected, and fails to reduce the actual rate of unemployment U below the new natural rate. Graphically, when the LRPC shifts rightward relative to the LL' locus, it intersects the LL' locus at a higher rate of inflation. The equilibrium SRPC shifts up correspondingly.

Barro and Gordon argue that the natural rate of unemployment rose in the USA between 1970 and 1985, and that the model thereby explains why the inflation and unemployment rates rose together over that period (an event sometimes called "stagflation"). It is not an intrinsic feature of the Kydland–Prescott model, however, that an increase in the natural rate increases the benefit of unexpected inflation. That result depends on Barro and Gordon's algebraic assumption that U^* is a fixed fraction of U_n. The result disappears (and yet the rest of the model's implications remain intact) if U^* equals U_n minus a fixed number of percentage points, because then the LL' locus will shift in parallel with shifts in the LRPC.[3]

The divergence of the most-desired or "target" unemployment rate U^* from the natural rate U_n is an essential feature of the model, in both the Kydland–Prescott and Barro–Gordon versions. Some commentators (e.g. Leijonhufvud 1986, pp. 38–9) have found the divergence paradoxical: why do individuals in the model, choosing the misery function as citizens, prefer an unemployment rate that cannot be obtained without fooling them into behaving sub-optimally as workers? Barro and Gordon attribute the divergence to policies that distort the labor market (unemployment insurance, income taxation), and make the natural rate of unemployment "too high." But how does this explain a seeming preference for being fooled? The seeming paradox can be resolved by considering that tax-funded unemployment insurance (or income taxation) creates a fiscal externality.[4] Citizen Jones sees the unemployment of his fellow citizens as having the negative effect of raising his own tax bill. It is not that Jones personally wants to be fooled,

---

[3] Barro and Gordon also assume that the public's misery depends on the absolute difference of the actual unemployment rate U from the target rate U^*, and that the absolute (percentage-point) differences of actual U from U_n are a linear function of unexpected inflation. The payoff from unexpected inflation, therefore, rises with any increase in the absolute difference between U_n and U^*. This result would disappear if the misery index, and the slope of the Phillips curve, were instead specified proportionally. An increase in U_n could then be represented, graphically, by a simple rescaling of the horizontal axis, with no impact on equilibrium inflation.

[4] I owe this resolution to Daniel B. Klein.

but that he wants *other* workers to be unemployed less to lighten his tax burden. Because he supports the unemployed, or benefits from the taxes that the employed pay, each citizen prefers that fewer of his fellow citizens be unemployed.

This account of U^*'s divergence from U_n suggests an alternative way to explain secularly rising inflation using the model. The size of the fiscal externality, and thus the size of the divergence of U^* from U_n, depends on the extent of the unemployment insurance program (or on marginal income tax rates). Increases in the divergence of U^* from U_n generate higher inflation in the model. Growing unemployment insurance (wider or longer coverage, or higher monthly payments), and rising marginal tax rates (up to 1982), thus provide an alternative explanation for historically rising inflation rates in the USA (up to 1982). The Reagan tax cuts reduced the fiscal externality, raised U^*, and thus lowered the Federal Reserve's incentive to inflate.

The inflation rate rises with an increase in the labor market's sensitivity to unexpected inflation

The larger the payoff from unexpected inflation in terms of a reduced unemployment rate, the larger the monetary authority's temptation to inflate. Graphically, a reduction in the steepness of the SRPCs moves the tangency point on each indifference ellipse in the direction of twelve o'clock. The LL' locus rotates counter-clockwise, and intersects the LRPC at a higher rate of inflation.

The inflation rate rises with increased public concern over unemployment, relative to concern over inflation

Greater relative concern over unemployment increases the monetary authority's temptation to inflate, and, thereby, raises the chosen inflation rate. Inflating more does not, however, give the authority any greater ability to reduce unemployment below the natural rate, so the realized unemployment rate does not fall. Graphically, increasing the weight given to unemployment relative to that of inflation in the misery function makes the social indifference ellipses taller. On each SRPC, the tangency with an indifference ellipse occurs at a higher inflation rate. The LL' locus consequently pivots counter-clockwise. The time-consistent equilibrium point M, where the LL' locus crosses the LRPC, occurs at a higher inflation rate.

Conversely, increasing the weight placed on inflation relative to that on unemployment makes the indifference ellipses squatter, rotates the LL' locus clockwise, and lowers the equilibrium inflation rate. Because it is only the shape of the ellipses (and not any absolute intensities of feeling assigned to them) that matters for the determination of the LL' locus and the equilibrium point M, it is only the *relative* (and not any absolute) weights placed on inflation and unemployment that matter.

Perhaps the most important positive implication of the model comes not from changing a parameter within the discretionary regime, but from a comparison across regimes:

The inflation rate rises with a shift from a rules-based regime to a discretionary regime (it becomes positive rather than zero)

A benevolent monetary authority, unable to precommit to zero inflation, is compelled to produce positive inflation. The shift to a discretionary regime means that the authority will pick the most-desired combination of inflation and unemployment, anew, each period. The authority cannot forswear the temptation to reduce unemployment with a little unexpected inflation, a temptation that is particularly strong when the expected inflation rate is zero. The rationally expected inflation rate, therefore, rises above zero. Graphically, discretion makes it impossible to sustain an equilibrium at point G, the best of the feasible equilibrium points represented by the LRPC. The public knows that if it expected zero inflation, the authorities would want to move to point B. The only time-consistent equilibrium occurs at point M. This point is further elaborated below, in connection with its normative implications.

As Barro and Gordon note, inflation has, historically, been higher since central banks abandoned the rules of the gold standard, despite the fact that fiat central banks have the means to produce the same, or lower, inflation. Although a strict gold standard is not the same as a money-growth or inflation-rate rule – it does not involve a precommitment to a particular rate of inflation or money growth because, as we have seen in chapter 2, those rates are determined by supply and demand conditions in the markets for gold and gold-redeemable money – it does entail a precommitment by money issuers not to be swayed to inflate by the Phillips tradeoff.

Policy Implications Under Discretion

In a discretionary regime of the Kydland–Prescott/Barro–Gordon sort, telling the monetary authorities to aim for zero inflation, or to produce low and steady money growth, is pointless. It amounts to telling the authorities not to optimize, given their constraints. The only way to influence central bank behavior toward the zero-inflation optimum, absent a binding rule, is to change one of the parameters discussed above. To reduce inflation requires one of three actions.

1   *Bringing the target rate of unemployment closer to the natural rate,* in light of the rationale for their divergence, would mean reforming unemployment insurance, or reducing marginal income tax rates, to reduce the fiscal externalities that cause the representative citizen to want his fellow citizens' unemployment rate to be less than the natural rate.

2   *Reducing the economy's responsiveness to unexpected inflation*: experience with highly variable inflation appears to have this effect (Lucas 1973), but no one would argue, on that ground, for deliberately erratic monetary policy. No other method of changing the slope of the SRPC is evident.

3   *Increasing the public's distaste for inflation* (which the central bank faithfully shares), relative to its distaste for an unemployment rate above the target rate: some economists have argued that the economics profession's emphasis on purely quantity-theoretic models of inflation, in which fully anticipated inflation is nearly harmless, have unfortunately lessened the economics profession's distaste for inflation. Milton Friedman's recent conjecture that the LRPC is positively sloped may be seen as an attempt to rebuild that distaste.[5]

A corollary of this last point is that any policy measure that makes an increase in rate of inflation less painful, for example a policy of indexing transfer payments, ends up increasing the total amount of inflation. In graphical terms, reducing the marginal misery cost of inflation means making the public's preference ellipses taller. Because it increases inflation, a palliative measure that reduces the marginal misery cost of inflation, such as indexing, actually increases the public's total misery cost given the Barro–Gordon algebra (Fischer and Summers 1989).[6]

An alternative to increasing the *public's* distaste for inflation is to give the central bank independence (allow it to have an objective function different from the public's), and to appoint individuals as central bankers who are less concerned about unemployment, relative to inflation, than the average citizen. The German Bundesbank was sometimes said to fit this prescription. Given that discretion is a trap, it is better for the public that the central

---

[5] For discussions of why inflation really is damaging, see Leijonhufvud (1981, chs. 9–10) and Yeager (1997).

[6] In the algebraic terms presented in the appendix to this chapter, the marginal cost of inflation is $(dZ/dgP) = 2bgP$. A policy that reduces the marginal-cost-of-inflation parameter, b, in the misery index increases misery Z once the induced increase in gP (which is squared in the misery index) is taken into account. From the equilibrium solution showing that gP is proportional to $1/b$, it follows that if b is halved, gP is doubled, $(gP)^2$ is quadrupled, and the total inflation misery $b(gP)^2$ is doubled.

bankers are more "hawkish" on inflation than the representative citizen. On this view, though giving the central bank independence is desirable *if* the central bank has discretion, it is second-best to precommitting the central bank to a non-inflationary policy.

Rules Versus Discretion

Kydland and Prescott (1977) have emphasized the model's normative implication for the constitutional choice among monetary regimes: discretion for the monetary authority yields a sub-optimal outcome. The sub-optimality of the time-consistent equilibrium in a discretionary regime, under the assumed conditions, can be seen by noting that point M is inferior to (is on a less central preference ellipse than) all points lower on the LRPC.

Conversely, the optimal outcome is *time-inconsistent*. Point G, the combination of the natural rate of unemployment and zero inflation, is the best point on the feasible set represented by the LRPC. However, a discretionary and benevolent monetary authority will abandon point G in pursuit of an even better outcome. If zero inflation were expected, the authority could choose any point on $SRPC_0$, and it would choose point B with positive inflation to minimize misery. The same temptation to inflate can be seen by noting that, at point G, the social indifference curves is vertical, indicating that the marginal misery cost of inflation is zero, while the marginal benefit of reducing unemployment below U_n is positive. With non-vertical SRPCs, G cannot be the best attainable point on its SRPC. The benevolent authority has an irresistible incentive to deviate from zero inflation when the public expects zero inflation.

A monetary policy rule, in contrast to discretion, allows the authority to reach an optimal outcome through pre-commitment to the preferred rate of inflation. The authority is bound to a formula that dictates the growth rate of some measure of the money stock, and, thus, dictates the inflation rate (absent shocks to real demand for that measure of money), without reference to the values of the unemployment rate or other real variables. The Phillips tradeoff can no longer tempt the authority, and monetary policy can be concerned exclusively with achieving the misery-minimizing value of the inflation rate, which is assumed to be zero. A credible pre-commitment of this sort eliminates the possibility of a monetary policy surprise, and thereby makes the public's expected inflation rate equal to whatever inflation rate the policy rule implies. The equality of the actual inflation rate to the expected rate becomes a constraint on the monetary authority, rather than an equilibrium condition, as it is under discretion.

The seemingly paradoxical conclusion emerges that rules, rather than restricting the monetary authority's ability to achieve its goals, are needed to *enable* the authority to achieve its goals. Under discretion, the public expects a positive rate of inflation, indeed, expects a rate so high that the authority is no longer tempted to go any higher for the sake of sub-natural unemployment. The best the authority can then achieve is point M, validating the public's expectation. Producing zero inflation under these conditions would generate a negative monetary shock, and would drive the economy southeast along $SRPC_M$ to a less-desired outcome with unemployment above the natural rate. Only a precommitment to zero inflation, which removes the authority's temptation to exploit the Phillips tradeoff, makes it possible for the public to expect zero inflation in equilibrium, and, therefore, makes it possible to achieve zero inflation without high unemployment.

The "time-consistency" case for rules is an important addition to the intellectual arsenal of rules advocates. There had previously been two standard arguments for rules, to be discussed in more detail in chapter 11.

1   The "Monetarist" argument, associated with Milton Friedman (1968), is that, even with the best forecasts available, a central bank has inadequate knowledge to stabilize the economy. Long and variable lags in the effects of monetary policy make it impossible for the central bank to move consistently, in the right direction, in a timely manner. A central bank unintentionally adds to instability when it pursues an active "stabilization" policy. Rules that prevent monetary policy activism thereby promote economic stability.

2   The "public choice" argument, associated with Geoffrey Brennan and James Buchanan (1981), is that a central bank, typically, faces incentives to pursue goals other than the low inflation desired by the public. A constitutional rule is needed to constrain the central bank to behave as the public wants.

The Kydland–Prescott/Barro–Gordon story shows that discretionary "optimal control" policy, with period-by-period decision making, can fail to attain the best attainable outcome even when there is no knowledge problem, and no malincentive problem. A sub-optimal outcome occurs, even if the monetary authority can perfectly predict the timing, and magnitude, of the effects of changes in money growth on the inflation and unemployment rates, and has a preference function identical to the public's.

The reason for the ill effect of discretionary policy, as Kydland and Prescott explain, is that agents with rational expectations respond to prospective changes in monetary policy, revising their inflation-rate expectations accordingly. A change in the expected inflation rate alters the parameters of the policy-maker's decision problem, and calls for further adjustments to policy. The sequence of such conjectural changes converges on a sub-optimal outcome. The outcome is sub-optimal because, in period-by-period decisions taking the discretionary regime (and its associated rational expectations) as given, the policy-maker cannot internalize the effect that the policy regime itself has on expectations, and, thereby, on the decisions of agents.

Kydland and Prescott offer several examples of the same basic problem in other contexts.

1   *Building on a flood plain*
Suppose that the high cost of building flood controls makes it best that no one build a house on a river plain subject to flooding (like the Mississippi River's). People know that once the houses are in place, however, the government will consider it worthwhile to build the flood controls (whose cost will not be fully charged to the benefiting houseowners). An inability to precommit to *not* building the flood controls results in houses being built on the flood plain, by assumption a sub-optimal outcome. (The same problem arises if we substitute, in place of building flood controls, a policy of after-the-fact disaster relief for flood victims.)

2   *Patents*
Suppose that it is better to award and protect patents than not to, because it creates an incentive to invent, even though patent holders can charge monopoly prices. A policy decision to nullify pre-existing patent rights, while promising to respect patents granted in the future, would appear to preserve the incentive to invent, while allowing past inventions to be used without paying monopoly prices to their inventors. Discretion therefore results in the nullification of old patents. However, since potential inventors rationally expect such a decision to be repeated in the future, an inability to precommit to respecting future patents would mean that no patentable inventions are forthcoming, again, by assumption, a sub-optimal outcome.

3   *Rent controls*
The application of rent controls to apartment buildings, even if new buildings are officially exempted, discourages investment in new apartment construction for the same reason.

The nature of the problem should be clear by now: discretion results in suboptimality because there is, in the nature of the case, no way to induce future policy-makers to consider the effect of their likely discretionary policy, via expectations, on the decisions of current agents. There is no way to convince perceptive agents, today, that if they were to expect a long-run optimal policy (zero inflation in the monetary example) to prevail tomorrow, they will not be cheated when tomorrow arrives, by the choice of what then seems the best policy (positive inflation). Some sort of rules, i.e.

binding precommitments, are need to internalize the externality from unconstrained future policy. In the case of money, "constitutional" rules (hard-to-change legal mandates) that can be credible include rules binding the central bank to zero inflation, to a fixed rate of money growth, to a fixed exchange rate[7] or a gold standard, or a rule abolishing the central bank, and completely removal of government from the production of money.[8] The time-consistency argument, by itself, does not determine which rule would be best.

If we take seriously the foregoing argument that discretion is simply a trap, a puzzle exists: if this is all true, why do most countries lack constitutional, or even legislated, monetary policy rules? Is it because rules are so hard to design? (Fixed exchange-rate rules certainly are not.) Or, is it because there is seldom an organized constituency for rules, the prospective benefits being so widely diffused, whereas an organized constituency opposes them, namely the central bankers, and their advisors, who derive importance from their discretion?

Subsequent Literature

A subsequent body of research on "monetary policy games" brings game-theoretic concepts, and solutions, to bear on modified versions of the problem of time-inconsistent discretionary policy. Barro and Gordon (1983a) consider a second-best way (rules being first-best) to avoid the sub-optimal outcome, based on strategic game-playing by the public. The public deliberately forms its inflation expectations in such a way as to punish the monetary authority for surprise inflation. If the authority "cheated" in the previous period, its "reputation" is diminished, and the public expects it to cheat again in the current period. By choosing high inflation-rate expectations, shifting up the SRPC, the public worsens the menu of options facing the monetary authority. The authority, recognizing this strategy on the part of

---

[7] I thus heard it argued, at a conference in the 1980s on whether Spain should join the European Monetary System, that fixing the exchange rate between the peseta and the Deutsche mark would beneficially provide the anti-inflationary discipline that Spain's central bank could not otherwise muster. To my surprise, it was an economist from the Spanish central bank who made the argument.

[8] McCallum (1997) provides a skeptical perspective on the relevance of the Kydland–Prescott model. He makes the important point that if there *is* a precommitment problem, it applies to the government and the central bank together. A monetary policy "rule" that the government is supposed to enforce will only relocate, and not eliminate, the problem, because the government may be in cahoots with the central bank, and choose not to enforce the rule. To solve the problem, the public must be able to enforce the rule against the government.

the public, is deterred from surprise inflation by the damage to its "reputation," and so, in equilibrium, it inflates less than at point M. A problem with this analysis, as Backus and Driffill (1985, p. 532) point out, is that the punishment strategy assigned to the public is arbitrary. Further, punishment would seem to be subject to a free rider problem: each individual would want to leave the burden of punishing to others, and would personally choose rational inflation-rate expectations.

Canzoneri (1985) considers a game in which the monetary authority has private information. In that case, there is an advantage as well as the time-inconsistency disadvantage to discretion.

Backus and Driffill (1985) provide a model in which the policy maker can be either of two types, "wet" (tempted to inflate) or "hard-nosed" (not tempted). The public has to guess which, because both types claim to be hard-nosed. A sequential game ensues in which a wet authority pretends to be hard-nosed, for a while, but ultimately cashes in on its reputation by inflating. Cuikerman and Meltzer (1986) give the monetary authority a preference function in which the key preference parameter (basically the misery weight on unemployment relative to inflation) shifts randomly over time. Because the public does not know the current value of the parameter, surprise inflation is possible (and Fed-watching becomes rational, which it would not be in the simple model with a perfectly informed public). Monetary policy has an inflationary bias, as in Kydland and Prescott, but there is no time-inconsistency problem. The authority's imperfect credibility is due, instead, to the public's imperfect information regarding the authority's inflation-proneness, an ambiguity the authority may itself choose to promote. Inflationary experience raises the public's estimate of inflation-proneness, much as in the Barro–Gordon and Backus–Driffill reputational models, making future stimulation more costly (in terms of inflation). However, because monetary control is imperfect, actual money growth is only a noisy indicator of the policy-maker's preferences.

Questions

1 According to the Kydland–Prescott / Barro–Gordon perspective, why does the inflation rate rise with a shift from a rules-based to a discretionary policy regime?

2 "Since stability of the price level is manifestly not society's only economic objective, what is the case for directing monetary policy solely toward that objective?" (Cooper 1988) How would Kydland and Prescott answer that question?

3 "A major contribution of Kydland and Prescott was the recognition that monetary policy involves the same issues about commitments as do such areas as patents." (Barro 1986)

(a) What monetary policy move, in this view, is analogous to the move to increase today's supply of goods by abolishing past patents?

(b) What cost does the lack of a commitment not to make such a move impose on the economy, parallel to the decrease in inventions, when inventors fear that current patents will be abolished later?

4 In the Barro–Gordon model, what inflation rate would the central bank choose if its most-preferred unemployment rate were equal to the natural rate?

5 "[G]overnments have not adopted precommitment strategies ('rules') to help them resist temptation; nor have they created incentive-compatible compensation schemes for their central bankers. Instead, they brought inflation down dramatically [in the 1980s] by purely discretionary policy decisions." (Blinder 1997).

(a) Suppose you wish to use the Barro–Gordon model to explain the fall in inflation since 1980. What are the various possible parameter shifts that could explain a decrease in the inflation rate? What would you look for, in other data, to determine which, if any, of these possible explanations is correct?

(b) Does the fact that US inflation was reduced to only 3 percent (from 14 percent), under a discretionary regime, weaken the case for rules as a strategy for avoiding inflation?

6 During the 1982 recession in the USA, when a reporter asked what it would take to ease the Fed's "tight" monetary policy, Fed chairman Paul Volcker reportedly replied that it would take his own impeachment.

(a) Why would a Fed chairman *want the public to believe* that he had such a single-minded devotion to lowering the inflation rate?

(b) Why might even such a strong declaration be ineffective at convincing the public?

7 Consider the usual Barro–Gordon model of how the inflation rate is chosen, but assume that the public, instead of having rational expectations, expects whatever inflation rate the monetary authority announces (no matter what happens). The authority knows that this is how the public forms its expectation. What inflation rate will the authority announce? What rate will it actually choose to generate, and what will be the resulting unemployment rate?

8 How can the time-inconsistency problem be used to argue that it serves the average citizen's interest to appoint central bankers who are especially "hawkish" on inflation, i.e. less willing than the average citizen to trade an increase in inflation for a reduction in unemployment?

9 "It might be argued that Italy has gained discipline by agreeing to align its exchange rate with the German mark [as part of its mem-

bership in the EMS]. This arrangement works because both countries are responsible for intervening according to clearly specified rules, because membership in the European Monetary System (EMS) is valuable, and because failure to comply with the rules of membership may lead to ejection from the [EMS]." (Calomiris 1995, p. 273)

(a) Assume that the Bank of Italy does gain "discipline" by agreeing to an exchange-rate alignment, i.e. that it loses discretion over monetary policy. Why might losing its discretion be a good thing from the point of view of the average Italian citizen, and even from the point of view of the Bank of Italy's governors?

(b) Why does it matter that the rules, defining what the Bank of Italy is to do as an EMS member, are clearly specified and strictly enforced?

Appendix: An Algebraic Version of the Model

This representation is based on Barro and Gordon (1983b), but with stochastic disturbances removed for simplicity.

Expectations-augmented Phillips curve

The expression for a deterministic linear Phillips Curve is

$$U = U_n \, c(gP - gP^e)$$

where

U = today's unemployment rate
U_n = the "natural" unemployment rate
c = the coefficient indicating the sensitivity of U to unexpected gP, corresponding to the flatness of the SRPC ($-1/c$ is the slope of the SRPC), $c > 0$
gP = today's actual inflation
gP^e = inflation expected for today

Social preference function

Defined over U and gP, the "misery index" is given by

$$Z = (U - U^*)^2 + b(gP)^2$$

where

Z   = the misery index
U^* = the "target" rate of unemployment
b   = the misery coefficient on deviations of gP from zero, $b > 0$

and the misery coefficient on squared deviations of U from target U has been normalized to one. We additionally assume

$$U^* = kU_n$$

where k is a constant, $0 < k < 1$. Note that Z rises as U departs from U^* in either direction; actual unemployment can be "too low" as well as "too high."

The policy-maker's instrument

The monetary authority has control over the inflation rate gP. This control follows from its control over the money growth rate gM, given the dynamic quantity equation

$$gM + gV = gP + gy$$

and the simplifying long-run assumptions that there are

1   no effects of a change in gM on gV, that is, no lag between changes in gM and changes in $(gP + gy)$, and
2   no effects of a change in gM on gy.

Thus, the economy is always on its long-run money demand curve, and the inflation rate always equals its steady-state equilibrium value. These assumptions are consistent with monetary policy always being correctly anticipated, and money demand shocks being absent, so that the economy always ends up on the LRPC. Barro and Gordon (1983b) make allowance for stochastic shocks to money demand, so that the authority controls instead only the *mean* inflation rate.

The policy-maker's objective

The monetary authority chooses gP to minimize the *PV* of the stream of future misery indices. This reduces to the one-period problem of minimizing Z, because under the assumptions of the model future U and gP^e are independent of today's gP. Any future period's U depends only on the contemporary values of U_n, gP, and gP^e, and not on today's gP. Any future period's expected inflation rate gP^e does not depend on today's gP, because gP supplies no new information on monetary authority's decision mechanism, or on the economy's structure (the shape of the SRPC), both of which are already perfectly known. Each period is independent; consequently, we do not need to subscript our variables by time.

Because Z depends on U, and U depends on gP^e, the policy-maker must calculate the public's gP^e. The public arrives at gP^e by a forecasting procedure which incorporates the same information on U_n which is available to the policy-maker, and the knowledge that gP will emerge from the policy-maker's minimization of Z. In other words, the public forms a rational expectation of gP by using the relevant theory. In contrast to Nordhaus' political business cycle theory, in which gP^e was formed adaptively by extrapolation, the policy-maker cannot take advantage of the public's having locked-in inflation-rate expectations.

If gP^e were given exogenously, and known to the policy-maker, the policymaker would simply choose the best (Z-minimizing) combination (U, gP) along the relevant SRPC. Instead, the public forms gP^e by forecasting the "best" (Z-minimizing) gP contingent on the information set of the policy-maker. In this sense, gP^e is "fixed" while the policy-maker chooses gP, but the public knows that in choosing gP^e.

(Nash) equilibrium policy

Equilibrium requires that

$$gP^* = gP^e$$

where gP^* is the chosen gP, that is, where gP^* minimizes Z given the information set. The equilibrium is a "Nash equilibrium" of the sort discussed in the economic theory of games: each side's choice is its best choice given the other side's choice. On one side of the monetary policy game, the policy maker chooses gP^* to minimize Z, given the gP^e chosen by the public. On the other side, the public, given that the policy-maker chooses gP^* according to the Z function, finds it optimal to choose the gP^e such that $gP^* = gP^e$. The public forms an expectation gP^e that it knows has the property that the monetary authority, facing that particular expectation, will choose to fulfill it. In brief, the public faces the authority with the inflation-rate expectation that gives the authority no incentive to produce a surprise.

We can solve for the public's choice of gP^e. Begin with the misery function

$$Z = (U - kU_n)^2 + b(gP)^2$$

Substitute for U from the Phillips equation

$$U = U_n - c(gP - gP^e)$$

yielding

$$Z = \{[U_n - c(gP - gP^e)] - kU_n\}^2 + b(gP)^2$$

Expanding the first squared expression, we have

$$Z = \{[(U_n) - c(gP - gP^e)]^2 - 2kU_n[U_n - c(gP - gP^e)] + (kU_n)^2\} + b(gP)^2$$

and expanding again

$$Z = (U_n)^2 - 2U_nc(gP - gP^e) + c^2(gP - gP^e)^2 \\ - 2kU_n[U_n - c(gP - gP^e) + (kU_n)^2] + b(gP)^2$$

Now, we maximize by setting the first derivative equal to zero.

$$0 = \frac{dZ}{dgP} = (-2U_nc + 2c^2gP - 2c^2gP^e + 2kU_nc) + 2bgP \\ = U_nc + c^2gP - c^2gP + kU_nc + bgP$$

Solving for gP

$$-bgP = -c(1 - k)U_n + c^2(gP - gP^e)$$

$$gP = \left(\frac{c}{b}\right)(1 - k)U_n - \left(\frac{c^2}{b}\right)(gP - gP^e)$$

Thus, the chosen inflation rate is

$$gP^* = \left(\frac{c}{b}\right)[-c(gP^* - gP^e) + (1 - k)U_n]$$

where $(gP^* - gPe)$ is the unexpected inflation. In equilibrium, unexpected inflation is zero, and we have

$$gP^* = gP^e = \left(\frac{c}{b}\right)(1 - k)U_n$$

where, to repeat,

c = sensitivity of U to unexpected gP, corresponding to the flatness of the SRPC

b = the misery coefficient on deviations of gP from zero

$(1 - k)U_n$ = the target U, below the natural rate

and the misery coefficient on squared deviations of U from target U has been normalized to one.

Where is this equilibrium value of the inflation rate? Given that b, c, $(1 - k)$, and U_n are all strictly positive, gP^* must be positive. As Barro and Gordon show,

$$gP^* = gP^e = 0$$

cannot be an equilibrium under discretion, even though it is the most preferred inflation rate on the LRPC. If expected inflation were zero, $gP^e = 0$, then positive inflation $gP > 0$ would reduce unemployment; this would present the policy-maker with a temptation to inflate. We can see this by noting that, under the assumed Z function, the marginal misery of inflation is zero when $gP = 0$, because

$$\frac{dZ}{dgP} = 2b(gP)$$

The marginal misery of unemployment (which is the marginal benefit of reducing unemployment),

$$\frac{dZ}{dU} = 2U - 2kU_n$$

is positive when $U = U_n$, given $k < 1$. Hence the marginal benefit of reducing unemployment exceeds the marginal misery of increasing inflation along the SRPC that faces the authority when $gP^e = 0$, and $gP = 0$ is not the best attainable point on the curve. Positive inflation would be chosen. Because $gP^e = 0$ is inconsistent with positive inflation being chosen, $gP^e = 0$ is not a rational expectation. Put another way, zero inflation is a "time-inconsistent" or "dynamically inconsistent" policy. The policymaker has an incentive to deviate from zero inflation when the public expects zero inflation. The time-consistent solution is the positive inflation rate solved for above. Given that zero inflation is the most preferred inflation rate on the LRPC, the time-consistent solution (a positive inflation rate on the LRPC) is suboptimal.

11
Monetary Rules

"Rules versus discretion for the central bank" has been the standard way of framing the debate over alternative monetary regimes since the 1930s, once it became clear that a discretionary regime was beginning to eclipse the rules of the gold standard. With the simultaneous rise of Keynesian economics, the pros and cons of discretion became identified with the pros and cons of "stabilizationist" or "counter-cyclical" monetary policy. Although the question of whether to have a central bank at all has been reopened since the mid-1970s (see Selgin and White (1994a), and chapters 12 and 13 in this book), proposals for fastening monetary policy rules onto the central bank continue to occupy center stage in debates over monetary reform.

Benefits and Burdens of Counter-cyclical Policy

In a "natural rate" economy, monetary policy is a potential source of deviations away from the natural rates of unemployment and output, conventionally shown as movements along the short-run Phillips curve (SRPC) and the short-run aggregate supply curve.[1] Such deviations are undesirable given that workers and producers want to make correctly informed decisions about job search and output, and prefer a less, to a more risky, macroeconomic environment. In such a world, what constructive role is there for monetary policy?

---

[1] The natural rates themselves can move for many reasons, such as shifts in the composition of the labor force, improvements in factor productivity, or raw material supply shocks.

The potential of counter-cyclical monetary policy does not lie in attempting to iron out *all* fluctuations of per capita real output around its historical trend. Monetary policy cannot usefully counteract swings due to technology or supply shocks that change the natural rate of output. The potential for monetary policy lies rather in avoiding the *component* of fluctuations that is attributable to monetary disequilibrium. In other words, the objective is not constancy of real output, but keeping the economy as close as possible to its natural rate of output. In a simple aggregate supply and demand framework, this means avoiding shifts in the aggregate demand curve, because aggregate demand shifts move the economy along the (upward sloping) short-run aggregate supply curve and, temporarily, off the long-run supply curve (which is vertical at the natural rate of output). When the economy is away from the natural rate of output, it is because agents are making misinformed decisions. The economy is regrettably discoordinated when real income is below, *or above*, its natural rate.

Viewing the task of monetary policy this way, and assuming that the sources of shifts in aggregate demand are variations in the quantity of money, M, or in the velocity of money V,[2] a successful counter-cyclical policy entails *offsetting changes in V with well-timed and correctly sized changes in M*. Activist monetary policy is a benefit on net if, and only if, it succeeds in this task.

Success is impossible if the economy rights itself faster than the monetary authority can ever respond to velocity shocks. Under strong-form rational expectations, the public anticipates any systematic monetary policy response to observable macroeconomic variables, and incorporates it into its pricing and output decisions, making monetary policy ineffective in stabilizing real income. Unanticipated policy can have a real effect, but its effect is not helpful: it only adds noise to the economy.

Success is not achieved in practice, even in conditions under which success is possible, if activist policy turns out to be cycle-amplifying, rather than cycle-dampening, because changes in money growth are poorly timed, or the wrong size. In the traditional monetarist diagnosis of typical central bank behavior, monetary policy moves are too often ill-timed, or ill-measured, because they act on the economy with a "long and variable lag." Forecasts of when a present change in monetary policy will begin to make an impact, and how far the economy will then be from its natural rate of output, are simply not good enough in the present state of knowledge. In too many cases, real output y has already returned, or nearly returned, to the

---

[2] When the "aggregate demand" curve is derived from the equation of exchange $MV = Py$ as the set of (P, y) pairs consistent with a given level of MV, then it is true, by construction, that the curve can only shift with a shift in M or a shift in V.

natural rate $y^\wedge$ by the time a positive boost arrives from higher money growth. The impact of policy is then to push y farther away from $y^\wedge$ rather than closer. To make things worse, the central bank tends, in practice, not to look ahead, i.e. to act in accordance even with the best forecasts available. Instead, it responds to political pressures to fight the current "number one evil" (Poole 1986).

Barro (1986) has pointed out another way in which discretion may be destabilizing: in contrast to the gold standard, discretionary fiat money regimes have contributed to real instability by "unanchoring" long-term price-level, and inflation rate, expectations. Changes in the expected inflation rate lead to changes in velocity, and thus create disturbances to aggregate demand.

In addition to arguments about the prospects for stabilization policy, a second strand of the traditional case for rules has come from concerns about the possible political (mal)incentives of monetary authorities. Public choice theorists identify discretion with the absence of a monetary constitution. Monetary authorities are free to pursue a political agenda, possibly seigniorage or political business cycles, contrary to the interests of the average citizen.

Since Kydland and Prescott (1977), the time-inconsistency problem has provided a third major strand to the case for rules. As we have seen, the Kydland–Prescott literature identifies discretion with the absence of a credible precommitment binding future monetary policy, leading to suboptimality in the form of excessive inflation. Unlike the traditional monetarist and public choice arguments, the suboptimality does not depend on the monetary authority's having too little information, or the wrong incentives.

Independence for the Central Bank

Before turning to specific monetary rules, we consider a distinct prescription addressed to some of the same concerns. Proposals for "an independent central bank" do not envision a monetary policy rule, but rather discretion vested in the hands of central bankers rather than elected officials. The basic motivation is to avoid the malincentive problem. Central bank officials are to be given greater insulation from control by elected officials, in the hope that this will better enable them to resist short-sighted demands for inflationary finance, election-year monetary stimulus, or artificially low interest rates. A non-partisan central bank, proponents hope, will pursue public-interest goals using scientifically favored techniques. The case for independence has been bolstered by comparative studies suggesting that countries with greater central-bank independence have experienced lower inflation rates.

While sharing the goal of low inflation, advocates of rules are some of the harshest critics of independence as a means. They argue that a central bank able to resist political demands is also able to resist public accountability for choosing the wrong goals, choosing the wrong techniques for attaining those goals, and using the techniques incompetently. Central bank officials are sometimes among the strongest advocates of independence. Critics fear that this is because the central bankers would find it comfortable to be answerable to no one.

Apart from whether it would be desirable, it is far from clear how much central bank independence from the legislative and executive branches is really possible. In the case of the Federal Reserve System, the President appoints its Governors. Congress created the agency, and can rewrite its mandate whenever it wishes, as it has, several times, over the years. To what extent can the Fed then afford to be unresponsive to pressures from Congress or the President?

Arguments for Rules

H. Geoffrey Brennan and James M. Buchanan (1981) define a "constitutional" monetary system as any regime that limits government's discretion regarding money, just as the First Amendment to the US Constitution limits the federal government's discretion regarding speech, press, and religion. Given such a broad definition, we then need to distinguish two very different sorts of constitutional regimes:

1 where a monetary authority is established with limited delegated powers prescribed in writing (this corresponds to the main body of the US Constitution), or otherwise generally understood, and binding, and
2 where government plays no monetary role, so that the provision of money is left to private enterprises bound by contract law (this corresponds to the First Amendment's injunction that "Congress shall make no law regarding . . .").

Both regimes impose limits on government, but very different sorts of limits.

Correspondingly, there are three basic schools of thought on the question of a monetary constitution.

1 The *discretionary central banking* school favors discretion or activism, and opposes the attempt to hem in the central bank with prescribed rules. In nineteenth-century Britain, the Banking School

opposed the limits on Bank of England note issue prescribed by Peel's Acts, though they favored the gold standard as a natural contractual constraint. In the twentieth century, the Keynesians have been the chief proponents of discretion.

2 The *constitutional central banking* school advises that the central bank should follow a specific formula. The nineteenth-century Currency School favored a 100 percent marginal reserve requirement on Bank of England notes. In the twentieth century, Monetarists, led by Milton Friedman, have offered much-discussed money supply formulas (considered below).

3 The "free banking" or *free market money* school favors decentralized and competitive money supply over central banking of either sort, and favors removing government from the monetary system. The nineteenth-century Free Banking School favored an end to Bank of England monopoly in London, and opposed the extension of Bank of England powers in the 1844 Act. In the twentieth century, the school was largely dormant until 1976 when F. A. Hayek's *Denationalisation of Money* (1990) was first published.

Before Friedman, Henry Simons (1936) had offered the classic case for rules. Simons made the preference for rules over discretion part of the "classical liberal" ideology, akin to the preference for "the rule of law" over arbitrary rule by authorities. Discretion creates uncertainty about, and subservience to, the whims of rulers. Simons declared that the ideal rule was to freeze M1, an ideal to which Friedman nearly returned. As a means to that end, Simons favored the "Chicago plan" banking reform which would make reserve requirements 100 percent. (Otherwise, M1 would vary as the currency-deposit ratio varies.) Freezing the money stock is a simple and clear rule, and would bring about a mild deflation as real income grows. Unfortunately, Simons noted, it does not accommodate changes in velocity that would cause the price level to vary. Its enforceability was in question because the 100 percent reserve requirement on demand deposits would encourage growth of near-monies. As a second-best short-term proposal, Simons favored a rule to stabilize the consumer price level.

Friedman's Proposals

Milton Friedman (1960, 1968) offered the "*k* percent rule" as part of a "framework for monetary stability." He doubted that the market by itself could provide a stable monetary framework, because he thought that US history showed fraud and overissue to be the typical outcome of free banking. Later, in light of evidence to the contrary, he reconsidered this view (Friedman and Schwartz 1986), and came closer to a "free banking school" viewpoint. In Friedman's (1960) view, it was up to the government to control the money stock M, by preventing counterfeiting, fraud, and bank runs that would over-expand or over-contract M.

Friedman's principal objection to having the gold standard play these roles, rather than a system of rule-bound fiat money, was the resource costs of the gold standard (as discussed in chapter 2). He added that an international gold standard (or any fixed exchange rate regime) makes the domestic money stock subservient to the balance of payments. For a country with a large international trade sector, fixed exchange rates might be worth it, but for a country like the USA, he considered it undesirable to make the domestic sector (then 95 percent of GNP) adjust to shocks in the international sector (5 percent). Fiat money, and floating exchange rates, allow an independent national monetary policy, which can, in principle, be devoted to pursuing a more stable money growth path than a gold standard would produce. (In practice, it has not turned out that way.) Floating rates also eliminate the chief rationale for harmful exchange controls and trade quotas, that they are needed to safeguard the nation's reserves.

In his 1968 Presidential address to the American Economic Association, Friedman elaborated his view of the benefits of rules over discretion. Because real variables tend toward their "natural rates," monetary policy cannot control real variables; it can only disturb them in the short run. The real interest rate can be disturbed through the liquidity effect, but is independent of monetary policy in the long run. The unemployment rate can be disturbed by surprise inflation, but the long-run Phillips curve (LRPC) is vertical at the natural rate of unemployment (this was not yet a widely accepted idea in 1968). The aggregate supply curve of real output is, likewise, vertical at the natural rate of output. In such a "natural rate" world, monetary policy is ultimately limited to controlling some nominal variable, such as the nominal money stock M, the price level P, the level of nominal income Y, or the nominal exchange rate. Unanticipated policy can disturb real variables away from their natural levels, but it is best to avoid such disturbances. The proper goals for monetary policy are, therefore, to provide a stable nominal anchor, and to avoid being itself a source of disturbances. Monetary policy should not try to offset changes in real money demand where the central bank cannot be sure of doing more good than harm (in light of the problem of long and variable lags).

The harm-minimizing proposal Friedman offered in 1960 was the "k percent rule": make some monetary aggregate (either H, M1, or M2) grow at the rate of k percent per year, where k is constant, month in and month out. The choice of which M to target is to be decided by which has the most stable velocity V, so that nominal income MV is relatively stable. Circa 1960, this criterion favored M2. The numerical value of k is to be chosen for its consistency with zero secular inflation. In terms of the dynamic equation of exchange,

$$gM + gV = gP + gy$$

Friedman's proposal involves solving (once and for all) for gM, having plugged in $gP = 0$ and appropriate long-run values for gV and gy. Looking back from 1960, Friedman found that gV was about -1 percent per year, and gy was about 3 percent. Together, these values indicated setting $gM = k$ at 4 percent per year.

Friedman rejected a price-level rule on the grounds that the link from ΔM to ΔP is too loose, the lags long and variable. An attempt to home in on P by trial and error may be destabilizing, i.e. involve over-shooting or endless oscillation.[3]

To supplement the k percent rule, Friedman offered measures to make M growth easier to control. Recalling the money-multiplier formula that $M = H(M/H)$, these measures were designed either to tighten the Federal Reserve's control over the monetary base H, or to reduce variability in the money multiplier M/H. In 1960, the vestiges of the gold standard remaining under the Bretton Woods system – the fact that foreign central banks could redeem dollars for gold – meant that the monetary base could be altered by foreign central bank redemptions. Friedman advocated severing this link between H and the gold stock (which was later done by President Nixon in 1971). The monetary base could also be altered at the initiative of domestic commercial banks, if the Fed felt compelled to honor their requests to borrow H from the Fed when the banks were otherwise unable to meet their reserve requirements. Friedman advocated eliminating discount-window lending of H, and instead imposing fines for reserve shortfalls. (This advice has not yet been adopted.)

To eliminate variability in M/H, Friedman, like Simons, suggested imposing 100 percent reserve requirements on all bank-issued components of the target aggregate. So that 100 percent reserves would not be onerous to banks, competitive interest is to be paid on commercial banks' reserve deposits on the Fed's books. Even if the 100 percent reserve requirement is not adopted, paying competitive interest on deposits at the Fed is advisable, because it would reduce the sensitivity of reserve ratios to market interest rates. (This proposal has not been adopted, presumably because

[3] For a specific price-level-stabilization rule that, its proponent argues, would not suffer from the over-shooting problem, see McCulloch (1991).

the Treasury and Fed would lose the income gained by the banks.) If 100 percent reserves are politically infeasible, Friedman advised at least making ratios uniform across all components of M2, so that shifts among accounts (e.g. from savings to checking) do not change the money multiplier. He also advised fixing the ratios permanently, so that the Fed, in its regulatory or revenue-gathering roles, does not interfere with its own monetary targeting.

Twenty-five years later, Friedman's (1987) prescription had evolved somewhat. His views on monetary theory and practice had not changed, and the goals remained the same: monetary policy should avoid being a source of disturbance, and should provide a stable nominal anchor. The specific proposals, however, had changed due to "public choice" considerations: a greater cynicism, if you like, nurtured by two-and-a-half decades of watching the Fed resist his and other proposals for monetary targeting. While Friedman still believed it would be desirable to stabilize the M whose V is empirically most stable, which points toward a relatively wide aggregate like M2, he noted that the Fed had been able to plead inability to hit M targets, and thus to avoid accountability. The best target for the sake of accountability is the narrowest: the monetary base. In light of the Fed's tendency to resist, or subvert, any restraint on its discretion, Friedman now viewed the generalized k percent rule as a "half-measure" because it leaves the Fed bureaucracy intact. With enforceability a leading concern, he now promoted a monetary base freeze as the "best real cure" for the instability of discretionary monetary policy.

Freezing the monetary base, H, eliminates the variability in money growth at the source. Moreover, it allows elimination of the Fed itself, hence banishes from the tent the "camel's nose" pushing for discretion. Without a positive growth path for any monetary aggregate to pursue, the Fed's Open Market Committee and bond traders could be released to seek employment elsewhere. The Fed's bank-regulatory and clearinghouse roles could also be eliminated, or transferred elsewhere. Reserve requirements, no longer needed for M targeting, could be phased out. Friedman suggested that commercial banks could again be allowed to issue currency. Though he did not say why this is desirable, it would buttress the H freeze, because it would allow banks to meet public shifts from deposits into currency without losing reserves of high-powered money (hence without contracting M). Thus, Friedman's later proposals moved him very close to, perhaps even into, the free-market money camp.

As Simons had, Friedman noted favorably that a base freeze would allow for a mild price deflation if real economic growth outruns innovations in the payment system that reduce demand for base money. For optimum-quantity-of-money reasons, a rising purchasing power of the dollar is beneficial to the base-money-holding public.

McCallum's Case for a Feedback Rule

Bennett McCallum (1989, pp. 336–51) has pointed out that activism (a regime in which the money growth rate responds to state of the economy) is not synonymous with discretion. Activism can be carried out according to a non-discretionary, pre-specified rule that holds at all times. It may then be possible to combine at least some of the potential stabilizing advantages of activism with the time-consistency advantages of rules. McCallum argues for a rule with feedback that would arguably avoid secular inflation more surely than a no-feedback k percent rule, and would also dampen price-level movements in the face of velocity and real income shocks. Given the lack of professional consensus on the macroeconomic "transmission mechanism," McCallum's objective is a modest feedback rule that "works" in the context of all the leading macro models: "a sensible monetary strategy would aim for a zero inflation rate on average and would not attempt to be highly ambitious with regard to its effect on cyclical variation of real variables. Most important . . . is the avoidance of abrupt changes in conditions due to monetary policy itself."

In Friedman's k percent rule for money growth, the value of k is set once for all time, with the hope that it will be consistent with zero inflation. Whether zero inflation actually obtains depends on whether the growth rate of velocity gV, and the growth rate of real income gy, turn out as expected. However, gV is hard to predict, in part because technical progress in the payments system occurs at seemingly random intervals. "Velocity drift" can drive the inflation rate away from zero. We have seen that Friedman assumed, by simple extrapolation of trend, gV of -1 percent and gy of 3 percent, and so recommended gM of 4 percent. McCallum notes that in fact, over the period 1954–1986, the realized value of gV was 2.5 percent per annum. Given realized gV was 2.5 percent, setting gM at 4 percent would have produced inflation gP of 3.5 percent, rather far from the zero inflation hoped for.[4]

McCallum proposes alternative rules with feedback to avoid the persistence of such prediction errors. Consider first a rule that, in contrast to the simple k percent rule, adjusts annual gM in response to changes in gV. The rule is formulated in terms of the M that the Fed directly controls, the mon-

---

[4] The rise in velocity, however, was not independent of the fact that the k percent rule was not followed. The main reason velocity rose over the period in question was that expected and actual inflation rose, and the main reason inflation rose was that money growth rose much higher than 4 percent per year. If money growth had been held to 4 percent per year, velocity would have risen less. The inflation rate may have missed zero, but it would have missed by less than 3.5 percentage points.

etary base, so the relevant V is the velocity of the monetary base. For this rule, we accept the assumption that gy is 3 percent, a value that McCallum notes has, in fact, obtained over almost all 20-year intervals (not counting World Wars or the Great Depression). Recalling again the dynamic equation of exchange

$$gM + gV = gP + gy$$

zero inflation ($gP = 0$) implies $gM + gV = 3\%$. The rule accordingly specifies

$$gM = 3\% - gV$$

where gV is the average over the previous four years (a period long enough to span the typical business cycle). Under this rule, nominal GNP will grow at 3 percent per year on average, even if velocity drifts, and inflation will be zero so long as real income growth gy is 3 percent.

McCallum also offers a slightly more complicated rule to deal with cyclical changes in gy. He reasons: "It seems likely . . . that cyclical fluctuations in real output and employment would be kept small if fluctuations in nominal GNP were minimized." Where Py denotes the natural log of nominal GNP and Py^* the "target" value of Py for the most recently observed period, the modified rule is

$$gM = 3\% - gV + .25(Py^* - Py)$$

Growth in the monetary base would be augmented when GNP is below path, and diminished when GNP is above path. The parameter value of .25 (which says that if nominal GNP is 1 percent below path, the central bank steps up money growth by one-fourth of one percentage point) was chosen to be small enough to avoid the problem of over-reaction that had concerned Friedman. McCallum reports that his simulation studies, nesting the policy rule in a variety of macro models, indicate robustly that following the rule would have yielded a more stable Py than the money growth path the Fed actually followed.

If McCallum's rule is a no-lose improvement over actual Fed policy, why has it not been adopted? The bureaucratic perspective, discussed in chapter 8, suggests that the Fed's officials will resist the imposition of rules because they value the prestige and importance that comes with discretion. There is no organized interest on behalf of imposing a rule. The subject of monetary policy rules is esoteric to the public, and to Congress. McCallum notes that post-Bretton Woods experience has not been so traumatic: although inflation did hit double digits, neither a Great Depression nor a hyperinflation has occurred in most countries. Central bankers in many countries have exercised their discretion to bring inflation down from double digits to a range of 3–4 percent, and now speak of their resolve to maintain "price stability." Under those circumstances, the public is unlikely to agitate for a major institutional experiment.

Simple Versus Complicated Rules

Friedman's proposal for freezing the monetary base, and abolishing the Fed, chooses a radical solution to the enforcement problem. Any rule allowing the central bank to remain in business must be enforced against a real-life agency staffed by experts in the field who naturally prefer to have the discretion to use their expertise. To survive, a rule must be resistant to amendment by a legislature that might defer to the central bank's expertise.[5] To be effective,

1 the rule must explicitly prescribe the central bank's operating routine in terms of variables and actions that outsiders can readily monitor,
2 someone must actually do the monitoring to detect any central bank departures from the rule, innocent or not, and
3 some disciplinary mechanism must penalize departures from the rule.

For example, there might be automatic dismissal for officials if performance within a specified range is not achieved; or cash bonuses only if targets are hit. It is difficult to find historical precedent for such a system of operating rules, monitoring, and penalties or incentives being applied to any government agency in any nation.

A cynic will note that the central bank itself has an incentive to make monitoring more costly for its would-be monitors. It can try to rationalize apparent deviations from the rule as really only matters of incorrect measurement, distortion in the aggregate being measured, or an emergency (if the rule has an emergency escape hatch). Monitoring, either by Congress or the public, is more difficult the more complex the rule. Serious concern for the monitoring and enforcement problems therefore favors a monetary aggregate rule over a price-level rule (P is harder to measure unambiguously). Within the set of monetary rules, it favors a no-feedback rule over a feedback rule, zero growth over positive growth, and a monetary base rule over

---

[5] Timberlake (1985) examines the legislative history of the Depository Institutions Deregulation and Monetary Control Act of 1980, and finds that Congress accepted, at face value, the Federal Reserve's most dubious claims of a need for expanded Fed powers.

an M1 or M2 rule. The monetary base can be prescribed tightly because the central bank controls it directly; a broader aggregate must be allowed to vary within a broader band because the money multiplier varies outside of central bank control. The base can be measured unambiguously on the central bank's balance sheet, whereas what should be included in M1 or M2 is subject to change with market innovations.

Thus the strong suit of the monetary base freeze is that it is the most *enforceable* of rules. It is the only rule that really is like a constitutional prescription of what government shall *not* do: it prescribes that the government shall not expand the sum of its fiat money. The base freeze requires no agency to administer it, hence avoids the "camel's nose under the tent" problem of having in place an agency that has an inherent interest in lobbying for greater discretion. The durability of the rule (were it to be adopted) matters, because a more durable rule will deliver more of the benefits of precommitment. If a rule is not expected to survive for long, then it will not reduce uncertainty about long-term inflation. A durable rule, by contrast, will reduce inflation uncertainty (as we have noted the gold standard did) and, thereby, reduce the resource costs devoted to filling the demand for inflation hedges. If the enforceability issue is paramount, the logic of banning the camel's nose from the tent can be taken even further. If even the frozen authorized issue is a dangerous precedent, this would suggest that the most durable rule removes money from government's hands entirely.

Questions

1 How might rules that *prevent* the central bank from pursuing counter-cyclical monetary policy actually promote *greater* cyclical stability?

2 How does the time-inconsistency argument for rules, as articulated by Kydland and Prescott, differ from the traditional monetarist argument offered by Milton Friedman?

3 Would freezing the monetary base mean greater, or lesser, volatility of interest rates?

4 "Monetary policy can be quite effective in controlling the price level, but not in increasing the average level of output or, in practice, reducing the size of variations in real output. Monetary policy should therefore concentrate exclusively on the task of keeping the price level stable."

    (a) Explain the reasoning behind the first sentence.

    (b) Does that reasoning actually support a price-level rule, as suggested by the second sentence? Does it support any other policy prescriptions just as much?

12

Competitive Supply of Fiat-type Money

F. A. Hayek's much-discussed monograph on the "denationalization of money" (Hayek 1990) predicted that, in the absence of legal barriers, the market economy would deliver a stable system of competing private irredeemable currencies. Currency issuers would compete for customers by promising stable purchasing power in terms of some basket of commodities. A vigilant financial press would help to enforce competitive discipline such that issuers would find it worthwhile to uphold their promises. If a currency's value was not as promised, Hayek's argument went, it would lose so many customers that the issuer would want to correct the situation quickly.

A distinguishing characteristic of the Hayekian regime is that it relies on mere *promises*. Reliance on enforceable *contractual guarantees* of purchasing power would be tantamount to a regime of redeemability, and a commodity (or multi-commodity) standard.

A weakness of Hayek's discussion, in light of the general problem of "time-inconsistency" identified by Kydland and Prescott (1977), is its failure to show that the issuer will not want to break its promise of stable purchasing power. The profitability of staying in business may not outweigh the profitability of spending into circulation larger sums of money than are consistent with keeping the promise. Guillermo Calvo (1978) and Bart Taub (1985) show, indeed, that overissue in the extreme (a hyperinflationary burst) can be profit-maximizing for issuers of irredeemable or fiat-type money. In their models, the one-shot gain from hyperinflation exceeds the present value of the stream of returns from any sustained lower path of issues. Aware that a profit-maximizing issuer would want to hyperinflate, agents with rational expectations will not want to hold a fiat-type money unless the issuer can enforceably precommit to a specified path for the quantity of its issues at all future dates.

In light of these results, the feasibility of private fiat-type money is doubtful. We cannot appeal to historical experience to reassure us that private issuers have solved the time-inconsistency problem with fiat-type money. All known private monies have been either full-bodied commodity monies (e.g. gold coins), or redeemable monies (e.g. gold-redeemable banknotes or dollar-redeemable deposits). Hayek's prediction that commodity money, and redemption contracts, would be dominated by fiat-type money in a competitive market is therefore not persuasive, without a theoretical resolution of the time-inconsistency problem facing private issuers of irredeemable money.

Even before Hayek wrote, Benjamin Klein had examined the feasibility, and efficiency, of the competitive supply of fiat money. Klein (1974, p. 424) addressed in particular "the possibility that firms may 'deceive' their customers by supplying more money than is anticipated." In summarizing his results, Klein claimed to have found feasibility even without contractual precommitment to a quantity path: "it is shown that if consumers and producers make the same estimate of the short-run profits from a policy of deception, then the equilibrium quantity of brand-name capital will insure that firms will not excessively overissue." Thus Klein's concept of "brand name capital" appeared to solve the time-inconsistency problem, at least in the context of Klein's model.

Taub (1985, p. 195), in reporting his contrary finding of non-feasibility, noted two differences between his and Klein's models. Klein had simply assumed a money demand function, and had imposed a particular form of non-rational expectations. Taub derived money demand from an overlapping-generations model, and imposed rational expectations.[1] It might be thought from Taub's discussion that Klein's feasibility result was perfectly valid, given Klein's assumptions. The question of which model, and which result, to "believe" would then simply depend on which assumptions were preferred.

A closer examination of Klein's model shows that, in fact, feasibility does not obtain, in the absence of perfect foresight. The concept of "brand name capital" does not solve the time-inconsistency problem in the case of fiat money. Even under Klein's assumptions, a private fiat money issuer would find it profit-maximizing to hyperinflate.

Klein's Model with Perfect Foresight

Klein proposes to examine the competitive supply of fiat money under perfect and imperfect foresight. Money is issued in distinct brands, with vari-

---

[1] John Bryant (1981), in a neglected paper, found that competitive provision of fiat money was either infeasible or inefficient. He also cited Klein, and implicitly contrasted Klein's model with his own overlapping-generations model.

ables for "brand j" money (issued by the jth firm in the industry) denoted by a subscript j. Under perfect foresight, all changes in the purchasing power of a currency are anticipated. The rising marginal cost of producing real balances of brand-j money (which here can be interpreted as the cost of endowing the money with greater transactions-facilitating properties) limits the profit-maximizing quantity of *real* balances produced, $(M/P)_j$. In profit-maximizing competitive equilibrium, where marginal cost equals price, the marginal cost of producing real balances equals the "rental price" obtained by the firm on its money. The equilibrium condition is

$$i_j - i_{M_j} = \text{MC}_j \tag{12.1}$$

where

i_j = the nominal interest rate on bonds denominated in money j
i_{M_j} = the nominal interest rate paid on balances of brand-j money
MC_j = the marginal cost of producing real balances of brand-j money

The left-hand side of equation (12.1), the difference between the two interest rates, can be considered the "rental price" of brand-j money: it indicates the yield differential (opportunity cost) consumers are willing to bear to hold brand-j money balances rather than bonds. (This equation is Klein's equation [5], with simplified notation.)

In Klein's theory, real money balances are not generally assumed to be costless to produce, because money has to be endowed with the capacity to render transactions-facilitating services. The real resource cost to firm j of producing real balances is an increasing function of the quantity of real balances produced (marginal costs MC_j are rising) in the area of the firm's chosen output. In the limiting case, where the MC of creating real balances *is* zero, the competitive outcome implies $i = i_M$, which is the "optimal quantity" of money outcome discussed in chapter 5.

We have already seen an equilibrium condition very much like equation (12.1), namely the equi-marginal condition for a competitive issuer of redeemable deposits (see chapter 3),

$$i_L - i_D = C_L + C_D + Q_D$$

The sum $(C_L + C_D)$, the marginal cost of intermediating loans into deposits, is the equivalent of MC_j, the cost of "producing money balances." In the case of irredeemable money, the marginal liquidity cost of bank liabilities Q_D is zero.

The total *nominal* balances produced of brand-j money, M_j, and the price level measured in j-money units, P_j, are individually indeterminate, but they are also of no consequence. The issuer's choice of the nominal unit in which to measure money j is akin to a soft-drink bottler's choice of whether to measure his output in liters or fluid ounces. Real price and quantity are independent of that decision.

The rate of monetary expansion gM_j and the inflation rate gP_j are likewise indeterminate and inconsequential *under perfect foresight*. For the public to hold money j, under perfect foresight and perfect competition, the potential impact of any anticipated inflation would have to be neutralized by an explicit interest yield i_{Mj} that fully compensates for future depreciation of money j's purchasing power. Rearranging equation (12.1),

$$i_{Mj} = i_j - MC_j$$

Assuming the Fisher effect to hold at every moment, and recalling that, under perfect foresight, the anticipated inflation rate equals the actual inflation rate, the nominal interest rate on money-j-denominated bonds equals the real rate of interest r plus the actual (and anticipated) inflation rate

$$i_j = r + gP_j$$

Given that the quantity of real balances $(M/P)_j$ does not change, the inflation rate equals the nominal money growth rate

$$gP_j = gM_j$$

Thus, by substitution

$$i_{Mj} = r - MC_j + gM_j \tag{12.2}$$

Equation (12.2) says that the explicit yield on money j must equal the real rate of interest minus the marginal cost of producing real money balances, plus full compensation for any (perfectly anticipated) dilution of the purchasing power of money j via money growth (Klein 1974, p. 427, n. 5). Essentially, any newly printed units of money j must be distributed to the holders of existing units, in proportion to their existing holdings, leaving holders indifferent to the printing up of new units. There is no profit to the firm from expanding the nominal money stock under this condition, and no loss either, given that real cost is a function only of real magnitudes (it is costless to add zeros to the currency).

This perfect-foresight analysis shows that the determinacy of real balances is what matters, and shows that hyperinflation is not the issuer's dominant strategy. It thereby counters the predictions of economists (Pesek, Friedman) who had argued that laissez-faire in fiat-type money must lead to an infinite price level. Those authors had discussed open competition in fiat money production as though it meant that open counterfeiting were permitted. Without *distinguishable* brands of money, as Klein points out, competition would, of course, drive the quality of private fiat-type monies to zero. "Competition" without distinguishable brands would drive to zero the quality of *any* good whose quality is not detectable at the point of sale. (If all producers could counterfeit identical Coca-Cola cans, the profit-maximizing strategy would be, to them all, to put water, rather than cola, in Coca-Cola cans.) But that does not show infeasibility where distinguishable brands are permitted.

Time-inconsistency problems do not arise in Klein's perfect foresight case, because promise-breaking, or deception, is ruled out by assumption. A perfectly foreseen would-be overissuer would never have any customers. A firm cannot decide, in the future, to deviate from an announced policy, because perfect foresight, in effect, collapses the future into the present.

Klein's Model with "Imperfect Foresight"

To analyze potential problems of time-inconsistency or deception, Klein moves on to an imperfect foresight case of a particular sort. This section will reconstruct his analysis. The next section will criticize it.

Klein now assumes that consumers do not know gP_j perfectly, but must form an estimate gP^*_j.[2] Under perfect foresight, as we saw in equation (12.2), higher rates of nominal money growth, and inflation, must be offset by a higher explicit interest yield i_{M_j}. Under imperfect foresight, consumers must likewise be compensated for higher anticipated inflation gP^*_j. In addition, to forestall deception, an issuer can and must offset a greater degree of misbehavior – larger discrepancies between anticipated and actual money growth – by a higher explicit interest yield. In equilibrium, high-confidence (low-discrepancy) monies will command a premium in the form of a higher "rental price," $i_j - i_{M_j}$.

Competitive equilibrium on the supply side implies that a higher-confidence money, earning for its producer a higher rental, will be produced at a higher marginal cost. The marginal cost of producing real balances of money j now has two components, combined in optimal fashion: the cost of providing greater transactions services, and the cost of increasing confidence.

---

[2] Klein (1974, p. 437) states that "in equilibrium the prior probability expected rate of price change distribution will have a variance," but the stochastic structure is never specified. The variance of the inflation rate plays no explicit role in the model.

The present value of the firm's rental stream, attributable to the public's confidence in its money, is the firm's "brand name capital," denoted β_j. Embroidering on Klein's discussion, the size of j can be represented as follows. If the firm owns assets earning i_j, and issues money paying i_{M_j} as its liability, its real income net of interest payments, π/P_j, is

$$\frac{\pi}{P_j} = (i_j - i_{M_j}) \left(\frac{M}{P}\right)_j \qquad (12.3)$$

To simplify, assume that the cost of providing services (but not the cost of generating confidence) is zero. In other words, assume that the cost of generating confidence is the only cost to finding people to hold the money. Then, the entire net income can be considered a stream of returns to the brand-name-capital asset β_j. Assuming β_j to be infinitely lived, and costlessly maintained, the present value of this infinite income stream is

$$\beta_j = \frac{(i_j - i_{M_j}) \left(\frac{M}{P}\right)_j}{r} \qquad (12.4)$$

(This is Klein's equation [6].) That is, the value of β_j is the capital value on which the stream of real income $(i_j - i_{M_j})(M/P)_j$ represents a normal rate of return.

To interpret this result, consider two extreme cases.

1   If confidence were also costless to produce, then, in competitive equilibrium, the value of β_j would have to equal zero. Intuitively, as confidence becomes unlimited, the value of confidence capital goes to zero, because confidence ceases to be scarce.[3] In this case

$$i_j - i_{M_j} = 0$$

or

$$i_j = i_{M_j}$$

There is no difference between the rate of return on bonds, and the rate of return on money. The outcome is the "optimum quantity of money" produced competitively: because the marginal cost of pro-

[3] Klein (1974, p. 435) notes that "if confidence were completely costless to produce, the value of the jth firm's brand-name capital . . . would vanish." That is, β_j goes to zero as confidence becomes non-scarce. Earlier, Klein (p. 425) had incorrectly suggested that β_j goes to infinity.

ducing real balances (by intermediating bonds into money) is zero in all respects, the opportunity cost of holding money (rather than bonds) is driven to zero.[4]

2   If, for some reason, the real interest payments on money are zero, so that nominal interest on money just equals the inflation rate

$$i_{Mj} = gP_j$$

then recalling from the Fisher equation that, in equilibrium,

$$i_j = r + gP_j$$

we get by substitution into equation (12.4) above that

$$\beta_j = \frac{[r + gP_j - gP_j]\left(\dfrac{M}{P}\right)_j}{r}$$
$$= \left(\frac{M}{P}\right)_j$$

Firm j's brand-name capital exactly equals the real quantity of its money in circulation. The stock of j-money corresponds to net wealth for its issuer, because it is a zero-interest, zero-maintenance cost "liability" that finances the ownership of financial assets.

Is the Equilibrium Rate of Inflation Bounded under Imperfect Foresight?

With foresight imperfect, the rate of monetary expansion can be higher than the public expects. The money issuer can adopt a time-inconsistent policy, or practice what Klein calls "deception." The profitability of staying in business must now be compared to the profitability of unbounded money growth. If the costs of producing nominal money balances are zero, and the anticipated inflation rate is systematically below the contemporaneous rate of money growth, then the profit-maximizing rate of monetary expansion would be infinite.[5] Infinite expansion of money j at a moment in time would mean

---

[4] Wallace (1983) derives a similar result. Klein, like Wallace, entirely begs the question of how explicit interest could be conveniently paid on currency. On the consequences of a significant cost of delivering interest on currency, see White (1987) and White and Boudreaux (1998).

[5] For a simple illustration of this point, see the rays in figures 7.5 and 7.6, showing seigniorage for an issuer facing fixed inflation expectations.

a one-shot confiscation of wealth from anyone who accepts money j. If potential acceptors of j-brand money recognized this outcome, however, they would refuse to accept money j, and $(M/P)_j$ would never become positive.

Klein argues that the hyperinflationary outcome is not inevitable, because there may exist a stable equilibrium where the issuer's temptation to deceive is curbed by the profit stream available from non-deception. In re-examining Klein's model, however, we will find that such an equilibrium is not globally profit-maximizing.

Klein (1974, p. 436, eq. 7) incorporates imperfect foresight by revising the equation for the jth issuer's real profit flow (equation 12.3 above) in basically the following way. The anticipated rate of inflation of the jth money, gP_j^*, is assumed to be incorporated in the nominal interest rate i_j, but not in the (pre-announced) interest yield on the jth money, i_{M_j}. Then, holders of the jth money will demand $gP_j^*(M/P)_j$ in rebates, as compensation for anticipated inflation of gP_j^*. Again, abstracting from the costs of producing transaction services and confidence,[6] the issuer's real profit becomes

$$\frac{\pi}{P_j} = (i_j - i_{M_j})\left(\frac{M}{P}\right)_j + gM_j\left(\frac{M}{P}\right)_j - gP_j^*\left(\frac{M}{P}\right)_j \tag{12.5}$$

where

$$\frac{\pi}{P_j} \qquad = \text{real profit}$$

$$(i_j - i_{M_j})\left(\frac{M}{P}\right)_j \quad = \text{net real interest income}$$

$$gM_j\left(\frac{M}{P}\right)_j \qquad = \text{gross real revenue from issuing new money, before rebates}$$

$$gP_j^*\left(\frac{M}{P}\right)_j \qquad = \text{the portion of new money that must be rebated to holders of existing } j\text{-brand money in order to compensate them fully for anticipated inflation, i.e. in order to keep real demand and thus } (M/P)_j \text{ from shrinking.}$$

To examine whether it is feasible that the profit-maximizing rate of monetary expansion is finite, we examine the implications of meeting the first-order (equi-marginal) conditions. The marginal profit of monetary expansion is:

---

[6] To incorporate these costs of producing real balances would mean adding a constant to equation (12.5). The marginal profit from nominal money growth (equation 12.6) would not be affected.

$$\frac{d\left(\frac{\pi}{P}\right)_j}{dgM_j} = \left(\frac{M}{P}\right)_j \left[d\left(\frac{i_j - iM_j}{dgM_j}\right) + 1 - \frac{dgP_j^*}{dgM_j} \right] \qquad (12.6)$$

where

$\dfrac{d(i_j - i_{M_j})}{dgM_j}$ = is the fall in rental price resulting from unanticipated inflation; hereafter we denote this term by u

$\dfrac{dgP_j^*}{dgM_j}$ = the degree to which current inflation rate expectations adjust to current money growth, hereafter denoted v

Klein appears to regard dgP_j^*/dgM_j as a constant. Implicitly, then, he assumes that inflation-rate expectations are determined by an equation of the form

$$gP_j^* = u + vgM_j \qquad (12.7)$$

Perfect foresight is represented by $v = 1$; imperfect foresight by $v < 1$.

Klein (1974, p. 436) notes that if the issuing firm can hold $(i_j - i_{M_j})$ constant as gM varies, so that $u = 0$, and, if expectations adjust less than fully, so that $v < 1$, then the marginal profit of monetary expansion "is always positive, and therefore the firm can make its current profit rate as large as it wants by merely making gM_j arbitrarily large ... The profit-maximizing rate of increase of money is therefore infinite." [7] Using our notation, if $u = 0$ and $v < 1$, then the marginal profit from faster monetary expansion is always positive ($u + 1 - v > 0$), and the firm is driven to inflate without limit. The issuer need not rebate all newly issued money to existing money-holders, but can keep and spend a share of it, $(1 - v)gM$. A higher rate of monetary expansion gM is then always more profitable, because the value of the non-rebated share $(1 - v)gM$ is larger.

Klein (1974, pp. 436–7) then denies that this outcome will actually obtain:

[7] Klein (1974, p. 436) refers to the case of $v < 1$ as a case where "there are lags in the adjustment of anticipations," but talk of "lags" is not appropriate in a one-period model. The adjustment of expectations is partial, but it is contemporaneous and not lagged, as Klein (p. 437 n. 17) elsewhere notes. For the same reason, it is not strictly correct for Taub (1985, p. 195) to speak of Klein's using "adaptive expectations." The expectations in question are not even really forward-looking. The distinction between Klein's two cases is not really perfect versus imperfect *foresight*; it is more a matter of perfect versus (supposedly) imperfect *perception* of *contemporaneous* money growth. We retain the terminology of foresight and anticipations, for convenience.

However, this argument assumes that the money firm's brand-name capital is
constant and so fails to consider the effect on consumer confidence and the
firm's demand from the policy of "deceiving" customers. . . . The higher the
actual rate [of monetary expansion] compared to the anticipated rate . . . the
lower will be consumer confidence. As β_j falls . . . $[i_j - i_{Mj}]$ must also fall to
keep [demand] constant. . . . Consumers can (and will) control $[d(i_j - i_{Mj})/$
$dgM_j]$ to prevent an infinite rate of growth of money.

He concludes (p. 438) that, as long as consumers do not underestimate the
short-run gain from deception, and make u too small in absolute value,
"wealth-maximizing firms will not inflate at an infinite rate."

Klein argues, in other words, that hyperinflation will not be profit-
maximizing, once we take into account the fact that money growth reduces
consumer confidence and, thus, reduces the rental price firm j can earn
on its money, i.e. once we drop the assumption that u is zero.

For maximum profit to occur at a finite monetary expansion rate, we
need

$$0 = (u + 1 - v)\left(\frac{M}{P}\right)_j$$

which implies

$$u = v - 1$$

and if $v < 1$, this requires $u < 0$.

Klein provides the first-order condition for maximum profit at a finite
inflation rate. He does not, however, inquire whether a local maximum, at
which the first-order conditions are met, is also a global maximum. We
return to the jth firm's profit function (equation 12.5). Because $[gM_j - gP_j^*]$
is directly proportional to gM_j, and the firm acts to keep $(M/P)_j$ constant, the
product

$$(gM_j - gP_j^*)\left(\frac{M}{P}\right)_j$$

(the sum of the second and third RHS terms in equation 12.5) grows without limit as gM_j grows. To keep π / P_j from also growing without limit, the
firm's rental stream (the first term on the RHS of equation 12.5) must become negative without limit. This requires that the rental price $(i_j - i_{Mj})$
become negative, and negative without limit as gM_j grows without limit. If
$(i_j - i_{Mj})$ is bounded below by zero, this condition cannot be satisfied. Maximum profit does not occur at a finite monetary expansion rate, but at an
infinite rate.

It is fairly straightforward to explain why the rental price $(i_j - i_{Mj})$ might be bounded below by zero. If the rental price becomes negative, then $i_{Mj} > i_j$. The yield on the jth money would exceed the yield on bonds denominated in the jth money. In this event, bond holders would entirely abandon bonds for money, as the yield on money overtook the yield on bonds. Only the money issuer would be left to hold j-denominated bonds.

If $(i_j - i_{Mj})$ does not fall below zero, the change in the rental stream cannot continue, indefinitely, to offset increasingly large money-printing revenue. Klein notes, in an aside, that "an infinite inflation rate [would be] implied . . . if the absolute value of $[d(i_j - i_{Mj})/dgM_j]$ never reached $[1 - dgP_j^*/dgM_j]$." The issue, however, is not whether this plateau $(-u = 1 - v)$ is ever reached; it is whether it can continue be occupied throughout the relevant range.

The implications of $(i_j - i_{Mj})$ being bounded below by zero are shown graphically in figure 12.1. Following equation (12.5), the real profit π/P_j at various rates of monetary expansion is the sum of two terms. The first term,

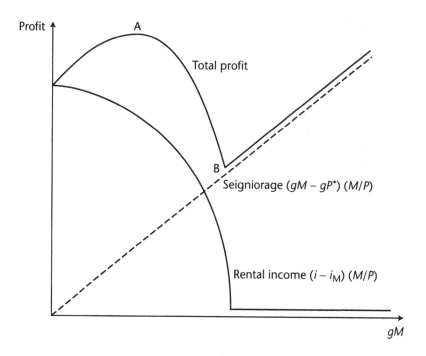

Figure 12.1 Unbounded monetary expansion: hyperinflation maximizes the issuer's profit when the public has imperfect foresight and the rental price on money is bounded below by zero

$$(i_j - i_{Mj})\left(\frac{M}{P}\right)_j$$

is represented by the negatively sloped curve. The second term

$$(gM_j - gP_j^*)\left(\frac{M}{P}\right)_j$$

is represented by the dashed ray, which comes from the origin under the simplifying assumption that the constant in equation (12.7) is zero. The slopes of the curves representing these terms are respectively u and $(1 - v)$. Klein never specifies a function relating the first term to the rate of monetary expansion. We have drawn the curve so that there is indeed a local equilibrium at point A, where $-u = 1 - v$. As the first term asymptotically approaches zero, u approaches 0, so that beyond point B, $-u$ is less than $1 - v$, and profit increases with the rate of monetary expansion. Beyond point B, the issuer can effectively travel out a ray, just as if there were absolutely fixed inflation-rate expectations. Profits are globally maximized with infinite monetary expansion and infinite inflation.

Klein argues that u will always be sufficiently negative, because "consumers will ... trade off higher levels of β_j, with correspondingly higher costs of holding cash balances $[i_j - i_{Mj}]$, against higher levels of unanticipated $[gM_j]$." As the jth firm (conjecturally) raises its money growth rate, it will forgo a higher rental price on its money. Consumers stand ready to pay a higher rental price for a money with a lower growth rate, precisely because they understand that, otherwise, the issuer would find hyperinflation profit-maximizing. Solving the problem of cheating, in this way, amounts to re-introducing perfect foresight through the back door. The public underanticipates money growth gM_j, but it knows exactly at each moment to what degree it is doing so (and by exactly how much it needs to lower the rental price it is prepared to pay as unanticipated money growth rises, in order to keep the issuer's profit from rising). To know exactly the discrepancy between actual and anticipated money growth is to know actual money growth; it is to have perfect foresight.

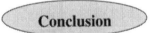

Conclusion

That a profit-maximizing private issuer of inconvertible money would hyperinflate means that the time-inconsistency problem bedevils private fiat-type money production even in Klein's model. The presence of "brand name capital" does not solve the problem.

Two solutions to the time-inconsistency problem with regard to money issue are available, but both entail a monetary regime unlike Klein's or Hayek's.

1   As Taub indicates, time-inconsistency could be eliminated, even with irredeemable currency, if it were feasible to write, and enforce, a contract stipulating the future quantity of money to be issued from now to eternity. The feasibility, and enforceability, of such a contract is doubtful, however.

2   The traditional approach to binding a private money issuer is to write a contract obligating the issuer to buy back his money at a pre-determined price, i.e. a redemption contract. At least for money, redemption contracts would appear to be cheap to write and enforce.

Both kinds of contracts are seen in non-monetary settings, for example where artists sell lithographs or firms sell "collectors' items." A producer, who is selling a good above its marginal cost of physical production, wants to make it credible that he will not later drive the resale value down by selling more at a lower price (Coase 1972). Purchasers of a lithograph, typically, prefer a quantity guarantee (the promise of a limited number of copies), accepting the risk of a decline in resale value in order to enjoy the potential for the lithograph to appreciate. Holders of a medium of exchange, by contrast, would understandably prefer a value guarantee.

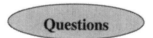

Questions

1   Under what conditions would private issue of fiat-type money reduce the opportunity cost of holding money (rather than bonds) to zero?

2   The time-inconsistency problem leads the fiat-money-issuing central bank in the Barro–Gordon model to a positive, but finite, inflation rate. Time-inconsistency leads the private issuer of fiat-type money in the Klein model to hyperinflation.

(a)   What accounts for this contrast?

(b)   Does the contrast indicate that a monopoly issue of fiat-type money is generally more trustworthy than competitive issue?

13

Cashless Competitive Payments and Legal Restrictions

Finance theorists Fischer Black (1970) and Eugene Fama (1980) have imagined a "cashless" competitive payments system (a system without a base money) as an analytical benchmark. Monetary economists Robert Greenfield and Leland Yeager (1983), and Kevin Dowd (1996), seriously propose adopting systems of this sort. Unlike the private fiat-type regimes imagined by Hayek and Klein, money issuers would adhere to a common unit of account, and would offer a form of redemption for their liabilities. By contrast to conventional banks, however, the medium of redemption (MOR) that banks keep in their vaults would be "separated" from the medium of account (MOA), some specified amount of which is the unit of account (UOA) in which money is denominated.

The Greenfield–Yeager Proposal

The GY proposal involves:

1. *laissez faire*, in the sense that government plays no money-issuing role,
2. a multi-commodity standard or MOA, to keep the price level more stable than under a gold or other single-commodity standard, and
3. "separation" of the MOA from the MOR: bank-issued money is denominated in the MOA bundle, but redeemable for an indexed quantity of something (anything) more convenient.

The GY reform relies on market-oriented, rather than governmental, payment institutions. The goals are price level stability, and the avoidance of monetary disequilibrium. By construction, there *is no base money*, so it cannot happen that an excess demand for base money arises and causes recession, or that an excess supply arises and causes inflation.

Fama calls a payments system that does not rely on any base money a "pure accounting system of exchange." In a PASE, banks transfer wealth, denominated in whatever unit, from account to account, but do not provide anything special called "money." Banks must settle by transfer of some non-money asset(s), unlike banks today, which use base money.[1] Fama suggests that any commodity whatsoever with a determinate relative price could function as the MOA.

Greenfield and Yeager give credit for parts of their inspiration to Black, Fama, and Robert Hall. Hall proposed the "ANCAP" standard as a more stable-valued medium of account. "ANCAP" is a bundle composed of ammonium nitrate, copper, aluminum, and plywood, in fixed weights. The ANCAP bundle tracked the CPI well up to 1980, when Hall made his proposal, but it should be noted that the ANCAP bundle did *not* continue to track the CPI well thereafter.[2]

One way to understand the GY proposal is to compare it to Irving Fisher's (1920) proposal for a "compensated dollar" scheme. Recall that under a gold standard P is measured in

$$\left(\frac{\$}{\text{oz Au}}\right)\left(\frac{\text{oz Au}}{\text{bundle}}\right)$$

Fisher proposed that government, as sole issuer of dollars, should periodically adjust the gold content of the dollar (the first ratio) to keep P stable as the second ratio varied. That is, reduce the gold content of the dollar if measured P falls (ppg rises), increase it if P rises (ppg falls), so P remains constant. There is a well-known problem with Fisher's scheme: if speculators think the next adjustment will reduce the gold content, they'll launch a speculative attack (run) on the dollar today.[3]

Greenfield and Yeager's proposal introduces several twists on Fisher.

---

[1] We use the term "banks" here to cover all manner of institutions that issue claims used in payments, whether debt-based like conventional demand deposits and banknotes, or equity-based like checkable mutual fund share accounts.

[2] Fernando Alvarez tracked the ANCAP bundle after 1980 for me.

[3] David Glasner (1989, pp. 227–48) discusses the Fisher plan, and (following Earl Thompson) proposes modifications (different from Greenfield and Yeager's) to avoid the speculative attack problem.

1   In the GY proposal, there is to be *continuous* adjustment of the redemption rate by indexing it to the prices of a bundle of continuously traded standardized commodities (inspired by Hall's ANCAP proposal) rather than to the CPI which is measured only monthly.

2   The redeemable media of exchange are to be issued by private firms rather than by government.

3   The MOA is to be separated from MOR (inspired by Black and Fama). Banks offer "indirect" (bundles-worth) redemption, rather than direct redemption with periodic redefinition of the UOA.

How is the price level determined in such a system? Following GY, call the UOA the "valun" (short for "value unit"). Denote it $\yen$. A $\yen$100 note is a claim to whatever amount of the MOR (say, platinum, chemical symbol Pt) is, at the moment of redemption, equal in market value to the goods comprising the bundle. Then P is measured in

$$\frac{\yen \text{ claims}}{\text{CPI bundle}}$$

Using the same kind of decomposition we've used for an ordinary single-commodity standard, P is measured in

$$\left(\frac{\yen \text{ claims}}{\text{oz Pt}}\right) \left(\frac{\text{oz Pt}}{\yen \text{ bundle}}\right) \left(\frac{\yen \text{ bundles}}{\text{CPI bundle}}\right)$$

The redemption rate ($\yen$ claims / oz Pt) varies continuously to keep constant the product of the first and second ratios. The price level P is then as stable as the third ratio. Unlike a gold standard, the valun standard insulates P from changes in the relative price of the MOR (the second ratio).

Is Bundles-worth Redemption Workable?

In a gold standard, claims for gold are redeemed directly for physically defined amounts of gold, so the MOA and the MOR are joined. The valun bundle that defines the UOA in the Greenfield–Yeager system, by contrast, never directly trades against anything. The individual goods in the bundle are bought and sold in organized markets, but it is no one's business to hold or transact in the physical bundle as such. What then ties the value of $\yen$ claims to the value of the goods comprising the $\yen$ bundle?

Norbert Schnadt and John Whittaker (1993) argue that the bundles-worth redemption scheme might self-destruct. If the sum of the market prices of the goods in the $\yen$ bundle happens to diverge from par, i.e.

$$\frac{\yen \text{ claims}}{\yen \text{ bundle}} \neq 1$$

arbitrage might make the system blow up, rather than return to par. Suppose the market price of the ¥ bundle rises momentarily to 102, but the ¥ price of platinum is unchanged. Banks with ¥-denominated liabilities are obliged to provide Pt equal in value to the ¥ bundle, i.e. to adjust the first ratio to keep

$$\left(\frac{\yen \text{ claims}}{\text{oz Pt}}\right)\left(\frac{\text{oz Pt}}{\yen \text{ bundle}}\right)$$

constant. With the second ratio up 2 percent in the market, they must now offer 2 percent more platinum per ¥100 claim. Schnadt and Whittaker worry that with arbitrage between the banks and the platinum market, this adjustment should make the ¥ price of platinum in the market fall: no one will pay more ¥ claims per oz Pt in the market than the rate obtainable at the bank. However, a fall in the market price of platinum compels the banks to adjust the redemption rate even further, offering even more ounces of platinum per ¥ claim, pushing the market price down further, and so on, *ad infinitum*.[4]

Other Concerns About the GY Proposal

Although GY call theirs "a laissez faire approach to monetary stability," their sort of separation of the MOA from the MOR is not the product of *laissez faire*. In a laissez-faire payments system, as analyzed in chapter 1, the MOA is naturally wedded to MOR, not divorced from it. Thus, there is no evolutionary tendency for base money (which is jointly MOA and MOR) to disappear.

GY's proposal to abolish base money appears to rest on the following *non sequitur*:

1   Base money has drawbacks (it allows inflation and monetary disequilibrium).
2   We can eliminate these drawbacks by eliminating base money.
3   Therefore, it would be a good thing to eliminate base money.

---

[4] Greenfield, Woolsey, and Yeager (1995) insist that the issue is a red herring; the GY system is stable. In reply, Schnadt and Whittaker (1995) reiterate their critique and argue that it has not been answered.

The conclusion does not follow because, while base money may have drawbacks, it may also have benefits that outweigh them.

Greenfield and Yeager appear to underappreciate the benefits of base money (an asset that combines the roles of MOA and MOR). Most familiarly, it provides the public a default-risk-free asset with defined UOA value that can be used as currency. However, suppose, not implausibly given the widespread use of banknotes in place of coin under specie standards, that the public is weaned from using base money as currency. Who then still does use base money? The banks do: they use base money for interbank settlement.

Why don't banks settle with other financial assets, as they could choose to do even in a system with base money, if, as GY suggest, they should be happy to do? It may be that base money survives as a settlement asset because it provides a low-cost medium for settlement, and that it provides a low-cost medium because it has an unambiguous UOA value. Base money has no bid-ask spread. With other assets, priced in but not constituting the UOA, settling banks would confront a bid-ask spread to be bridged. If a bank with $1m adverse clearings is to fork over $1m in IBM shares, the question arises: is that $1m as valued at the currently bid (lower) price or the currently asked (higher) price? If the bid price, the sending bank has to pay more than $1m to replace the shares in its portfolio. If the ask price, the receiving bank receives less than $1m when it liquidates the shares. Bid-ask spreads on widely traded financial assets may be tiny in percentage terms, but interbank settlement involves huge sums of money – billions of dollars a day in the USA, for example – so it would add up.

The Legal Restrictions Theory

A distinct group of economists, also taking a finance-theoretic approach, have developed the "legal restrictions theory" of money demand. Their analytical approach bears some similarities to the "cashless" model because it predicts that, under *laissez faire*, the payment system would operate without base money as we currently know it.

The LRT begins with a long-standing question in monetary theory: Why do individuals hold non-interest-bearing currency when it is dominated in rate of return by interest-bearing bonds with the same default risk? Unsatisfied by traditional appeals to "transaction frictions," because such "frictions" have proven hard to model, and have no role in the "frictionless" arbitrage models that have proven fruitful in finance theory, Neil Wallace (1983) answers: individuals who hold an asset dominated in rate of return must be constrained by legal restrictions. The LRT thus offers a "non-coexistence" prediction: in the absence of relevant legal restrictions, non-interest-bearing currency cannot coexist with higher-yielding equal-risk assets. In a fully arbitraged equilibrium, either nominal interest rates are zero on *all* assets, or all "currency" pays competitive interest. Either way, there is no difference between currency and bonds

The legal restrictions theory has some striking implications:

1   If FR (Federal Reserve) notes were identical in yield to T-bills (Treasury bills), open market operations would be irrelevant, merely an exchange of one government bond for another.
2   The spread between the yield rates on T-bills and FR notes measures how binding the legal restrictions are at any moment.
3   In marketing FR notes and T-bills with different yields, the Fed and Treasury together are practicing price discrimination. Big savers (who are in a better position to take their business elsewhere) receive a higher return than small currency-holders.

Bryant and Wallace (1980) reach the conclusion that legal restrictions, alone, explain coexistence of non-interest-bearing notes with interest-bearing bonds by beginning with three finance-theoretic postulates:

1   Assets are valued only in terms of explicit payoff distributions.
2   Anticipated equal actual payoffs.
3   "Under laissez faire, no transactions costs inhibit . . . the law of one price," including the equalization of yields on equal-risk assets.

The first assumption means that we cannot (as standard monetary theory does) view base money as providing an implicit "service yield". The third assumption means we cannot talk about money reducing "frictions" in the transactions system.

It follows from the three postulates that cases in which distinct money survives, despite being dominated in rate of return, "are to be explained by deviation from laissez faire." Interest-bearing bonds would drive out non-interest-bearing FR notes if not for legal restrictions. An obvious objection is that T-bills are much too big ($10,000 minimum) to use as currency. Wallace notes that private intermediaries could, however, easily "split" large T-bills into their own small bonds. The intermediary's balance sheet might have a $10,000 T-bill on its asset side, and 1000 individual $10 interest-bearing notes on its liability side. Assuming that the intermediary's marginal costs are similar to the 1 percentage point of yield that competitive no-load mutual funds charge for their services, competition in T-bill-splitting would ensure that the small-denomination notes pay an interest rate within 1 percentage point or so of the T-bill rate.

If the demand for non-interest-bearing currency disappears, and FR notes consequently become worthless, what serves as the UOA? Wallace suggests, in passing, the gold ounce. The LRT postulates do not rule out the survival of non-interest-bearing gold coins, because even government bonds under a gold standard cannot equal their freedom from default risk. Nor does it rule out gold as the MOR. Hence, the LRT does not quite predict the Greenfield–Yeager cashless competitive payments system.

Historical Evidence on the Non-coexistence Prediction

Wallace cites two historical cases where bonds have, to some extent, been used in payments: US "Liberty Bonds" during World War I, and bills of exchange among nineteenth-century Manchester merchants. In neither episode, though, were bonds a *commonly* accepted medium of exchange.

As evidence contrary to the LRT, several authors (Makinen and Woodward 1986; Gherity 1995; Woodward 1995) have noted historical cases (French government bearer bonds during World War I, interest-bearing Confederate Treasury and US Treasury notes during the US Civil War) where the government issued small-denomination bearer bonds, yet these bonds did not circulate, much less drive out non-interest-bearing currency. Instead, the bonds coexisted with ordinary currency. The US Treasury notes actually circulated at par, until accrued interest became large, at which point they were withdrawn from circulation and held as savings vehicles.

Perhaps the most telling evidence against the LRT non-coexistence prediction is that, in historical episodes of competitive note-issue, without any relevant legal restrictions, for example in early nineteenth-century Scotland, interest-bearing notes did *not* drive out ordinary banknotes. Scottish banks did pay 3–4 percent interest on deposits, and on promissory notes (which were like transferable certificates of deposit), while charging 4–5 percent for loans. So, it was neither the case that all interest rates were close to zero, nor that the Scottish banks simply had a high cost of intermediation. Interest was paid on deposits and promissory notes at a rate only about 1 percentage point below loan rates, exactly Wallace's estimate of the competitive spread. But the interest-bearing promissory notes did not circulate. The circulating medium consisted of non-interest-bearing banknotes. We have seen in chapter 3 that the circulation of non-interest-bearing notes does not imply unlimited profits for banks, because costs are bid up (the profits are returned to consumers) via non-price competition.

In the absence of legal restrictions, how *can* non-interest-bearing currency survive? It can survive because the costs of collecting, or delivering, interest can easily exceed the interest to be delivered on currency. Wallace supposes that notes would accumulate interest the way zero-coupon bonds do, trading each day at the (rising) present discounted value of the redemption amount. This method of collecting interest can, however, easily be more bother than it is worth. Consider a $10 bill. At 5 percent annual interest, it yields 50 cents a year, or less than 1 cent a week. If the note turns over once a week, is it worth the time and effort to perform the present-value calculation in order to collect a penny's interest? More generally, for any positive collection cost, there is *some* threshold note denomination, below which the potential interest is not worth the bother.

Imaginative authors have proposed other devices for paying interest on currency: have lottery drawings on banknote serial numbers, denominate notes in a proprietary unit that appreciates in real terms. However, these devices have not been used historically, so they probably do not deliver interest cheaply enough. In the future, digital currency may be developed that will deliver interest at negligible cost. If so, then competition *will* produce interest-bearing currency. The only remaining demand for base money will come from banks that use base money as an interbank settlement medium.

Questions

1 "There is no reason to expect the most efficient MOA [medium of account] to be the same as the most efficient MOEs [media of exchange] or the most efficient MORs [media of redemption], and there is certainly no reason to impose more than one function on any one good." (Dowd 1989)
   (a) What might it mean for one MOA to be more efficient than another?
   (b) Are there, in fact, any reasons to expect market forces to separate the MOA from the MOR? If so, is this inefficient?
2 The government of the Confederate States of America in 1862 issued bearer bonds in a CS$100 denomination, paying interest of 7.3 percent per year or exactly 2 cents per day. Previously, it had issued a fixed quantity (up to a legislated ceiling amount) of non-interest-bearing currency notes, in denominations up CS$100. Neither liability was currently redeemable, and neither was legal tender. At this time, a nonfarm employee earned about CS$1.15, so CS$100 was a large denomination.
   (a) What does the legal restrictions theory predict about the coexistence of the 7.3 percent bonds with the non-interest-bearing currency notes?
   (b) Does the *contrary* theory that predicts the non-circulation of small-denomination bearer bonds because of the cost of com-

puting accrued interest or present value, apply to this case?

(c) Suppose the public treated the 7.3 percent bonds as a substitute for the currency notes. What was the implication for the Confederate government's seigniorage?

3 (a) What sort of historical evidence appears to conflict with the legal restrictions theory's non-coexistence prediction?

(b) Provide an alternative explanation for co-existence that does not conflict with the historical evidence.

(c) Why might a proponent of the legal restrictions theory find the alternative explanation unappealing?

References

Alchian, A. 1977: Why money? *Journal of Money, Credit, and Banking*, 9 (February, Part 2), 133–40.

Alesina, A. and Sachs, J. 1988: Political parties and the business cycles in the United States, 1948–1984. *Journal of Money, Credit, and Banking*, 20 (February), 63–82.

Allen, S. D. 1986: The Federal Reserve and the electoral cycle. *Journal of Money, Credit, and Banking*, 18 (February), 88–94.

Alonso, I. 1996: On avoiding bank runs. *Journal of Monetary Economics*, 37 (February), 73–87.

Armentano, D. T. 1982: *Antitrust and Monopoly: Anatomy of a Policy Failure.* New York: John Wiley & Sons.

Auernheimer, L. 1974: The honest government's guide to the revenue from the creation of money. *Journal of Political Economy*, 82, 598–606.

Axelrod, R. 1984: *The Evolution of Cooperation.* New York: Basic Books.

Backus, D. and Driffill, J. 1985: Inflation and reputation. *American Economic Review*, 75 (June), 530–8.

Bagehot, W. 1873: *Lombard Street: A Description of the Money Market.* London: Henry S. King.

Bailey, M. J. 1956: The welfare cost of inflationary finance. *Journal of Political Economy*, 64 (April), 93–110.

Baltensperger, E. 1972: Economies of scale, firm size, and concentration in banking. *Journal of Money, Credit, and Banking*, 4 (November), 467–88.

Bannock, G., Baxter, R. E. and Rees, R. 1974: *A Dictionary of Economics.* Harmondsworth, UK: Penguin.

Barro, R. J. 1972: Inflationary finance and the welfare cost of inflation. *Journal of Political Economy*, 80 (Sept.–Oct.), 978–1001.

Barro, R. J. 1983: Inflationary finance under discretion and rules. *Canadian Journal of Economics*, 16 (February), 1–16.

Barro, R. J. 1986: Rules versus discretion. In C. D. Campbell and W. R. Dougan (eds), *Alternative Monetary Regimes*, Baltimore: Johns Hopkins University Press, 16–30.

Barro, R. J., and Gordon, D. B. 1983a: Rules, discretion and reputation in a model of monetary policy. *Journal of Monetary Economics*, 12 (July), 101–21.

Barro, R. J., and Gordon, D. B. 1983b: A positive theory of monetary policy in a natural rate model. *Journal of Political Economy*, 91 (August), 589–610.

Becker, G. S. 1993: A proposal for free banking. In L. H. White (ed.) *Free Banking*, vol. III, Aldershot, UK: Edward Elgar, 20–25.

Besen, S. M., and Farrell, J. 1994: Choosing how to compete: strategies and tactics in standardization. *Journal of Economic Pespectives*, 8 (Spring), 117–31.

Black, F. 1970: Banking and interest rates in a world without money: the effects of uncontrolled banking. *Journal of Bank Research*, 1 (Autumn), 9–20.

Blinder, A. S. 1997: What central bankers could learn from academics – and vice versa. *Journal of Economic Perspectives*, 11 (Spring), 3–19.

Bordo, M. D. 1984: The gold standard: myths and realities. In Barry N. Siegel (ed.), *Money in Crisis: The Federal Reserve, the Economy, and Monetary Reform*, Cambridge, MA: Ballinger, 197–237.

Bordo, M. D. 1990: The lender of last resort: alternative views and historical experience. *Federal Reserve Bank of Richmond Economic Review*, (January/February), 18–29.

Bordo, M. D. (1993): The gold standard, Bretton Woods, and other monetary regimes: A historical appraisal. *Federal Reserve Bank of St Louis Review*, (March–April), 123–91.

Bordo, M. D. and Ellson, R. W. 1985: A model of the classical gold standard with depletion. *Journal of Monetary Economics*, 16 (July), 109–20.

Bordo, M. D. and Redish, A. 1987: Why did the Bank of Canada emerge in 1935? *Journal of Economic History*, 47 (June), 405–17.

Boyer-Xambeu, M.-T., Deleplace, G. and Gillard, L. 1994: *Private Money and Public Currencies: The 16th Century Challenge*. Armonk, NY and London: Sharpe: xvi, 231.

Brennan, H. G. and Buchanan, J. M. 1981: *Monopoly in Money and Inflation*. London: Institute of Economic Affairs.

Browning, J. and Reiss, S. 1988: *Encyclopedia of the Economy, Wired*, March, April, May. Also on-line at www.hotwired.com/special/ene.

Brunner, K. and Meltzer, A. H. 1971: The uses of money: money in the theory of an exchange economy. *American Economic Review*, 61 (December), 784–805.

Bryant, J. 1981: The competitive provision of fiat money. *Journal of Banking and Finance*, 5, 587–93.

Bryant, J. and Wallace, N. 1980: *A Suggestion for Further Simplifying the Theory of Money*. Photocopy, Federal Reserve Bank of Minneapolis and University of Minnesota.

Bryant, J. B. and Wallace, N. 1983: A price discrimination analysis of monetary policy. *Research Department Staff Report 51*, Federal Reserve Bank of Minneapolis.

Buchanan, J. M. and Stubblebine, W. C. 1962: Externality. *Economica*, n.s. 29 (November), 371–84.

Burns, A. R. 1927: Early stages in the development of money and coins. In T. E. Gregory and H. Dalton (eds) *London Essays in Economics in Honour of Edwin Cannan*, London: Routledge.

Cagan, P. 1956: The monetary dynamics of hyperinflation. In M. Friedman (ed.) *Studies in the Quantity Theory of Money*, Chicago: University of Chicago Press, 25–117.

Calomiris, C. W. 1995: Comment. In George Edward Durell Foundation, *Money and Banking: The American Experience*, Fairfax, VA: George Mason University Press.

Calomiris, C. W. and Khan, C. M. 1991: The role of demandable debt in structuring optimal banking arrangements. *American Economic Review*, 81 (June), 497–513.

Calvo, G. A. 1978: Optimal seignorage from money creation: an analysis in terms of the optimum balance of payments deficit problem. *Journal of Monetary Economics*, 4, 503–17.

Canzoneri, M. B. 1985: Monetary policy games and the role of private information. *American Economic Review*, 75 (December), 1056–70.

Click, R. W. 1998: Seigniorage in a cross-section of countries. *Journal of Money, Credit, and Banking*, 30 (May), 154–71.

Coase, R. H. 1972: Durability and monopoly. *Journal of Law and Economics*, 25, 143–9.

Congdon, T. 1981: Is the provision of a sound currency a necessary function of the state? *National Westminster Bank Quarterly Review*, (August), 2–21.

Cooley, T. F. and Hansen, G. D. 1989: The inflation tax in a real business cycle model. *American Economic Review*, 79 (September), 733–48.

Cooper, R. N. 1988: Toward an international commodity standard? *Cato Journal*, 8 (Fall), 315–38.

Cowen, T. and Kroszner, R. 1990: Mutual fund banking: a market approach. *Cato Journal*, 10 (Spring/Summer), 223–37.

Cowen, T. and Kroszner, R. 1994: *Explorations in the New Monetary Economics*. Oxford: Basil Blackwell.

Cribb, J. (ed.) 1986: *Money: From Cowrie Shells to Credit Cards*. London: British Museum Publications.

Cuikerman, A. 1986: Central bank behavior and credibility: some recent theoretical developments. *Federal Reserve Bank of St Louis Review*, (May), 5–17.

Cuikerman, A., and Meltzer, A. H. 1986: A theory of ambiguity, credibility, and inflation under discretion and asymmetric information. *Econometrica*, 54 (September), 1099–128.

David, P. A. 1985: Clio and the economics of QWERTY. *American Economic Review*, 75 (May), 332–7.

De Grauwe, P. 1997: *The Economics of Monetary Integration* (3rd edn). Oxford: Oxford University Press.

de Roover, R. 1948: *Money, Credit, and Banking in Mediaeval Bruges*. Cambridge: The Mediaeval Academy.

de Roover, R. 1974a: What is dry exchange? A contribution to the study of English mercantism. In J. Kirshner (ed.), *Business, Banking, and Economic Thought in Late Medieval and Early Modern Europe*. Chicago, University of Chicago Press, ch. 4.

de Roover, R. 1974b: New interpretations of the history of banking. In J. Kirshner (ed.), *Business Banking and Economic Thought in Late Medieval and Early Modern Europe*. Chicago, University of Chicago Press, Ch. 5.

Diamond, D. W. and Dybvig, P. H. 1983: Bank runs, deposit insurance, and liquidity. *Journal of Political Economy*, 91 (June), 401–19.

Dingle, T. 1988: *Aboriginal Economy*. Fitzroy, Victoria: McPhee Gribble/ Penguin Books.

Dowd, K. 1988: Option clauses and the stability of a laissez faire monetary system. *Journal of Financial Services Research*, 1, 319–33.

Dowd, K. 1989: *The State and the Monetary System*. New York: Philip Allan.

Dowd, K. 1991: The evolution of central banking in England, 1821–1890. In F. Capie and G. E. Wood (eds) *Unregulated Banking: Chaos or Order?*, London: Macmillan, 159–95.

Dowd, K. 1992a: Models of banking instability: a partial review of the literature. *Journal of Economic Surveys*, 6, 107–32.

Dowd, K. (ed.) 1992b: *The Experience of Free Banking*. London: Routledge.

Dowd, K. 1996: *Competition and Finance*. New York: St. Martin's Press.

Dwyer, G. P., Jr and Saving, T. R. 1986: Government revenue from money creation with government and private money. *Journal of Monetary Economics*, 17, 239–49.

Edgeworth, F. Y. 1888: The mathematical theory of banking. *Journal of the Royal Statistical Association*, 51 (March), 113–27.

Fama, E. F. 1980: Banking in the theory of finance. *Journal of Monetary Economics*, 6 (Jan), 39–57.

Fama, E. F. 1983: Financial intermediation and price level control. *Journal of Monetary Economics*, 12 (July), 7–28.

Fischer, S. and Summers, L. H. 1989: Should governments learn to live with inflation? *American Economic Review*, 79 (May): 382–7.

Fisher, I. 1920: *Stabilizing the Dollar*. New York: Macmillan.

Fleming, M. 1994: *The Choice of Monetary Standards: Evolution and Efficiency*. PhD dissertation, University of Georgia.

Freeman, S. 1989: Fiat money as a medium of exchange. *International Economic Review*, 30 (February), 137–51.

Friedman, M. 1953: Commodity-reserve currency. In *Essays in Positive Economics*. Chicago: University of Chicago Press, 204–50.

Friedman, M. 1960: *A Program for Monetary Stability*. New York: Fordham University Press.

Friedman, M. 1968: The role of monetary policy. *American Economic Review*, 58 (March), 1–17.

Friedman, M. 1969: The optimum quantity of money. In *The Optimum Quantity of Money and Other Essays*. Chicago, Aldine.

Friedman, M. 1982: Monetary policy: theory and practice. *Journal of Money, Credit, and Banking*, 14 (February), 98–118.

Friedman, M. 1987: Monetary policy: Tactics versus strategy. In J. A. Dorn and A. J. Schwartz (eds) *The Search for Stable Money*, Chicago: University of Chicago Press, 361–82.

Friedman, M. and Schwartz, A. J. 1963: *A Monetary History of the United States*,

1867–1960. Princeton: Princeton University Press.

Friedman, M. and Schwartz, A. J. 1986: Has government any role in money? *Journal of Monetary Economics*, 17 (January), 37–62.

Fullarton, J. 1845: *On the Regulation of Currencies* (2nd edn). London: John Murray.

Gandal, N. and Sussman, N. 1997: Asymmetric information and commodity money: tickling the tolerance in medieval France. *Journal of Money, Credit, and Banking*, 29 (November, Part I), 440–57.

Gherity, J. A. 1995: The option clause in Scottish banking, 1730–65: A reappraisal. *Journal of Money, Credit, and Banking*, 27 (August), 713–26.

Giles, M. 1996: Safe banking. *Economist*, 339 (Apr 27), S27–S32.

Glasner, D. 1989: *Free Banking and Monetary Reform*. Cambridge: Cambridge University Press.

Glasner, D. 1997: *Classical Monetary Theory and the Quantity Theory*. Manuscript, Bureau of Economics, Federal Trade Commission.

Goodfriend, M. and King, R. A. 1988: Financial deregulation, monetary policy, and central banking. In W. S. Haraf and R. M. Kushmeider (eds) *Restructuring Banking and Financial Services in America*, Washington: American Enterprise Institute, 216–53.

Goodhart, C. A. E. 1988: *The Evolution of Central Banks*. Cambridge: MIT Press.

Goodhart, C. A. E. 1989a: Central banking. In J. Eatwell, M. Milgate, and P. Newman (eds) *The New Palgrave: Money*, New York: W. W. Norton, 88–92.

Goodhart, C. A. E. 1989b: *Money, Information and Uncertainty* (2nd edn). London: Macmillan.

Gorton, G. 1985a: Clearinghouses and the origin of central banking in the United States. *Journal of Economic History*, 45 (June), 277–83.

Gorton, G. 1985b: Bank suspension of convertibility. *Journal of Monetary Economics*, 16 (September), 177–93.

Gorton, G. 1988: Banking panics and business cycles. *Oxford Economic Papers*, 40 (December), 751–81.

Gorton, G. 1989: *Public Policy and the Evolution of Banking Markets*. Unpublished ms., University of Pennsylvania.

Gorton, G. and Mullineaux, D. J. 1987: The joint production of confidence: endogenous regulation and nineteenth century commercial-bank clearinghouses. *Journal of Money, Credit, and Banking*, 19 (November), 457–68.

Gramm, W. P. 1974: Laissez-faire and the optimum quantity of money. *Economic Inquiry*, 12 (March), 125–32.

Greenfield, R. L. 1994: *Monetary Policy and the Depressed Economy: As Illustrated by the Period 1929–1933*. Belmont, CA: Wadsworth.

Greenfield, R. L., and Yeager, L. B. 1983: A laissez-faire approach to monetary stability. *Journal of Money, Credit, and Banking*, 15 (August), 302–15.

Greenfield, R. L., Woolsey, W. W. and Yeager, L. B. 1995: Is indirect convertibility impossible? A comment. *Journal of Money, Credit, and Banking*, 27 (February), 293–7.

Greenspan, A. 1997: Fostering financial innovation: the role of government. In J. A. Dorn (ed.) *The Future of Money in the Information Age*, Washington, DC: Cato Institute, 45–50.

Grier, K. 1987: Presidential politics and federal reserve independence. *Southern Economic Journal*, 54, 475–86.

Grilli, V. U. 1988: Seigniorage in Europe. *Yale Economic Growth Center Discussion Paper*, 565 (October), 45.

Gurley, J. G. and Shaw, E. S. 1960: *Money in a Theory of Finance*. Washington: Brookings Institute.

Haslag, J. H. 1996: Honest money is the best policy. *Federal Reserve Bank of Dallas Southwest Economy*, 3, 6–9.

Hayek, F. A. 1978: *The Denationalisation of Money* (2nd edn). London: Institute of Economic Affairs.

Hayek, F. A. 1990: *Denationalisation of Money: The Argument Refined* (3rd edn). London: Institute of Economic Affairs.

Heilemann, J. 1994: Can the BBC be saved? *Wired*, 2.03 (March), 101–103, 140–2.

Hellwig, M. 1985: What do we know about currency competition? *Zeitschrift fur Wirtschafts- und Socialwissenschaften*, 5, 565–88.

Hume, D. 1970: Of the balance of trade. In E. Rotwein (ed.) *Writings on Economics*, Madison: University of Wisconsin Press, 60–77. First published in 1752.

Humphrey, T. H. and Keleher, R. E. 1984: The lender of last resort: a historical perspective. *Cato Journal*, 4 (Spring/Summer), 275–318.

Huo, T. M. and Yu, M. T. 1994: Do bank runs exist in the Diamond–Dybvig model? *Journal of Institutional and Theoretical Economics*, 150 (September), 537–42.

James, F. C. 1938: *The Growth of Chicago Banks*. New York: Harper and Brothers.

Kagin, D. H. 1981: *Private Gold Coins and Patterns of the United States*. New York: Arco Publishing.

Kane, E. 1980: Politics and Fed policymaking: the more things change the more they remain the same. *Journal of Monetary Economics*, 6 (1980), 199–211.

Katz, M. L. and Shapiro, C. 1994: Systems competition and network effects. *Journal of Economic Perspectives*, 8 (Spring), 93–115.

Keil, M. W. 1988: Is the political business cycle really dead? *Southern Economic Journal*, 55 (July), 86–99.

Keynes, J. M. 1935: *A Treatise on Money*, vol. I. London: Macmillan.

Khan, M. S. and Knight, M. D. 1982: Unanticipated monetary growth and inflationary finance, *Journal of Money, Credit, and Banking*, 14 (August), 347–64.

Kiguel, M. A. and Neumeyer, P. A. 1995: Seigniorage and inflation: the case of Argentina. *Journal of Money, Credit, and Banking*, (August), 672–82.

Kindleberger, C. P. 1986: International public goods without international government. *American Economic Review*, 76 (March), 1–13.

King, R. G. and Plosser, C. I. 1986: Money as the mechanism of exchange. *Journal of Monetary Economics*, 17 (January), 93–115.

Kiyotaki, N. and Wright, R. 1989: On money as a medium of exchange. *Journal of Political Economy*, 97 (August), 927–54.

Klein, B. 1974: The competitive supply of money. *Journal of Money, Credit, and Banking*, 6 (November), 423–53.

Klein, B. 1975: Our new monetary standard: the measurement and effects of price uncertainty, 1880–1973. *Economic Inquiry*, 13 (December), 461–84.

Kydland, F. E. and Prescott, E. C. 1977: Rules rather than discretion: the inconsistency of optimal plans. *Journal of Political Economy*, 85 (June), 473–91.

Leijonhufvud, A. 1981: *Information and Coordination*. New York: Oxford University Press.

Leijonhufvud, A. 1986: Rules with some discretion. In C. D. Campbell and W. R. Dougan (eds) *Alternative Monetary Regimes*, Baltimore: Johns Hopkins University Press, 38–43.

Liebowitz, S. J. and Margolis, S. E. 1990: The fable of the keys. *Journal of Law and Economics*, 33 (April), 1–25.

Liebowitz, S. J. and Margolis, S. E. 1994: Network externality: an uncommon tragedy. *Journal of Economic Pespectives*, 8 (Spring), 133–50.

Lin, S. 1989: *Optimal Monetary Policy in a Stochastic Overlapping-generations Economy*. Unpublished, Brown University.

Livingston, J. 1986: *Origins of the Federal Reserve System: Money, Class, and Corporate Capitalism, 1890–1913*. Ithaca: Cornell University Press.

Lucas, R. E., Jr 1973: Some international evidence on output-inflation tradeoffs. *American Economic Review*, 63 (June), 326–34.

Lucas, R. E., Jr 1987: *Models of Business Cycles*. Oxford: Basil Blackwell.

Macaulay, H. H. 1983: *Is Money a Public Good?* Unpublished, Clemson University.

MacRae, C. D. 1977: A political model of the business cycle. *Journal of Political Economy*, 85 (April), 239–63.

Makinen, G. E. and Woodward, G. T. 1986: Some anecdotal evidence relating to the legal restrictions theory of the demand for money. *Journal of Political Economy*, 94 (April), 260–5.

Markowitz, M. J. 1993: Fractional reserve versus 100% reserve banking. In *Bankers and Regulators*. Irvington-on-Hudson, NY: Foundation for Economic Education, 73–6.

McCallum, B. T. 1978: The political business cycle: an empirical test. *Southern Economic Journal*, 44 (January), 504–15.

McCallum, B. T. 1983: On the role of overlapping-generations models in monetary economics. *Carnegie-Rochester Conference Series on Public Policy*, 22 (Autumn 1985), 13–45.

McCallum, B. T. 1989: *Monetary Economics: Theory and Policy*. New York: Macmillan.

McCallum, B. T. 1997: Crucial issues concerning central bank independence. *Journal of Monetary Economics*, 39 (June), 99–112.

McClure, J. H., Jr and Willett, T. D. 1988: The inflation tax. In T. Willett (ed.) *Political Business Cycles: The Political Economy of Money, Inflation, and Unemployment*, Pacific Research Institute for Public Policy Book series, Durham and London: Duke University Press: 177–85.

McCulloch, J. Huston 1982: *Money and Inflation: A Monetarist Approach* (2nd edn). New York: Academic Press.

McCulloch, J. H. 1991: An error-correction mechanism for long-run price stability. *Journal of Money, Credit, and Banking*, 23 (August, Part 2), 619–24.

McDonald, G. 1987: *Australian Coin and Banknote Market Guide*. Umina Beach, NSW: privately published.

Meiselman, D. I. 1986: Is there a political monetary cycle? *Cato Journal*, 6 (Fall), 563–79.

Melitz, J. 1974: *Primitive and Modern Money*. Reading, MA: Addison-Wesley.

Meltzer, A. H. 1986: Some evidence on the comparative uncertainty experienced under different monetary regimes. In C. D. Campbell and W. R. Cougan (eds) *Alternative Monetary Regimes*. Baltimore: The Johns Hopkins University Press, 122–53.

Meltzer, A. H. 1998: What is money? In G. Wood (ed.) *Money and the Economy*. Aldershot: Edward Elgar.

Melvin, M. 1988: Monetary confidence, privately produced monies, and domestic and international monetary reform. In T. Willet (ed.) *Political Business Cycles: The Political Economy of Money, Inflation, and Unemployment*, Pacific Research Institute for Public Policy Book series Durham and London: Duke University Press: 435–59.

Menger, C. 1892: On the origin of money. *Economic Journal*, 2 (June), 239–55.

Menger, C. 1936: Geld. In F. A. Hayek, (ed.) *The Collected Works of Carl Menger*, vol. IV, London: London School of Economics and Political Science. Unpublished English translation by Albert Zlabinger, 1–116.

Minford, P. 1985: Interest rates and bond-financed deficits in a Ricardian two-party democracy. *Centre for Economic Policy Research Discussion Paper*, 79 (November), 24.

Morrell, S. O. 1983: *Exchange, Money, and the State*. Unpublished, Auburn University.

Mulligan, C. B., and Sala-i-Martin, X. X. 1997: The optimum quantity of money: theory and evidence. *Journal of Money, Credit, and Banking*, 29 (November, Part 2), 687–715.

Mullineaux, D. J. 1987: Competitive monies and the Suffolk bank system: a contractual perspective. *Southern Economic Journal*, 53 (April), 884–98.

Negroponte, N. 1996: Being local. *Wired*, 4.11 (November), 286.

Nichols, D. A. 1974: Some principles of inflationary finance. *Journal of Political Economy*, 82: 423–30.

Niehans, J. 1978: *The Theory of Money*. Baltimore: Johns Hopkins University Press.

Nordhaus, W. D. 1975: The political business cycle. *Review of Economic Studies*, 42 (April), 169–90.

Noyes, A. D. 1910: *History of the National Bank Currency*. Washington: Government Printing Office.

Nozick, R. 1974: *Anarchy, State, and Utopia*. New York: Basic Books.

O'Driscoll, G. P. Jr 1986: Deregulation and monetary reform. *Economic Review*, Federal Reserve Bank of Dallas (July), 19–31.

Patinkin, D. 1965: *Money, Interest, and Prices* (2nd edn). New York: Harper & Row.

Pearce, D. W. (ed.) 1986: *The MIT Dictionary of Modern Economics* (3rd edn). Cambridge: MIT Press.

Poole, W. 1986: Monetary control and the political business cycle. *Cato Journal*, Winter, 685–99.

Richards, D. J. 1986: Unanticipated money and the political business cycle. *Journal of Money, Credit, and Banking*, 18 (November), 447–57.

Richards, R. D. 1965: *The Early History of Banking in England.* New York: Augustus M. Kelley.

Ritter, J. A. 1995: The transition from barter to fiat money. *American Economic Review,* 85 (March), 134–49.

Rockoff, H. 1984: Some evidence on the real price of gold, its costs of production, and commodity prices. In M. D. Bordo and A. J. Schwartz (eds) *A Retrospective on the Classical Gold Standard, 1821–1931,* Chicago: University of Chicago Press, 613–44.

Rolnick, A. J. and Weber, W. E. 1994: Inflation and money growth under alternative monetary standards. *Working Paper 528,* Federal Reserve Bank of Minneapolis Research Department.

Romer, C. D. 1986: Is the stabilization of the postwar economy a figment of the data? *American Economic Review,* 76 (June), 314–34 .

Rothbard, M. N. 1995: Fractional reserve banking. *The Freeman,* 45 (October), 624–27.

Sachs, J. (1987): The Bolivian hyperinflation and stabilization. *American Economic Review, Papers and Proceedings,* May, 279–83.

Salerno, J. T. 1987: Gold standards: true and false. In J. A. Dorn and A. J. Schwartz (eds) *The Search for Stable Money,* Chicago: University of Chicago Press, 241–55.

Samuelson, P. A. 1968: What classical and neoclassical monetary theory really was. *Canadian Journal of Economics,* 1 (February), 1–15.

Samuelson, P. A. 1969: Nonoptimality of money holding under laissez-faire. *Canadian Journal of Economics,* 3 (May), 324–30.

Santomero, A. M. 1984: Modeling the banking firm: A survey. *Journal of Money, Credit, and Banking,* 16 (November 1984, Part 2), 576–602.

Schmidtz, D. 1991: *The Limits of Government: An Essay on the Public Goods Argument.* Boulder and Oxford: Westview Press: xviii, 197

Schnadt, N. and Whittaker, J. 1993: Inflation-proof currency? The feasibility of variable commodity standards. *Journal of Money, Credit, and Banking,* 25 (May), 214–21.

Schnadt, N. and Whittaker, J. 1995: Is indirect convertibility impossible? A reply. *Journal of Money, Credit, and Banking,* 27 (February), 297–8.

Schuler, K. 1992: The world history of free banking. In K. Dowd (ed.) *The Experience of Free Banking,* London: Routledge, 7–47.

Schwartz, A. J. 1986: Alternative monetary regimes: The gold standard. In C. D. Campbell and W. R. Dougan (eds) *Alternative Monetary Regimes,* Baltimore: The Johns Hopkins University Press, 44–72.

Scitovsky, T. 1954: Two concepts of externalities. *Journal of Political Economy,* 62 (April), 143–51.

Selgin, G. 1988: *The Theory of Free Banking.* Totowa, NJ: Rowman and Littlefield.

Selgin, G. 1994a: On ensuring the acceptability of a new fiat money. *Journal of Money, Credit, and Banking,* 26 (November), 808–26.

Selgin, G. 1994b: Free banking and monetary control. *Economic Journal,* 104 (November), 1449–59.

Selgin, G. 1997a: E-money: friend or foe of monetarism? In J. A. Dorn (ed.) *The Future of Money in the Information Age,* Washington, DC: Cato Institute, 97–100.

Selgin, G. 1997b: *Network Effects, Adaptive Learning, and the Transition to Fiat Money.* Manuscript, University of Georgia.

Selgin, G. and White, L. H. 1987: The evolution of a free banking system. *Economic Inquiry*, 25 (July), 439–57.

Selgin, G. and White, L. H. 1994a: How would the invisible hand handle money? *Journal of Economic Literature*, 32 (December), 1718–49.

Selgin, G. and White, L. H. 1994b: Monetary reform and the redemption of national bank notes, 1863–1913. *Business History Review*, 68 (Summer), 205–43.

Selgin, G. and White, L. H. 1995: National bank notes as a quasi-high-powered money. In *Money and Banking: The American Experience*. Fairfax, VA: George Mason University Press, 169–99.

Selgin, G. and White, L. H. 1996: In defense of fiduciary media – or, we are not devo(lutionists), we are misesians! *Review of Austrian Economics*, 9(2), 83–107.

Selgin, G. and White, L. H. 1997: The option clause in Scottish banking: a comment. *Journal of Money, Credit, and Banking*, 29 (May), 270–7.

Selgin, G. and White, L. H. 1999: A fiscal theory of government's role in money. *Economic Inquiry* (in press).

Shah, P. J. 1997: The option clause in free-banking theory and history: a reappraisal. *Review of Austrian Economics*, 10: 1–25.

Shugart, W. F. II, and Tollison, R. D. 1983: Preliminary evidence on the use of inputs by the Federal Reserve system. *American Economic Review*, 73 (June), 291–304.

Simons, H. C. 1936: Rules versus authorities in monetary policy. *Journal of Political Economy*, 44, 1–30.

Sjaastad, L. A. 1976: Why stable inflations fail: an essay in political economy. In M. Parkin and G. Zis (eds) *Inflation in the World Economy*. Manchester: Manchester University Press, 73–95.

Smith, A. 1981: *An Inquiry into the Nature and Causes of the Wealth of Nations*, edited by Campbell, R. H., Skinner, A. S. and Todd, W. B., Indianapolis, Liberty Classics. First published in 1776.

Smith, V. C. 1990: *The Rationale of Central Banking*. Indianapolis: Liberty Press. First published in 1936.

Sumner, S. 1993: Privatizing the Mint. *Journal of Money, Credit, and Banking*, 25 (February), 13–29.

Taub, B. 1985: Private fiat money with many suppliers. *Journal of Monetary Economics*, 16 (September), 195–208.

Timberlake, R. H. 1978: *The Origins of Central Banking in the United States*. Cambridge: Harvard University Press.

Timberlake, R. H. 1984: The central banking role of clearinghouse associations. *Journal of Money, Credit, and Banking*, 16 (February), 1–15.

Timberlake, R. H. 1985: Legislative construction of the monetary control act of 1980. *American Economic Review*, 75 (May), 97–102.

Tobin, J. 1980: Discussion [of Wallace 1980)]. In J. H. Kareken and N. Wallace (eds) *Models of Monetary Economies*, Minneapolis: Federal Reserve Bank of Minneapolis, 83–90.

Toma, M. 1982: Inflationary bias of the Federal Reserve system: a bureaucratic perspective. *Journal of Monetary Economics*, 10, 163–90.

Usher, A. P. 1943: *The Early History of Deposit Banking in Mediterranean Europe*. Cambridge: Cambridge University Press.

van Dun, F. 1984: "Public goods" from the market. *Economic Affairs* (July–September), 28–31.

von Mises, L. 1980: *The Theory of Money and Credit*. Indianapolis: Liberty Classics. First published in 1912.

Vaubel, R. 1984: The government's money monopoly: Externalities or natural monopoly? *Kyklos*, 37, 27–58.

Wagner, R. E. 1977: Economic manipulation for political profit: macroeconomic consequences and constitutional implications. *Kyklos*, 30, 395–410.

Wallace, N. 1980: The overlapping generations model of fiat money. In J. H. Kareken and N. Wallace (eds) *Models of Monetary Economies*, Minneapolis: Federal Reserve Bank of Minneapolis, 49–82.

Wallace, N. 1983: A legal restrictions theory of the demand for "money" and the role of monetary policy. *Federal Reserve Bank of Minneapolis Quarterly Review* (Winter), 1–7.

Wärneryd, K. 1990: Legal restrictions and monetary evolution. *Journal of Economic Behavior and Organization*, 13 (January), 117–24.

West, R. C. 1974: *Banking Reform and the Federal Reserve, 1863–1923*. Ithaca: Cornell University Press.

White, L. H. 1987: Accounting for non-interest-bearing currency: a critique of the legal restrictions theory of money. *Journal of Money, Credit, and Banking*, 19 (November), 448–56.

White, L. H. 1989: *Competition and Currency: Essays on Free Banking and Money*. New York: New York University Press.

White, L. H. 1990: Competitive monetary reform: A review essay. *Journal of Monetary Economics*, 26 (September), 191–202.

White, L. H. (ed.) 1993: *African Finance: Research and Reform*. San Francisco: ICS Press.

White, L. H. 1995: *Free Banking in Britain* (2nd edn). London: Institute of Economic Affairs.

White, L. H., and Boudreaux, D. J. 1998: Is nonprice competition in currency inefficient? *Journal of Money, Credit, and Banking*, 30 (May), 252–60.

Williamson, S. D. 1996: Sequential markets and the suboptimality of the Friedman rule. *Journal of Monetary Economics*, 37 (June), 549–72.

Woodward, G. T. 1995: Interest-bearing currency: evidence from the Civil War experience: A comment. *Journal of Money, Credit and Banking*, 27, August, 927–37.

Wriston, W. 1996: The future of money [Interview]. *Wired*, 4.10 (October), 141–3, 200–05. Also available online at www.wired.com/wired/4.10/features/wriston.html.

Wynne, M. 1997: The economics of one dollar. *Southwest Economy* (Federal Reserve Bank of Dallas), (July/August), 1–5.

Yeager, L. B. 1968: Essential properties of the medium of exchange. *Kyklos*, 21, 45–69.

Yeager, L. B. 1983: Stable money and free-market currencies. *Cato Journal*, 3 (Spring), 305–26.

Yeager, L. B. 1997: The costs, sources, and control of inflation, in L. B. Yeager (ed.) *The Fluttering Veil: Essays on Monetary Disequilibrium*. Indianapolis: Liberty Fund, pp. 33–84.

Index

advertising, 135
Alaska, 38
Alchian, Armen, 9
Alesina, Alberto, 189–92
Allen, Stuart D., 188
Alvarez, Fernando, 143
"ancient and honorable" gold parity, 41
antitrust, 116
Argentina, 103, 104, 163, 165
Aristotle, 2
Armentano, Dominic, 117
Auernheimer, Leonardo, 158, 159, 162, 171
Australia, 38
autarky, 6
automatic teller machine, 13, 16
Axelrod, Robert, 15
Ayr Bank, 83

Backus, David, 208
Bagehot, Walter, 14, 71–5, 81, 82, 86
Bailey curve, 149–50
Bailey, Martin J., 143, 144, 148–50, 153, 155, 156, 162, 163, 165, 171, 177
Bailey, Samuel, 2
balance sheet, 54, 56, 65
Baltensperger, Ernst, 56, 134
bank clientele, costs of cultivating, 60, 134
bank examination, 78

Bank of Canada, 85
Bank of England, 20, 70–5, 81–6, 173, 219
  charter debate, 82
Bank of Italy, 210
Bank of Montreal, 85
Bank of Scotland, 83
bank optimization problem, 56
bank runs, *see* runs on banks
bank shareholders, 122, 127, 128, 131
  extended liability for, 82, 131
  limited liability for, 81
banker's bank, 18, 71–5, 80, 82–5, 88
  defined, 71
Banking School, 218
banknotes, 3, 6, 7, 13–26, 46, 53, 69, 73, 77, 80, 81, 84, 95–7, 103, 105, 228, 241, 244, 246, 247
bankruptcy, 121
bank-issued money, 11–14, 18, 20, 21, 26, 30, 50, 53–6, 66, 67, 88, 110, 114, 117–19, 143, 154
  demand for, 80
Barro, Robert J., 155, 160, 161, 163, 193–5, 199–211, 214, 217, 239
barter, 1–4, 8, 9, 24, 93, 94, 105
Baumol, William, 111
bearer bonds, 246–8
Becker, Gary S., 119
Besen, Stanley M., 102

bid–ask spread, 23
Black, Fisher, 240–2
Blinder, Alan S., 209
Bolivia, 165, 166
Bordo, Michael D., 27, 33, 39, 76, 85, 123, 133
Boudreaux, Donald J., 134
Boyer-Xambeau, M.-T., 140
branch banking, 22, 83, 133
brand-name capital, 228, 232, 233, 236, 238
Brennan, H. Geoffrey, 205, 218
Bretton Woods system, 43, 221, 224
British Broadcasting Corporation, 89
British Linen Company, 83
Browning, John, 25
Brunner, Karl, 95, 97
Bryant, John, 155, 228, 245
Buchanan, James M., 92, 205, 218
bureaucracy, 173
bureaucratic aspect of central banks, 138, 173, 175, 176, 179, 224
Burma, 163
Burns, Arthur R., 11

Cagan, Phillip, 148–50, 159, 163, 166–9, 171
California, 20
    gold strike of, 1848, 38
Calomiris, Charles, 210
Calvo, Guillermo, 227
Canada, 76, 79, 80, 85, 86, 133, 163
    Dominion notes, 85
Canadian Bankers Association, 85
Canzoneri, Matthew B., 208
capital adequacy, 127, 128, 131, 136
capital gains, 108
capital levies on money-holders, 158, 160–2
capital requirements, 78
Caplan, Bryan, 90
cashier's checks, 13, 78
"cashless" payment system, 240, 244, 246
central bankers, interests of, 207
central banks and central banking, 12, 19, 27, 40, 43, 49, 53, 54, 67–9,
    70–86, 95, 113, 133, 138, 142, 143, 165, 173, 177, 179, 202–9, 215–21, 224–6
    discretion of, 40, 49
    independence of, 179, 217
    "natural" development of, 72, 73
cheating, 159, see also time-inconsistency
checking accounts, 96, see also deposits: transferable
"Chicago Plan" of banking reform, 219
Chile, 163
Civil War, American, 20, 84, 85, 246
classical liberalism, 219
clearinghouse associations, 17, 18, 21, 22, 23, 48, 71–86, 132
clearinghouse certificates, 77, 78
clearings, 14–22, 36, 50, 55, 57, 61–5, 77
    adverse, 57, 61–3, 67
    positive, 62, 65, 66
Coase, Ronald H., 239
codification of standards, 99
coinage, 11, 26, 27, 32, 34, 42, 48, 95, 117
coins, 9, 11, 12, 20–55, 90, 95–7, 103, 117, 118, 137, 139, 140, 141, 228, 244, 246
Colorado, 38
commercial banks, regulation of, 71, 77–9
commodity money, 9, 26–7, 39, 48, 74, 80, 81, 94, 110, 111, 117, 119
commodity standard, generic definition of, 26
commonness of money, 94, 101
    as a public good, 92
Confederate Treasury bonds, 246, 247
Congdon, Timothy, 72
consensus on a medium of account, 98
consumer welfare, 88
contagion effects of bank runs, 79, 121, 123, 131, 133
convergence to a common money, 93–6, 105, 118
Cooley, Thomas F., 48
Cooper, Richard N., 208
copper, 103

copyright law, 102, 103
counterfeiting, 220, 231
counter-cyclical monetary policy, *see*
    stabilization: macroeconomic
country banks, 72, 77, 82, 86
Cowen, Tyler, 129, 136
credibility, 162, 204, 207, 217
Cuikerman, Alex, 208
currency board, 75
Currency School, 219
cyanide process, 38

David, Paul A., 93, 102, 106
De Grauwe, Paul, 104
de Roover, Raymond, 97
de Tracy, Destutt, 2
debasement, 41, 97, 140, 141
deception, 231, 233, 234, 236, *see also*
    time-inconsistency
default risk, 81
deflation, 110, 113–16, 219, 222
Deleplace, G., 140
denationalization of money, 227
depletion effect in gold mining, 33, 34,
    36, 39, 50
deposit insurance, 123, 127–9, 132, 133
deposit transfer, 12, 13, 18, 26, 96, 97
deposits, 26, 33, 38, 45–7, 53, 54, 56, 57,
    59, 60–2, 65–8
    non-run-prone, 128–30
    run-prone, 123, 127, 128, 131, 136
    transferable, 228, 229, 241, 246
Deutsche Bundesbank, 203
devaluation, 41
Diamond, Douglas, 122, 123, 126, 127,
    132, 136
Diamond–Dybvig model, 123–8,
    130–2, 136
digital currency, 14, 247, *see also* smart
    cards
direct exchange, 4, 6, 8, *see also* barter
discretion for policy-makers, 193, 202–8,
    214, 215, 217–20, 222–6
    in flood control policy, 206
    in monetary policy, 138, 194, 202,
    204–8, 215, 217, 218, 222, 223, *see*
    also monetary policy

in patent policy, 209
    in rent control policy, 206
diseconomies of scale, 134
disinflation, 185
division of labor, 6, 7
doughnuts, chocolate, 89, 91, 102
Dowd, Kevin, 1, 18, 20–3, 69, 79, 82,
    127, 130, 133, 136, 240, 247
Driffill, John, 208
Dwyer, Gerald P. Jr, 170
Dybvig, Phillip H., 122, 123, 126, 127,
    132, 136

economies of scale, 125, 134, *see also*
    natural monopoly
economies of standardization, 94, 99,
    117, 118
Edgeworth, Francis Y., 133
Edinburgh, 17
Egypt, 163
electronic funds transfer, 13
electronic money, *see* digital currency or
    smart cards
Ellson, Richard W., 33
England, 71, 73, 75, 81–3, 95, 119
equation of exchange, 113, 145
    dynamic, 211, 221, 224
euro, 23, 104
Europe, 96, 97, 104
European Central Bank, 23
European Monetary System, 153, 207,
    210
evolution of monetary institutions, 1, 11,
    12, 20, 70, 101, 243
excess supply of money, *see* over-issue
exchange rates
    fixed, 207
    floating, 220
expectations
    adaptive, 182, 184, 212
    rational, 185, 187–9, 193, 194, 198,
    200, 205, 206, 209, 216, 227, 228
external drain, 62, 63
external effects, 96, 106, 109
    negative, 121, 123, 135
    on the purchasing power of money,
    107, 108

pecuniary, 108, 109
positive, 90, 91, 92, 105, 106, 109, 114, 120
technological, 108, 109

Fama, Eugene F., 134, 240–2
Farrell, Joseph, 102
Federal Reserve, 70, 75, 84, 85, 132, 173–9, 188, 201, 208, 209, 218, 221–5, 245
  scapegoat role of, 174
  secrecy of, 175
Federal Reserve Act, 84
Fed-watching, 40, 173–6, 208
fiat money, 3, 11, 12, 18–20, 24, 26, 39, 42, 43, 48–50, 52, 54, 67, 68, 81, 100, 103, 110–16, 120, 138, 141–3, 146, 154, 155, 202, 217, 220, 226
  private issue of, 54, 110, 114, 117, 118, 227–39
fiduciary media, see bank-issued money
financial statements, 78
"fire-sale" losses, 122, 130
fiscal motive for government intervention, 80, 81, 85
Fischer, Stanley, 203
Fisher, Irving, 113, 230, 233, 241
Fisher effect, 148, 230, 233
Fleming, Michele, 10
float, 15, 81, 134, 142
forced tender, 19
Fort Knox, 34, 51
fraud in banking, 219, 220
free banking, 53, 68, 79
Free Banking School, 219, 220
free rider problem, 90, 92, 94, 102, 103
Freeman, Scott, 116
Friedman, Milton, 33, 43–8, 51, 54, 108, 110, 112, 114, 116, 118, 130, 175, 176, 203, 205, 219–26, 230
Fullarton, John, 60, 61

Garber, Peter, 141
Gates, Bill, 25
general equilibrium, 3, 5
Germany, 104, 163, 186, 203, 210
Ghana, 163

Gherity, James A., 246
Gillard, L., 140
giro, 13
Glasner, David, 1, 61, 97
gold, 2, 3, 9, 10, 11, 17, 20, 21, 23, 24, 26–51, 54, 55, 100, 101, 103, 104, 110, 117
  demand for, 28–38, 43, 48, 51, 55
  discoveries of, 35
  mining of, see mines and mining
  purchasing power of, 27–45, 50, 51, 55
  rushes, 50
  stock of, 29, 30, 31, 45, 50
  supply of, 28, 30–9, 43, 44, 51, 55
gold standard, 22–4, 27, 29, 31, 33, 34, 36, 39–44, 46–9, 51, 53, 55, 100, 103, 104, 110, 202, 207, 215, 217, 219–21, 226, 240–2, 246
  benefits of, 39
  definition of, 46
  definition of the unit of account under, 28
  resource cost of, 33, 42–50, 52, 220
Gold Standard Corporation, 103
Goldfinger, Auric, 34, 51
goldsmiths, 12, 14
Goodfriend, Marvin, 74
Goodhart, Charles A. E., 2, 72–4, 86
Gordon, David B., 193–5, 199, 200, 202–5, 207–11, 214, 239
Gorton, Gary, 76–9, 84, 132
Gramm, W. Phil, 107, 110
Great Britain, 2, 10, 14, 184, see also UK
Great Depression, 85, 132, 224
greenbacks, 68
Greenfield, Robert L., 20, 23, 142, 240–4, 246
Greenfield–Yeager proposal, 240–4, 246
Greenspan, Alan, 137
Gresham's Law, 10
Grier, Kevin, 188
Grilli, Vittorio U., 153
Guinea (West Africa), 142
Gurley, John G., 12

Hall, Robert, 241, 242
Hansen, Gary D., 48
Haslag, Joseph H., 51
Hayek, Friedrich A., 118, 219, 227, 228, 239, 240
Heilemann, J., 89
Hellwig, Martin, 92, 109–11, 114
high-powered money, 74–7, 79–81, 84
Hodgskin, Thomas, 2
Humphrey, Thomas H., 74
Humphrey–Hawkins Act, 175
hyperinflation, 39, 48, 118, 155–8, 160, 163, 165, 166, 224, 227, 228, 230, 234, 236, 238, 239
 dynamics of, 158

Iceland, 163
illiquidity, 57, 58, 63, 64, 66
income tax, 196, 200, 201, 203
independence for a central bank, 203, 204, 217, 218
indexation, 23
 effect on inflation, 203
indirect exchange, 4, 6, 7, 8, 24, see also barter
indirect redemption, see redemption, indirect
inflation, 39, 40–51, 91, 103, 104, 113, 116, 138, 144–79, 180–214, 217, 218, 220–4, 226, 230, 231, 233–9, 241, 243
 anticipated, 159, 181, 182, 193, 197, 198, 202–5, 212, 214, 217, 229–31, 233, 234
 impact on national income, 164
 "menu costs" of, 196
 time-varying policy, 162
 unanticipated, 180, 189, 193, 204, 205, 207, 208, 220, 235
 uncertainty about, 226
 welfare burden of, 48, 143, 164, 178
inflationary bias of the Federal Reserve, 176–9
inside money, 12
insolvency, 121, 122, 129–33, 135, 136
interest rates, 76, 79, 83, 84, 143, 151, 153, 154, 174, 175, 217, 221, 226

interest-bearing currency, 14, 112, 135, 245–7
interest-rate risk, 23
intermediation, 12, 66, 152
internal drain, 74, 75
invisible hand, 1, 3, 70, 101
irredeemable money, 19
Israel, 103, 163, 165
Italy, 153, 163, 166

Kagin, Donald H., 11
Kane, Edward, 173–6
Katz, Michael L., 102
Keil, Manfred W., 184, 187
Keleher, Robert E., 74
Kennedy, John F., 192
Keynes, John Maynard, 8
Keynesian economics, 49, 215, 219
Khan, Mohsin S., 161, 165
Kiguel, Miguel A., 163
King, Robert E., 9, 74
Kirzner, Israel, 101
Kiyotaki, Nobuhiro, 3
Klein, Benjamin, 40, 114, 118, 228–39
Knight, Malcolm D., 161, 165
Kroszner, Randall, 20, 129, 136
Kydland, Finn E., 193–5, 200, 202, 204–8, 217, 226, 227
Kydland–Prescott model, 194–9

Laidler, David E. W., 106
Laffer curve, 144, 149
Lebanon, 166
legal tender, 19, 100, 140
"legal restrictions theory" of the demand for money, 60, 244–8
Lego brick standard, 96
Leijonhufvud, Axel, 101
lender of last resort, 71, 74–6, 79, 80, 82, 84–6, 123, 132, 133
 as co-insurance among banks, 76
 Bagehot's rules for, 75
 definition of, 74
 prerequisites for, 75, 76
 private, 77
liability rules, see bank shareholders
Liebowitz, Stanley, J., 102

Lin, Shoukang, 116
lines of credit, 106
liquidation, 121, 124, 128, 130
liquidity, *see* marketability
liquidity cost, 56–9, 61, 65
Livingston, James, 85
"lock-in" problem, 102, 105
London, 17, 21, 71, 72, 82, 83
Lucas, Robert E. Jr, 49, 203

MacRae, C. Duncan, 180, 189
Makinen, Gail E., 246
Malta, 74, 163
Manchester, 246
Margolis, Stephen E., 102
market failure, 90, 94, 96, 99, 105, 132
marketability, 5–7, 9, 11, 14, 16, 24, 26,
    94
Markowitz, Morris J., 69
maturity of new corporate debt, 40
McCallum, Bennett, 187–9, 193, 207,
    223–4
McClure, J. Harold, Jr, 164
McCulloch, J. Huston, 2, 4, 24, 140, 144,
    149, 155
McDonald, Greg, 11
medium of account, 7, 8, 20, 21–3, 27,
    54, 98–105, 240–4, 247, *see also*
    unit of account
medium of exchange, 1–12, 21, 24, 90–6,
    98, 99, 101, 103–5, 120, 129, 130,
    239, 242, 246, 247
medium of redemption, 20, 26, 54, 240,
    242–7
Meiselman, David I., 188
Melitz, Jacques, 9
Meltzer, Allan H., 40, 41, 95, 97, 119,
    208
Melvin, Michael, 118
Menger, Carl, 1–3, 5–7, 9–11, 14, 19, 25,
    92, 93, 95–7, 99, 101, 103, 118, 119
mines and mining, 29–38, 42–4, 48, 55,
    110, 111, 117
    technical progress in, 38, 50
Minford, Patrick, 192
mints and minting, 27, 30, 32, 36, 41, 42,
    97, 117, 139–41

monopoly of, 140
    private, 11, 19, 24, 91, 96, 99, 117
misery index, macroeconomic, 195–200,
    203, 210–14
Mondex, 13
Monetarism, 49, 175, 205, 216, 226
monetary disequilibrium, 107, 241, 243
monetary equilibrium, 108
monetary expansion, rate of, 144–66,
    172, 176–9, 230, 233–8
monetary policy, 71, 73, 79–81, 84, 85
    activism in, 176
    activism versus discretion in, 223
    constitutionalism in, 218, 219
    rules versus discretion in, 88
monetary policy rules, 27, 193, 198, 202,
    204–10, 215, 217–20, 223–6
    base freeze, 222, 226
    enforcement of, 225, 226
    k-percent, 179, 207, 219–23
    with feedback, 223–5
monetary stability, 91–2
money multiplier, 67
money-changers, 12
monopoly of currency issue, 11, 19, 71,
    73, 75, 80, 82, 84–6, 88, 91, 119,
    134, 135
Montreal, 85
moral hazard, 75, 76
Morrell, Stephen O., 94
Mulligan, Casey B., 115, 116
Mullineaux, Donald J., 73, 78, 79
multi-commodity standard, 20, 23, 54,
    227, 240
mutual funds, 245
    money-market, 129, 131, 136
mystique of gold, 40

Nash equilibrium, 198, 212
National Banking system of the USA, 68,
    77, 84, 85, 132, 133
natural monopoly, 11, 54, 72, 73, 116,
    117, 118, 119, 121, 133, 134
natural rate hypothesis, 187, 191, 220
"natural" system of banking, 72, 73, 86
network effects, 93, 94, 101, 102, 103,
    117

Neumeyer, Pablo Andres, 163
New England, 86
New York, 17, 22, 72, 77, 78
New Zealand, 38, 186
Nicaragua, 163
Nichols, Donald A., 154
Niehans, Jurg, 7
Nixon, Richard M., 192, 221
nominal income stabilization, 67
"non-optimality of money holding under
    laissez-faire", 109, 110
non-price competition, 60, 63, 64, 81,
    134, 135, 143, 246
Nordhaus, William D., 180, 184–95, 198,
    212
Nordhaus–MacRae model, 180–4
Northern Ireland, 20
note dueling, 15
note-changers, 14, 15
note-exchange system, 17
note-holding clientele, 59, 60
Noyes, Alexander Dana, 84
Nozick, Robert, 3

O'Driscoll, Gerald P., Jr, 99
"official price" of gold, 28
optimal quantity of money, 106, 108,
    113, 114, 115, 116, 120, 196, 222,
    229, 232
optimal taxation, 115
option clause, in deposit and note
    contracts, 129, 130
origin of money, 1–3, 99
outside money, 11, 12, 13, 14, 16, 18, 22,
    74, 110, 114, 118
overlapping-generations model of
    money, 228
over-issue, 60–6, 219, 227, 228
    in-concert, 62–6, 68

panics, banking, 68, 74, 76–9, 84, 85,
    121, 123, 130–3, 136
    defined, 121
par acceptance, 14–16, 17, 54, 83
Paraguay, 163
Parnell, Henry, 68
"partisan" theory of monetary policy,

180, 189–92
patent law, as a pre-commitment, 206
paternalism, 98
Patinkin, Donald, 30
Patterson, William, 81
pawn shops, 106
Peel's Act of 1844, 75, 82, 83, 95, 119,
    219
Peru, 163
Pesek, Boris, 230
Philadelphia, 78
Phillips curve, 180, 181, 189, 191,
    193–5, 197–205, 207, 210–12, 214,
    215, 220
Plosser, Charles I., 9
Poland, 163, 165
policy ineffectiveness, 187
political business cycle, 138, 180–94,
    198, 212
Portugal, 163
precommitment
    by a central bank, 160, 161, 202,
        205–7, 209
    by a private money issuer, 227, 228,
        239
Prescott, Edward C., 193–5, 200, 202,
    204–8, 217, 226, 227
price index, 98
price level, 23, 27, 33, 36, 37, 39, 41, 44,
    50, 51, 62, 67
    anchor for, 39, 40
    determination of, 27, 242
    stability of, 80, 100, 119
    unpredictability of, 39
price-level stabilization, 221, 226, 227,
    241
    as a public good, 91
price-specie-flow mechanism, 55, 61, 66
primitive monies, 9
private goods, 89, 102
prospecting, 33, 37, 38
Public Choice, 205, 217, 222
public good(s), 88–102, 105, 116, 119
    defined, 89
public receivability, 19
purchasing power of money, 54
purchasing-power risk, 40

"pure accounting system of exchange", 241
pyramiding of reserves, 79

quantity theory of money, 203

Reagan, Ronald, 201
real income, growth of, 45, 47, 114, 146
redeemability, 13, 14, 20, 21, 22, 142, 227–9, 240, 242, 247
  as a contractual solution to time-inconsistency, 239
  indirect, 20–3, 242
redemption, 14–21, 23, 26, 27, 46, 47, 53, 54, 59, 69, 81, 86, 122, 123, 128–130, 228, 239, 240, 242, 247
Redish, Angela, 85
reflux of excess currency, 60, 61
regulation of commercial banks, 77, 80, 84, 85, 86, 88, 154
  by clearinghouse association, 77
Regulation Q, 134, 135
Reiss, Spencer, 25
rental price of money, 229, 231, 235–8
reputation, in monetary policy, 207, 208
reserve ratio, 21, 46, 64
reserve requirements, 78, 143, 150–5, 166, 174, 177, 222
  effects on inflation, 153
  effects on seigniorage, 150–2, 169, 170
reserves, 15, 17, 19–22, 42, 46–8, 51, 53–9, 61–8, 71–7, 79, 80, 83, 85, 86, 122, 123, 130, 133, 143, 151–3, 169, 170
  centralization of, 72, 74, 83, 86
  fractional, 46, 50, 69, 74, 77, 132, 136
  one-hundred percent, 45, 50, 69, 77, 219, 221
  optimal holding of, 55, 68
Richards, Daniel J., 188
Richards, R. D., 14
Ritter, Joseph A., 3
Rockoff, Hugh, 37, 38, 41
Rolnick, Arthur J., 39, 48
Romer, Christina D., 49
Rothbard, Murray N., 46

Royal Bank of Scotland, 83
rule of law, 219
rules for monetary policy, see monetary policy rules
runs on banks, 84, 121–33, 135, 136, 220
  defined, 121
  triggering of, 122, 132

Sachs, Jeffrey, 166, 189–92
Sala-i-Martin, Xavier, 115, 116
Salerno, Joseph T., 51
Samuelson, Paul A., 106, 107, 110
Santomero, Anthony M., 12
Saving, Thomas R., 170
Schmidtz, David, 89, 93
Schnadt, Norbert, 242, 243
Schuler, Kurt, 74
Schwartz, Anna J., 130, 220
Scitovsky, Tibor, 108, 109
Scotland, 16, 21, 47, 79, 83–4, 130, 133, 246
seigniorage, 11, 41, 42, 115, 138–72, 176–9, 188, 189, 196, 217
  countries that rely heavily on, 163
  defined, 139
  different measures of, 142
  maximization of, 141, 144, 146–9, 159–69, 172, 178
  nominal versus real, 141
  received by commercial banks, 143
  short-run versus long-run, 156
  tax base for, 144, 145, 152, 153, 155, 164, 165
  tax rate, 144, 145, 149, 155, 165
  time-varying policy, 164
  under a specie standard, 139
Selgin, George, 1, 3, 11, 15, 20, 46, 54, 63, 67, 68, 84, 139, 215
separation of monetary functions, 240
settlement, interbank, 14, 17, 18, 21, 22, 23, 71, 244, 247
Shapiro, Carl, 102
Shaw, Edward S., 12
shell money, 9, 12, 103
"shock absorber" role of money balances, 165
Shugart, William F. II, 177, 178

silver, 3, 7, 9, 10, 11, 20, 26, 27, 39, 48,
    54, 98, 101, 103, 117, 139–42
Simons, Henry C., 219, 221, 222
Simpsons, The, 89
six-partner rule of 1708, 82, 83
Sjaastad, Larry A., 161, 162
smart cards, 13, 14, 53, 59, 69
Smith, Adam, 1, 2, 6, 7, 83
Smith, Vera C., 53, 73, 84, 85, 72
social convention, 2, 8, 11, 92
"social economies of scale" in use of a
    money, 117–18
South Africa, 38
Soviet Union, 20, 104
Spain, 163
specialization, 4, 6
specie, 18–20, 139
spontaneous order, 99, see also invisible
    hand, social convention
stabilization, macroeconomic, 49, 88
    as goal of monetary policy, 205, 215,
    217, 221, 226
stagflation, 185
state theory of money, 2, 7, 8
Stubblebine, W. Craig, 92
Suffolk Bank clearing system, 15, 16, 73,
    86
Summers, Lawrence H., 203
Sumner, Scott, 134
"sunspot" theory of bank runs, 122, 131,
    132
suspension of payments, 19, 128, 130
Sweden, 10, 133
switching between monetary standards,
    19, 20, 23, 98, 100–5
Switzerland, 133, 163

Taub, Bart, 227, 228, 235, 239
tax on holding money, 48
Timberlake, Richard H., 76, 77, 85
time-consistency, 198, 201, 202, 204,
    205, 207, 214, 223
time-inconsistency, 138, 226–8, 231,
    233, 238, 239
Tobin, James, 111
Tollison, Robert D., 177, 178
Toma, Mark, 176–9

transaction costs, 93, 94, 106
Treasury, Canadian, 85
Treasury, US, 75, 84, 142, 154, 174, 176,
    177, 179, 245, 246
Treasury bills, 154

Uganda, 163
UK, 187; see also Great Britain
underweight coins, 140
under-issue, 60, 65
unemployment, 138, 174, 180–205,
    208–11, 214, 215, 220
    natural rate of, 180, 181, 189–94,
    196–205, 209, 212, 214–17, 220
unemployment insurance, 200, 201, 203
uniformity of money, 10, 24, 95, 105,
    117
unit of account, 7, 8, 18, 19, 20, 22, 23,
    24, 27, 28, 40, 54, 96, 98, 99, 100,
    101, 102, 103, 104, 105, 120, 240,
    244, 246
    proprietary, 98, 99, 103
USA, 10, 16, 19, 27, 43, 47, 49, 68, 69,
    75, 77, 79, 80, 84–5, 103, 119, 132,
    133, 141, 153–5, 163–5, 173, 176,
    178, 186, 190, 192, 200, 201, 209,
    218, 220, 244
Usher, A. P., 14

"valun" unit of account, 242
van Dun, Frank, 89
Vaubel, Roland, 90–4, 98, 105, 106, 108,
    114, 117, 119, 134
velocity of money, 44–8, 67, 113, 114,
    145, 146, 216, 217, 221–4
    variations in, 216, 219
Volcker, Paul, 209
von Mises, Ludwig, 3, 22, 50

Wagner, Richard E., 188–9
Wales, 82
Wallace, Neil, 3, 155, 233, 244, 245, 246
wampum, 9
Wärneryd, Karl, 1
wear and tear on gold, 30, 33, 34, 39, 42,
    44, 48, 51
Weber, Warren E., 39, 48

West R. C., 85
White, Lawrence H., 1, 11, 15, 23, 26, 46, 53, 60, 70, 82, 84, 88, 96, 98, 105, 117, 121, 127, 130, 133, 134, 138, 139, 142, 173, 193, 215
Whittaker, John, 242, 243
Willett, Thomas D., 164
Williamson, Stephen D., 116
Woodward, G. Thomas, 246
Wright, Randall, 3

Wriston, Walter, 69
Wynne, Mark, 137

Yansane, Kerfalla, 142
Yeager, Leland B., 3, 20, 23, 98, 100, 102, 108, 240–4, 246
Yugoslavia, 163, 165

zero inflation, 193, 196, 197, 202, 204, 205, 207, 214, 223